4400504

MANAGERS
MUST
LEAD!

Revised Edition

MANAGERS MUST LEAD!

Ray A. Killian

amacom

A Division of American Management Associations

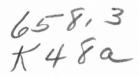
Library of Congress Cataloging in Publication Data

Killian, Ray A
  Managers must lead!

  Includes index.
  1. Personnel management. 2. Supervisors.
I. Title.
HF5549.K48 1979   658.3   78-23709
ISBN 0-8144-5482-8

First Printing

TO
Betty, Ray, Jr., and Ann
whose cooperation and understanding
made possible the writing of this book
and
John M. Belk and associates, whose
contributions and activities are
reflected in these pages

Contents

Foreword

RAY Killian's *Managers Must Lead!* occupies a unique position in the literature on managerial leadership. It is the only book I know of that gets right to the heart of the matter and discusses the types of everyday operating situations that call for individual leadership skills on the part of the manager.

Other books in this area tend to fall into one of two categories. Some concentrate on the *managerial styles* of leadership. Such books put emphasis on the manager's personality, values, philosophy, and attitudes toward subordinates. While it is true that such factors strongly influence a manager's general approach to leading and supervising, they do not deal with the skills required to manage successfully in the specific interpersonal situations which the practicing manager runs into in his or her daily work.

A second category of managerial leadership books deals with a cookbook approach to the subject. These books feature the "10 keys to successful (delegation, motivating, communicating, coaching. . . . and so forth)." Again, although some of these checklists are useful as general principles, they do not come to grips with what managers typically must do to lead successfully in their daily work situations.

This book gets to the core of managerial leadership, the types of management situations that practitioners encounter in their daily work activities. As a result, the book is useful in focusing on the key interpersonal situations in management that are most successfully handled through personal leadership.

In addition, the book concentrates heavily on the supervisory aspects of leadership. This involves the daily give and take of delegating, directing, measuring, and motivating, along with developing subordinates on the job.

Author and publisher have made a strong effort to put this revised edition into nonsexist language. As a result, it is useful to either the female or male manager who seeks to improve skills in leading those who report to them.

The book is particularly useful for the following:

- □ For training and management development specialists who want to build "real world" expertise into their training programs.
- □ For individual managers who want to polish their skills in interpersonal leadership.
- □ For individual contributors and technical specialists who are moving into management and who must now obtain objectives with and through people.
- □ For students in human resources management courses in business schools, where an effort is made to balance academic theory with real-world applications.

Robert F. Pearse
Boston University
August 1978

Preface

THIS book has been written expressly for the ambitious supervisor who is seriously dedicated to climbing the ladder of management success. It deals specifically with those keys to management growth that are based on job results obtained through people, who also benefit proportionately from their contribution.

The book will be of greatest benefit to the man or woman who is willing to recognize that management leadership consists of certain identifiable tools and techniques and that these can be mastered through intelligently applied effort. It is aimed at the rising executive who is seeking practical guides for effective human achievement. Its premise is that effective leadership must render a genuine service to the employee and the enterprise and by doing so deserves to increase its influence, leadership role, and job-related personal benefits.

The rule-of-thumb, hit-or-miss method of supervisory leadership is outmoded, and neither management nor employees will tolerate its haphazard handling of people or its uncertain results. Rather, the demand today is for leadership that is skillful in applying tested techniques that ensure complete utilization of every resource at its command—recognizing that if employees fail to make contributions equal to their fullest potential, a share of the blame belongs to leadership. Why? Because leadership has failed to meet its responsibility of providing sufficient knowledge, skills, motivation, and overall direction.

Leaders want to get right down to facts—facts proved by successful experience. These pages offer specific guides and principles, supported by illustrative examples, for dealing with the very real world of everyday human problems. The book is based on more than 30 years of firing-line experiences in handling all types of situations, involving all levels of employees and management in a variety of types and sizes of companies, as well as in a great many two-way leadership and supervisory training sessions.

Consideration is given to the traditional concepts of human relations, but equal attention is focused on firm, unvarying adherence to reasonable standards of job performance. Consideration is also given to the latest behavioral science techniques of job enrichment and coping with changing life styles. Although the challenge to be persuasive is significant, management has not surrendered its basic prerogatives; it cannot rely solely on voluntary performance. The employee has an obligation—of which he or she must be made fully aware—to respond substantially to appropriate leadership as it relates to job performance.

The basic principles of human relations and of the achievement of results through people are fairly universal. Thus, the guides in this book apply with equal validity to all leaders whose accomplishments hinge on motivating people effectively. Whether a new first-line supervisor or an experienced executive, the reader will discover recommendations that are realistic, practical, and innovative.

This book has been written in an easy-to-understand, conversational style. It can provide an excellent self-training program. It is ideal as a textbook for college and company courses, each chapter supplying the subject guides for one or more sessions. It can serve as a realistic reference for supervisors and would-be supervisors who are concerned with goal achievement—both for themselves and for their employees—right now.

Mastery of this material will not guarantee management success or growth. The book does, however, represent a map of the road that was traveled by many who are top executives today. It can, therefore, open the door to opportunity. But the degree to which individuals apply themselves and succeed will be determined by the degree to which they are able to take advantage of that opportunity and increase their ultimate management contribution.

The supervisor's future achievement is in his or her own hands. It is possible to learn to manage effectively. The genius of leadership is effort applied intelligently and persistently according to a workable master plan.

Ray A. Killian

Publisher's Note

"Memo to all department heads: Be sure that every employee brings his . . . er, her . . . their report to. . . . Scratch that. Be sure that all employees bring their report . . . reports. . . ."

THE executive writing that memo is having a problem. Ray Killian had the same problem in revising this book. For 12 years *Managers Must Lead!* has been a useful book for business executives. The many changes that have taken place in the management field since the original publication in 1966 have made a revision necessary.

One of the significant changes that Mr. Killian had to deal with in preparing the current edition was the new awareness of the problems and rights of women. Increasing numbers of women have entered almost every field of professional activity, from finance and medicine to engineering and even the military. In fact, Mr. Killian was so aware of the importance of women in the business world that he wrote *The Working Woman,* a book published by AMACOM in 1971. It was one of the first management books in support of women's job rights.

Despite important progress in legislation, employment, and compensation for women, much remains to be done before we can talk of a truly nonsexist society. One major obstacle to the elimination of sex discrimination is the English language. Authors and editors concerned about the issue struggle continually to avoid unintentional linguistic bigotry. This is especially true in management books, where we are repeatedly confronted by such traditional words as chairman, businessman, salesman, and foreman. Predictably, replacing these terms by their nonsexist equivalents, chairperson, businessperson, and so on, has drawn criticism—of a valid sort from those who find the substitutes awkward, and of a less valid sort from those who refuse to acknowledge that a problem exists.

A more pervasive problem exists in the conventionally accepted use of the masculine pronouns he, him, his, and himself to refer to a person regardless of sex. Often is it possible to rephrase such examples using the plural; in other cases, careful authors resort to the use of *he or she* or *he/she* in their inflected variants.

Mr. Killian, in revising his book, took great pains to give women full representation, using whatever techniques he could. The results, by his admission, were often cumbersome to the extreme. Confronted with the same problem, other authors who are sensitive to the issue of discrimination against women include a disclaimer in their preface, stating that although they continue to use the masculine pronouns to refer to both sexes, they do not thereby intend any violation of the rights of women. Mr. Killian, with us, felt that such disclaimers do not solve the problem but merely postpone its solution.

Some readers will say that we are overstating the problem. After all, what counts is not what we say but what we do. But we maintain that language can act as a self-perpetuating mechanism for preserving prejudice. Past ways of thinking are handed down to us through language and continue to exert a subtle yet powerful influence over our actions. Unless we make a conscious effort to break out from the constraints imposed on our thinking by our inherited language, stereotypes will stay with us.

As a publisher of books for management education, we are acutely aware of the need for a set of common-gender pronouns for referring to a person regardless of sex, and since English does not offer us the forms we need, the only way to fill this gap in the language is to construct them. Language should not become a straightjacket; it must respond—and historically has responded—to the needs of its users.

But there is a difficulty here. Language cannot be mandated; it must ultimately be accepted by the community of its users. At least two facets will determine this acceptance. One, any new forms proposed must be such that English speakers can accept and use them; that is, they must be pronounceable and should not offend one's sense of esthetics. Second, there must be a certain amount of open-mindedness on the part of the language users to consider such proposals. It is easy to reject any innovation on the basis that it is "ugly," "unnatural"—or simply new.

In the spirit of a constructive solution, we introduce in this book a set of common-gender pronouns to be used for generic reference. We cannot claim that they are "English" words, but they can become part of the English language if the reader considers the issue serious enough. The forms we have selected are:

hir (to be pronounced like the word *here* and replacing
    the forms *he/she* and *him/her*)
hirs (replacing *his/her* and *his/hers*)
hirself (replacing *himself/herself*)

Let us try an example:

The applicant can learn a lot about *hirself* from a good interview. *Hir* is talking about *hirs* favorite subject.

We are aware that there have been other proposals to introduce common-gender pronouns, and most of them seem acceptable insofar as they are pronounceable and not necessarily offensive to our ears. How then does one choose among them? Should the deciding factor be philological soundness, esthetics, or something else?

If we can agree on the need to adapt the English language to the trend of our society, we should not let arguments over specifics cloud the issue. Therefore, before we go on to justify our own choice, we would like to make it clear that we are interested in solving a problem, not in defending a solution. Any other choices that can win a higher chance of general acceptance will be welcomed and seriously considered.

With this in mind, let us look at the problem of choice. We feel that the ultimate decision must be based on the needs of present language users, for it is they who will accept or reject any new form. Philological soundness is of secondary importance, because speakers are ordinarily not aware of the history of their language.

The needs of the language user, we believe, dictate a form that is (1) short, preferably a single syllable (this would eliminate proposals like *heshe* and *himmer*), (2) clearly related in its sound to the masculine and feminine pronouns of modern English, and (3) easy to pronounce.

The form we have selected, *hir,* meets all three criteria. It is monosyllabic, it is no more difficult to pronounce than the word *here,* and it is based on the simple phonetic equation:

$$(hi:) + (h\partial r) = (hi\ :r)$$
$$he \qquad her \qquad hir$$

Finally, this form happens to have some historical justification as well. The Middle English word for *her* was *hire.* Even more to the point, the possessive *hers* at that time was spelled first *hires* and then *hirs.*

One final note on our proposal. It will have been noticed that we suggested not four but three pronouns; that is, one and the same form, *hir,* serves as both nominative (*he/she*) and objective (*him/her*). This is not because we could think of no separate form to replace the nominative *he/she.* Rather, we feel that in introducing new forms into the language, one should pay attention to the overall grammatical system and the trends observable in that system. English is no longer a case language. In fact, the only vestiges of the old case distinctions are found in the pronoun system. In short, then, to propose separate nominative and objective forms for common-gender English pronouns would mean to introduce an essentially archaic distinction into the language. The case distinction is indicated by word order.

In closing, we would like to thank the author, Ray Killian, for his cooperation. Writing a book means a great investment of time and effort, and it is understandable that authors do not want to risk losing the rewards of their labor by subjecting themselves to possible negative criticism or offending their readers. Mr. Killian felt strongly enough about the issue to accept the risk.

Publishing is a business which we believe has special social and educational responsibilities. We are grateful to Mr. Killian for helping us attempt to meet those responsibilities, and hope that other authors and publishers analyze their own sense of responsibility to this issue.

The art of developing human relationships is the best known and the most inefficiently practiced of all human skills.

Keys to Getting Results Through People

EXECUTIVE Vice President John Barbour: I'm in favor of giving the promotion to Fred Morton. He knows how to get his people to produce and how to build a team.

General Manager David Helms: I agree that Fred is a good man, but he hasn't been with us nearly as long as several of the others who are expecting this promotion.

Mr. Barbour: David, you're probably right. But let me ask you, what do we spend the most money for around here? Payroll—that's what gets the largest share of the budget. Now, which one of the supervisors out there is getting the best return for those payroll dollars? Fred Morton, that's who. Fred has demonstrated during the past two years that he knows how to get along with people. He keeps his people satisfied; and what's more important, he gets the best results. His people are well trained, he has practically no turnover, he's firm, but they still think he's a great guy. He knows everyone in the department, and he always seems to know how his people will react and exactly what they can be expected to do.

Mr. Helms: Yes, when you put it that way, I begin to see what you mean.

Mr. Barbour: What's more, a man with that kind of track record deserves a bigger job, and the company needs what he can contribute. He develops people and makes money for us. We want more of both. David, you talk with Fred Morton and tell him that as of the first of the month he will be plant superintendent. Anyone who can handle people the way he does *deserves* a bigger job. In the meantime we'll have the necessary meetings to make the announcement.

It was in this manner, and for these reasons, that Fred Morton became plant superintendent of the Marion Manufacturing Company. He had been a foreman for only two years and was promoted over three senior foremen, *because he knew how to get results through people.*

Yes, leaders must be able to predict with a reasonable degree of accuracy the reaction, job performance, and overall contribution of other people. Their actual success depends on their ability to anticipate those responses and to exert those influences that will result in the reactions and job performance that will contribute most to the desired goals. This book is concerned primarily with the application of this fundamental principle to human achievement.

Job Behavior Is Predictable

It *is* possible to predict human behavior. The industrial firm and the gasoline company predict percentages of honesty before they extend credit. The bank teller greets customers graciously, thanks them for their business, and invites them back, because this will result in a more favorable customer reaction. The bank recognizes that a favorable reaction is desirable, and has learned how to bring it about.

Being able to anticipate and predict what people will do and how they will react has tremendous potential. It means that, on the basis of *hirs** knowledge of human behavior and of the specific group of people under *hirs* jurisdiction, the supervisor is able to forecast job performance, attitudes, reactions—and results. This ability should lead *hir* to exert the kind of influence that will bring about the desired job performance and encourage *hir* to enlarge on the favorable influences and minimize the negative ones.

The leader must also recognize that in order to achieve certain established goals, specific reactions must take place and a certain

---

*The reader is strongly urged to read the Publisher's Note on our use of these original words. They have been italicized in the first two chapters to give you time to adjust to their use throughout the text.

level of job performance is required. It follows, then, that *hirs* knowledge of people should enable *hir* to ensure that these reactions and this performance will occur. In essence, *hir* is predicting human behavior and then bringing to bear those influences that will lead to desirable activity.

Because experience has proved that certain procedures are most effective in achieving a favorable response, definite fundamental rules have emerged that can be used as guides. Disregarding these rules will lead to poor results. The quest for maximum results through people must begin with an understanding of goals, and then proceed logically through a series of steps, as follows:

1. It begins with an identification of the exact results desired, including production goals, economical use of resources, and maintenance of favorable working relationships. Once this picture has been clarified, the process involves determining the quantity and quality of activity that must occur before these results can be achieved.
2. Accomplishment is based on achieving a certain level of job activity. Jobs must be performed, and energy must be applied to the problem. The supervisor determines what must be done to accomplish the desired results and how people must be influenced to apply themselves most efficiently.
3. The greatest opportunity for leadership lies in influencing performance. Here, the supervisor applies *hirs* knowledge of people and human skills to exert the appropriate influence in order to bring about the specific activity needed to achieve the desired results.
4. The supervisor next focuses on the individual and group resources at *hirs* disposal. Because *hir* must work with the strengths and weaknesses of individuals, *hir* seeks to employ only the most qualified people available. *Hir* determines the most effective way of working with each member of the group and tries to utilize each person's maximum potential. Then, as part of the continuing job environment, *hir* sets into motion those factors that are most effective in causing the individual and the team to engage in those activities most likely to help achieve the goal.

Once this process is understood and applied, the supervisor should achieve maximum results through people. However, the degree of success depends on the leader's skill in influencing particular job performance. This influence, in turn, depends on a thorough understanding of people and their basic behavior patterns, together with the leader's ability to bring this understanding to bear on the problems at hand.

The Human Factors in Achievement

Paradoxically, despite automation, executives are becoming increasingly aware of the critical need for people who willingly and skillfully apply themselves to their jobs. The problem is not one of machines but of people. When a machine is needed for a particular job, one can be bought or designed. If it does not function properly, a skilled mechanic can repair it without delay or difficulty. The power of the machine can be increased, or the device can be rewired to change its output. However complicated the machine, it is still relatively simple compared to the challenges of altering the input/output of the human component in job performance. Yet this is precisely the responsibility of the supervisor. It can be handled successfully only when the rules of the "human game" are recognized and followed.

The Vital Impact of Human Cost and Influence

In addition to the supervisor's concern with basic leadership and human relations, *hir* must respond to the decisive impact of human cost and influence as they relate to all activities and results. In many companies, the cost of human time (employee presence on the job), including payroll, benefits, and personnel-support services, represents at least 70 percent of every operating expense dollar. In addition to cost, human decisions and contributions determine what is produced, its quality and cost, how much is sold, and whether the overall effectiveness of the particular operation will assure the continuing profitability of the larger organization.

Supervisors exert the major influence on how efficiently this 70 percent component is utilized for the benefit of the individual employee and the company. They must avoid human waste and, as skillfully as possible, use all available leadership tools and techniques to achieve the goals that have been set for the particular unit under their jurisdiction. In essence, that is top management's basic expectation for satisfactory performance of supervisory personnel.

The Humanizing Revolution

Today, approximately 90 percent of human failures on the job are the result of a breakdown in human relations. The individual fails to make the proper adjustments in *hirs* association with others and thus becomes less effective in the group, develops a negative attitude toward *hirs* job, and loses confidence in *hirself*. As a result, *hirs* job performance declines.

A recognition of this problem has led management to seek the most promising solutions. It was discovered long ago that slave labor and brute force are too costly and inefficient. In 1776, Adam Smith offered a hint in *An Inquiry into the Nature and Causes of the Wealth of Nations*. His theory was that management should treat its employees with consideration and understanding. This approach, he reasoned, would in turn cause the employee to give the job *hirs* maximum effort. The theory was fine, but managers did not consider it necessary to cultivate the goodwill of employees because, in the early years of the Industrial Revolution, the available workers far outnumbered the number of jobs to be filled.

During the early 1920s, industrial engineers began to look in earnest for the most effective methods of achieving productivity. They had only limited success, because there was still a surplus of labor. Then, during World War II, almost 25 percent of the workforce was drafted into the armed services. Hence, the manager who was tempted to discharge a slow, insufficiently trained or inadequately motivated employee was forced to realize that there might not be anyone else to fill the position. As a result, the search for the most effective way to get people to produce began in earnest.

The procedure that was eventually developed was actually a restatement of the human relations concepts taught in the New Testament. It hinged on the importance of every human life, the need for human dignity, consideration for the individual, and an attempt to conduct the total enterprise in such a manner as to merit each person's maximum contribution.

Clarence Francis, while chairman of General Foods, best expressed this new philosophy with these words:

> You can buy a man's time, you can buy a man's physical presence at a given place, you can even buy a measured number of skilled muscular motions per hour or day. But you cannot buy enthusiasm, you cannot buy initiative, you cannot buy loyalty, you cannot buy the devotion of hearts, minds, and souls. You have to earn these

things. . . . It is ironical that Americans—the most advanced people technically, mechanically, and industrially—should have waited until a comparatively recent period to inquire into the most promising source of productivity; namely, the human will to work. It is hopeful, on the other hand, that this search is now under way.

It was this search for the key to "the human will to work" that caused the humanizing revolution in the relationship of manager and managed in the industrial world. It led to the programs of training of human relations for all levels of management. It led to a revamping of employee benefits and the entire structure of the business organization. In fact, the pendulum swung so far in this direction that supervisors were concentrating more on understanding people than on meeting production schedules. This caused Malcolm McNair, Havard Business School professor, to state:

> The world's work has to be done, and people have to take responsibility for their own work and own lives. Too much emphasis on human relations encourages people to feel sorry for themselves. It makes it easier for them to slough off responsibility, to find excuses for failure, and to act like children. When somebody falls down on a job, but does not behave in accordance with codes, we look into his psychological background for factors that may be used as excuses. Undue preoccupation with human relations saps individual responsibility, leads us not to think about the job anymore and about getting it done, but only about people and their relations.

Emphasis on a benevolent managerial philosophy is no panacea. It has significant value and must be a part of the process of getting results through people, but it is not an excuse for accepting less than every individual's best. A proper balance must be maintained and should include fairness, firmness, and a consideration for the individual's feelings. However, it should be clear at all times that an employee is being paid to make a contribution and that the expectation of certain results is not unreasonable. It is also good human relations not to retain an individual on the job if *hir* fails to live up to *hirs* responsibilities after management has made every reasonable effort to provide the necessary job ingredients.

The supervisor, then, has the challenge of balancing a consideration for the individual with maintenance of a high standard of productivity. This requires skillful leadership and awareness of the human aspects.

The Fine Art of Working with People

Employees are free to apply or not to apply themselves fully to the task at hand. It requires effort to harness the human will to get a job done in the prescribed manner. This means that the company must engage in those activities and practices that offer the best chance of achieving maximum results through people.

In applying this philosophy, management accepts the responsibility of providing job knowledge through training. It accepts the challenge of motivating through fair pay, forms of competition, and enlightened leadership. It seeks to provide a favorable job environment, machines, systems, and a functional organization which offers the employees the most productive framework in which to exert their efforts.

It follows that if production schedules fall behind or sales quotas are not met, the employee is not necessarily at fault; management must also accept its rightful share of the blame for the failure, and must make an objective evaluation of the situation and change what needs to be changed.

Supervisory Guides to Effective Human Relations

Perhaps no activity has a more significant common denominator than the basic needs and feelings of people. The prudent supervisor builds upon this foundation, but at the same time *hir* makes individual adjustments to suit individual lifestyles. The human leadership program should have these two cornerstones:

1. *Operate from a base of merited credibility.* There is no place in long-range, positive human relationships for the slick operator or the fast talker, for sleight of hand or for fakery. The supervisor must at all times be honest and forthright, and *hir* must deal fairly with *hirs* employees.
2. *Job-related activities should be mutually beneficial.* The concept of getting work done through others presupposes that one person will control and direct the activity of other people, not because one person is better than another but simply to assure that assigned responsibilities achieve desired results.

This attempt to influence or persuade should bring about mutually beneficial results. The supervisor should not seek to satisfy his own needs at the expense of others. The practice of effective long-range human relations is built on the premise that positive job performance is beneficial to the employee as well as to the company.

Results Depend on Adherence to Guides

Achievement is dependent on appropriate leadership, and leadership in turn depends on the capacity to influence job-related behavior. Both the leader and the follower require identifiable patterns within which to function, and frameworks in which to operate.

The supervisor who expects to get results through people must deliberately give attention to effective human relations, must develop a broad understanding of human nature and of the practice of certain supervisory rules, and must follow a deliberate course of action. George Halsey summed up the idea best in *Supervising People* when he stated: "It has been demonstrated time and time again that almost any person of normal intelligence and sincere desire to be of service to people can acquire considerable skill in the art of supervising people if he will study its principles and methods and apply them thoughtfully, conscientiously, and persistently."

Appropriate supervision brings about the best results when it is an intelligent, thoughtful, planned, deliberate, and continuing process. Just as the athlete practices long hours and concentrates on every phase of the game, so must the supervisor. People are complex, their reactions are often puzzling, and their relationships might be confusing. The supervisor's capacity for predicting behavior and anticipating job performance can be *hirs* most valuable asset as *hir* seeks maximum goal achievement. The facts, the guides, and the information are available. It is up to the supervisor to take the initiative and utilize these materials as efficiently as possible in performing *hirs* duties.

Legal Responsibilities Involved in Supervising People

All management personnel, from first-line supervisors to the president, are legal agents of the company, and their decisions and actions can have a major legal impact on the entire company. Overt acts, failure to act, or neglect of legal obligations can subject the company to a variety of charges, investigations, and costly fines.

Every supervisor should be familiar with the basic requirements of the following laws and the company's policies for compliance.

Fair Labor Standards Act

This law is primarily concerned with minimum rates of pay, overtime pay, child labor, time records, executive exemptions, and other related requirements.

Equal Pay Act of 1963, as Amended

This law states that an employer must pay male and female employees equally if both are performing work which requires equal skill, effort, and responsibility, and which is performed under similar working conditions.

Title VII of the Civil Rights Act of 1964, as Amended

This law forbids an employer from discriminating on the basis of race, color, religion, sex, or national orign in any aspect of employment—hiring, firing, promotions, transfer, benefits, and terms and conditions of employment.

Age Discrimination in Employment Act of 1967 (Amended in 1978)

This states that an employer cannot discriminate on the basis of age in any aspect of employment—hiring, firing, promotion, transfer, benefits, and terms and conditions of employment. This particularly applies to employees between the ages of 40 and 70.

Occupational Safety and Health Act

This law sets forth specific requirements regarding the physical conditions under which employees are permitted to work. It is concerned with the construction of the building housing the job; rest room and water facilities; chemical, mechanical, electrical, and other types of potential hazards; the width of stairways; the height of stacked materials; and a multitude of other factors affecting the general health and safety of employees on the job.

In addition to these laws, many companies and supervisors must be concerned with the union contracts that contain specific provisions supported by local and federal law.

Many companies are operating with voluntary or government-imposed affirmative action guides and quotas. These generally require that equal job opportunities be given to blacks, veterans, the handicapped, and to women. Supervisors should be aware of company goals and requirements related to affirmative action, because they are expected to implement these policies in their particular area of responsibility.

Although these are only a few examples, they are sufficient to show the vital concern supervisors must have for legal compliance. Most companies have written statements of policy pledging strict conformity with all laws. The company often adds the statement that legal compliance must be achieved, but that at the same time, the quality of human resources and of all products and services must also be improved.

High Risk and Added Requirements

It is acknowledged that people-related decisions by supervisors at every level often entail high risks in employee relations and legal compliance. The risk of costly mistakes can be minimized by guaranteeing that every supervisor thoroughly understands the requirements of these laws and the company policies that specify how they are to be observed.

Supervisors must also be increasingly concerned with documentation, or keeping a written record of all the details of every decision concerning an applicant, employee, or former employee. Decisions regarding such considerations as employment, job placement, work assignment, promotion, transfer, pay change, and discharge may be challenged by the employee directly, or by making charges to a shop steward or to an outside government agency. Supervisors are unlikely to remember, at some later date, all the reasons behind these decisions. Therefore, it is essential that supervisors take care to create and retain sufficient written records to justify and defend every decision.

Supervisors must be especially careful to guarantee that all employees receive equal treatment and consideration in situations that relate to legal compliance. Policies must be interpreted and administered with equity for every category of employee, regardless of sex, age, or race. The criteria used for the evaluation of pay increases, promotions, and discharges must be standardized. Job requirements, rewards, and penalties must be administered without discrimination.

Restraint and Controls of Supervisory Action

These requirements force companies to put more restraints on supervisory action, so that decisions and actions often must be checked beforehand with higher management or with legal counsel, or both. As a result, the supervisor's freedom of action is restricted, and *hir* finds it difficult to make many final decisions. Companies and supervisors must now adjust to operating profitably in a restricted, legalistic, and overly documented system.

Compliance makes it virtually mandatory for supervisors to utilize all the tools and skills of professional management. They must be skilled in every area of administrative responsibility: position descriptions, job-performance reviews, compensation, benefit administration, communications, career planning, human resource planning, training and development, and a variety of other management skills that provide for a structured, objective personnel framework. The utilization of an overall system provides a more dependable basis for making nondiscriminatory decisions.

Personal Responsibility for Legal Compliance

Although the company will assume considerable initiative and responsibility for posting legally required notices and providing legal guidelines, individual supervisors should make it a point of keeping abreast with these matters. Disrupted employee relations or legal problems created by the supervisor can have a negative impact on *hirs* career. For example, one nationwide company has stated: "Government regulations, employee relations, and affirmative action are so vital to the bottom-line success of this company that managers will be evaluated, compensated, and promoted based partially on how well objectives are achieved in these areas."

In addition to being concerned with efficiency, productivity, and basic human relations, supervisors must also be vitally involved in carrying out their legal responsibilities. Most of the guides and recommendations which will be provided in this book must be administered within the framework of government regulations and specifically related company policy. These provisions place restraints on supervisory action, necessitate additional record keeping, and are often considered a hindrance to supervisory activity, but in the final analysis, they can help guarantee equity in all human activity in the workplace and thereby bring about a stronger, more cohesive team effort on the part of the employees.

The responsibility for controlling and directing human lives is the most sacred trust of leadership.

2

Leadership for Goal Achievement

THE ability to influence PEOPLE and direct their energies toward desirable goal achievement is the most significant factor in the success of people and enterprises. How high an individual rises on the corporate ladder will depend on *hirs* effectiveness in leading others toward established goals. No business can achieve competitive superiority without leadership superiority.

In the final analysis, the only real advantage one organization has over another in a competitive economy where each can buy essentially the same products and machinery is the quality of management and of its human resources. Leadership decisions determine who is employed, how they are trained, what supervision they are given, and how well they perform on the job. Leadership decisions determine whether the company will grow, what products or services it will offer, and what direction it will take. In truth, the most vital factor in every business and industrial enterprise is the caliber of its management leadership.

Leadership Can Be Exciting

Although leadership carries a heavy burden of responsibility, it can be exciting and rewarding. It offers the stimulation of command, organization, and accomplishment; the sense of game participation; and the satisfaction of winning that some people experience in sports. The more leaders enjoy it, the more time, attention, and resourcefulness they will devote to it. A keen anticipation of excitement, opportunity, and all the human compensations which come with quarterbacking the team increase immeasurably their chances of becoming real "pros" in the big leagues of management.

Leadership can be a completely stimulating activity. For example, consider the young man in his late thirties who was one of the principal heirs to a multimillion-dollar business. From a financial standpoint, it was not necessary that he work; however, he enjoyed the stimulation of decision making and sought the satisfaction of accomplishment. His associates marveled at his devotion to the almost endless number of business and civic projects to which he applied his seemingly limitless resources of time and energy. He was a successful leader by every criterion, and much of his accomplishment was attributable to his enthusiastic attitude toward every activity he undertook.

What is leadership and how can it be developed? In *Twelfth Night*, Shakespeare said that "some are born great, some achieve greatness, and some have greatness thrust upon them." Since the chance that greatness will be thrust upon most of us is remote, those who seek to achieve greatness—or leadership—must identify the qualities of leadership and then devote maximum attention to improving the skills necessary for the application of those leadership qualities.

Leadership is largely a rational process which becomes the foundation for subsequent action. Popularity is not its chief end: Leadership concentrates on effective relationships with others and maintains their respect, but is at all times oriented toward purposeful forward movement and achievement.

Recognizing Leadership

Leadership can be measured by the amount of influence one individual has over the behavior or job performance of others. If this influence is significant, the leadership is effective. If the influence is slight, then there is almost no leadership—the supervisor has failed to influence others sufficiently. On the other hand, the successful leader is able to bring sufficient influence to bear on the activities of others to move them toward the desired results.

It is obvious that the supervisor or business leader cannot hope to become successful without the attributes of leadership. The individual who emerges from the group to a position as first-line supervisor and continues up the ladder to top executive responsibility is the one who has learned how to be an effective leader and how to extend *hirs* influence to an ever-increasing number of people.

The Many Forms of Leadership

Concepts of successful leadership have changed rapidly in recent years. In the era of rugged individualism and authoritarianism, leadership consisted of physical strength and a show of force. Today, broader education, labor unions, government regulations, improved standards of living, and the concept of individual dignity demand enlightened techniques and relationships.

Effective leaders must utilize today's rules—the old ways not only are ineffective but often result in negative reactions. The modern leader must operate from a solid foundation of knowledge, usually based on formal education, company-initiated programs, and techniques founded on successful experience. *Hir* must lead through persuasion, through example, and through services rendered.

Historically, great leaders have come in assorted sizes and shapes. Some exerted leadership through political position, some through mental brilliance, some through creativity, and still others through effective organization. Yet they all shared certain qualities which can be identified and used for developing effective leadership in business and industry.

During World War II, when our nation was confronted with the need for thousands of leaders in both industry and the armed services, it was discovered that no one knew either what leadership consisted of or how to identify potential leaders. Since no criteria had been established, it was impossible to select potential leaders or to develop an effective training program for them.

Experiments revealed that leaders emerge when there are problems to be solved. In the absence of problems, people remain an undirected mass; but when difficulties arise, they frequently accept the leadership of someone who can offer them acceptable solutions.

The common mental picture of leadership is that of a great orator speaking before a crowd, or a corporation president at the head of a conference table. However, supervisors who talk over the roar of machines as they explain a change of production schedule are leaders in their own right. Regardless of the circumstances in which it occurs, leadership denotes dynamic action, movement, activity, organization, purpose, goals, and human resourcefulness. Leadership functions best when it is initiating action and when it is maintaining order and direction.

The Action Functions of Leadership

The need for leadership and its principal characteristics can best be understood by examining its functions and goals.

Leadership renders a service. This is the most significant single statement that can be made about leadership. No leadership is exercised when employees are serving supervisors—it only begins to function when the supervisor begins to serve the employees by making *hirs* superior knowledge available to them, increasing motivation, and creating favorable attitudes toward the job. The quantity and quality of results should increase as a direct consequence of this service. The supervisor moves individuals toward fulfillment of their maximum potential, thus increasing their value to themselves and to the enterprise. A leader thus multiplies the contribution of every individual under *hirs* jurisdiction.

Leadership should serve the interests of the total activity as well as those of the individual. Managers who become outstanding leaders are those who put their knowledge and skills at the disposal of their employees. People are willing to follow a leader who helps them achieve mutually beneficial goals.

Leadership makes decisions. Movement and progress are initiated and continued through a series of decisions. Indecisiveness results in no movement—only in waiting for someone who is capable of making the right decision and is willing to do so.

The sales promotion department of a large company was beset by constant employee turnover and internal dissatisfaction. During an exit interview, one employee revealed that the principal source of dissatisfaction was that the department head was not a satisfactory decision maker. Because he delayed making most decisions until the last possible moment, he put everyone in the department under strain and made it almost impossible to produce satisfactory work.

An important function of everyone who supervises is the process of decision making to meet both individual and project needs. This must not be reckless, but must entail careful evaluation of the facts.

The leader practices successful techniques of decision making in order to keep resources concentrated on the task at hand and to maintain satisfactory progress of the entire project.

Leadership elicits response. The very nature of modern leadership requires persuasion. The environment in which leadership is forced to operate, even in the company framework, depends on people who are capable of persuading other people, rather than issuing edicts or threats.

Sufficient human energy will be applied to a task only by those who respond willingly. This will happen only when a supervisor has been able to convince them of the advantages of their response. An important function of leadership, then, is to communicate to others sufficient understanding to elicit this response.

For example, the industrial supervisor who seeks to promote safety must be prepared with facts, figures, reasons, and a conviction that safety is essential. Then the supervisor must get others to see the importance of safety procedures and equipment, in order to gain their willing participation. Leadership functions only when it gives others sufficient understanding of the task at hand to motivate them to accomplish that task.

Leadership achieves results. The criterion for good leadership is whether it achieves the desired result. For all practical purposes, leadership is guiding human energy in a definite direction for a specific purpose. Leadership that does not succeed at this is like a ship that does not deliver its passengers and cargo safely into port—it has rendered a disservice because it has consumed resources without subsequent benefit.

Great movements in history—and successful companies—have aimed their arrows at great targets. But it was not aiming or shooting the arrow that left the mark; it was hitting the target. Supervisors today leave their mark by hitting their targets with results.

Leadership is a willingness to be different. Leaders are ordinary human beings who excel through a willingness to practice harder and longer, master their skills more thoroughly, and engage in those activities which achieve goals. This often involves a different level of discipline and of performance from that practiced by nonleaders.

Profile of the Effective Leader

The following list of activities is not a stereotype or a rigid mold into which effective leaders must fit—it is a set of guidelines for those who seek to enlarge the scope of their own contribution and influence.

Leaders maintain respect. It has been asked many times and debated at many levels: What should the relationship be between the supervisor and the supervised? Either overfamiliarity or detachment can be detrimental to the group's mutual aims. The appropriate relationship can be summarized in one word—respect. Leaders must respect the individuality, the dignity, and the needs of everyone in the group. They must deserve and receive the respect of others because of what they are and what they do. Unless leaders have this respect, their attempts to lead will be disregarded. The instinct, the impulse to turn toward another person for direction begins with confidence, builds on respect, and eventually becomes a willingness to follow. The supervisor who expects to lead must create the proper relationship with the group and retain their acceptance of the people in the group in order to gain their acceptance of *hirs* leadership.

Leaders work effectively with people. Working with people is leadership in action. Human resources are the principal asset of leaders, and it must therefore follow that their own contribution to the group effort will be dependent on their success in utilizing those resources.

Effective leadership must be based on identification and skillful implementation of all the established principles of good human relationships, beginning with a knowledge of the fundamentals of psychology and proceeding to a blueprint for effective team utilization. It is at the same time a recognition that everyone is an individual and must be dealt with as an individual, an identification of the response or job performance required for results, and a willingness to exert the appropriate influence in order to bring about this type of job behavior.

Effective relationships with others involve the use of facts and a rational approach. But they must also go the extra mile—which is often the most decisive one—and make maximum use of subjective appeal. This type of appeal involves an understanding of ourselves in order to elicit the desired reactions in others. It is generally recognized that response to a sales appeal is based more on a subconscious emotional reaction than on a conscious rational process. It follows that most successful leaders have learned to practice the art of subjective appeal. Just as the advertiser knows the appeal of status, acceptance, and belonging, so must the production or office supervisor learn that emotional appeal can be used beneficially in motivating people.

Leaders are responsive to the needs and desires of others. Leaders must be sufficiently responsive to both the immediate and the long-range needs and desires of others. They cannot be all things to all people, but neither can they lead in a free society without being sensitive to the desires of those who are expected to follow.

Leaders are knowledgeable. Leadership hinges on knowing a great deal about a subject and being able to supply the answers needed by one's employees, whose willingness to follow depends on the leader's ability to supply answers—and answers will be forthcoming only if the leader functions from a base of expert knowledge. The leader must understand the total situation: its past, present, and future; how it affects others; and how it is affected by other influences. *Hir* must command broad general information, know the details of systems and of procedures, and understand the techniques involved in the business enterprise.

Leaders possess superior motivation. From the standpoint of achievement, knowledge and ability are of no value until they are galvanized by motivation. Leaders should have an intense desire to get things done and to involve others in this activity. They must recognize that they cannot motivate others until they are personally convinced and stimulated into action. Motivation not only sets energy into motion but is responsible for keeping it moving, and it should be able to bring everyone else to the same point of energetic action.

Leaders know how to motivate others on the basis of self-interest. Likewise, leaders can increase their own motivation by identifying and enlarging on those things that are to *their* self-interest as well. Leaders who are not highly motivated themselves are not likely to motivate others. Since self-motivation is indispensable to success, leaders who want to accomplish results through other people must recognize that people's desire to contribute is directly related to their conception of how this contribution will benefit them.

Leaders exhibit confidence and enthusiasm. These qualities are closely identified with the essentials of leadership. Enthusiasm is contagious. It spreads to all those within its sphere of influence. However, it cannot be spread unless it is first possessed by the leader.

Many managers who seem to be following all the rules of effective leadership fail to reach their maximum potential because they do not possess—or have been unable to transfer—the qualities of enthusiasm and confidence. These qualities inspire other people to work with more dedication, hold on a little longer, and have more respect for the one who leads them, and these factors often mean the difference between success and failure.

Leaders utilize every resource. The automobile that does not use the energy potential of every ounce of fuel has wasted power, reduced efficiency, increased operating costs, and slowed forward progress. Similarly, the leader who accomplishes most and moves fastest is the one who recognizes and utilizes every available resource. Those who fail to do so not only impede progress but also waste potential— people, machines, money, goodwill, organization, public relations. The superior leader recognizes the contribution each resource can make and then skillfully weaves them all into a smoothly functioning pattern that moves toward goal achievement.

Leaders capitalize on the organizational environment and the leadership of others. Part of the potential available to individual leaders is the organizational environment in which they work and the leadership of others who can contribute to their accomplishment. They must determine exactly where their duties and responsibilities fit into the larger organizational structure—the people who supervise them, those on their own level, and those they supervise. A clear understanding of this function reveals what their responsibilities are—as well as what is beyond their jurisdiction—and gives them an opportunity to improve their working relationship with people on all levels of the organization.

The effective leader utilizes the leadership potential of other leaders. *Hir* learns from them, profits from their mistakes, and enlarges on their successes in order to move forward in *hirs* own area of concern. *Hir* does this by working within the acceptable framework of company organization and proper human relationships.

Leadership, then, has many attributes and qualifications. In addition to those already mentioned, other important aspects include reliability, ambition, judgment, moral courage, competitive spirit, the will to win, poise, and a willingness to work longer and harder than most followers.

Guides to the Practice of Leadership

The practice of leadership involves taking certain identifiable steps which, if performed skillfully, will result in maximum leadership influence and goal achievement. If these guidelines are disregarded, the results will not reach desired levels. The late Chester I. Barnard, former president of the New Jersey Bell Telephone Company and an outstanding thinker on management, suggested the following four factors in leadership behavior:

1. The determination of objectives.
2. The manipulation of means.
3. The instrumentality of action.
4. The stimulation of coordinated action.

The ten-step guide of leadership achievement which follows embodies these factors. This guide can be applied to most activities where the leader must utilize human resources to get the job done:

1. *Establish goals.* Activity has no value until the reason for it has been identified. Leadership implies movement in some direction— but toward what destination? The first step is to determine the desired result. This could mean getting $100,000 in orders for the sales team, meeting a production quota for the assembly line, or winning the pennant for a major league ball club. In each case, planning, appropriate use of resources, and follow-through cannot be completed until the goal has been clearly identified. Once this has been done, everything else should focus on what is necessary to accomplish the required end.

2. *Communicate understanding of goals.* Once the leader has a clear understanding of the goal, *hir* must use adequate means to communicate this understanding to the people who will help *hir* achieve the desired result. This could entail a simple explanation or an elaborately planned meeting and a lengthy presentation. In any case, the leader must take account of the fact that others' interest and responses are directly related to their understanding of the goal.

3. *Justify the effort and response requested.* After the goal is understood, its achievement requires response and effort from the group. This response may not be forthcoming without special effort by the leader. *Hir* must carefully gauge the amount of effort which will be needed, establish a clear picture of the job performance necessary, and set an appropriately devised program into motion, making certain to keep employees informed of the reasons for the goal and the potential benefits to those involved in the project. Success by its very nature hinges on the reaction of both the individual and the team. It is therefore a leadership responsibility to justify this response and bring it to bear effectively on the situation.

4. *Provide a roadmap to the goals.* Identifying and understanding the goals provide only the foundation for their achievement. Leadership must furnish the roadmap which indicates the proper paths to follow, the correct turns to take, and practical steps each person

can take to accomplish the company objectives. This roadmap must offer all the information necessary for progress, and to a degree that minimizes uncertainties, delays, and distractions.

5. *Set resources into motion.* Battles have been lost, production schedules missed, and golden opportunities wasted because of inertia. Successful leadership recognizes that resources must be set into motion in the correct direction—things must be made to happen, effective teams must be organized, and initiative must be provided.

6. *Keep oriented toward the goal.* Undirected energy will fail to reach the target. When resources have been set into motion, the leader is responsible for keeping them oriented toward achievement of the desired results.

7. *Provide answers and set the example.* The best way to show people where to go is to lead them. The best way to get an enthusiastic response is to be enthusiastic. The best way to provide answers is to exert the effort necessary to find the answers. People are willing to follow the leader only when *hir* shows the desire to lead them toward their goal.

8. *Evaluate and improve all activities.* When a ship crosses the ocean, it has a destination. But its speed, position, course, and progress must be evaluated and adjusted often during the crossing to make certain it will reach the desired port. Human activity, too, seldom arrives at its goal without periodic appraisal of progress and adjustment of direction. The leader's responsibility is to provide this appraisal and determine what adjustments must be made.

9. *Recognize and commend progress.* People need to know how they are getting along and what progress they are making. The leader's responsibility is not so much to find fault as to guide *hirs* human and material resources toward the desired goal. Often, the most effective way to speed up what is being done it to give recognition and commendation to those who deserve it, and thus spur them to greater effort.

10. *Reward goal achievement appropriately.* Only the short sighted leader fails to reward those who have contributed to the achievement of the goal. Proper rewards are the best assurance of future response and achievement. These rewards may be monetary or material, but of equal importance are ego satisfaction and recognition of individual contribution. The individual who gives this type of recognition acquires a reputation as a good leader, increases his chances of success for *hirs* current project, and builds a sound foundation for future achievement.

Keys to Improved Leadership

An essential characteristic of leadership is a striving for constant improvement. It follows that leaders themselves must constantly try to increase their own contribution. This does not occur by accident, but must be the result of a deliberate and carefully planned approach. Experience has shown that when leaders improve their knowledge and skills by following the rules, they increase their total contribution potential.

Be willing to accept additional leadership. A department head in a large general office was asked to assume responsibility for an additional segment of the work. Her reaction was that she didn't want it: She felt that she already had too much to look after, and that she couldn't take on additional work because she didn't have enough people or equipment to do it. What she failed to recognize was that if she agreed to do more work, the company expected to provide the necessary people and equipment. Yet this same woman was dissatisfied with her progress and salary.

Leaders who rise rapidly to higher positions of responsibility have one trait in common—a willingness to accept additional responsibility. Too many people make excuses for themselves by saying that they have too much to do already, that it will be too much trouble, or that is someone else's job. The successful leader recognizes that the only way to make a greater contribution is to accept greater leadership and work responsibility and, of course, to discharge that responsibility efficiently.

Surround yourself with capable people. All successful leaders realize somewhere along the way that they cannot handle all the details of their work themselves. The wise ones choose capable people to help get the job done. The abilities of these people do not detract from the leader's role; they contribute to it. And as their contributions increase, the leader reaches higher levels of accomplishment.

Be dissatisfied. The fatal blow to progress is self-satisfaction. When leaders become smug about what they have accomplished, it is almost certain that they will make no further progress. Most executives look for leaders who are dissatisfied in their present positions in the hope that this dissatisfaction will bring about continuing improvement and growth.

After discussion, it was decided not to promote a line executive to the position of branch manager because he was too satisfied to bring sufficient drive to the job. The man was a college graduate, had a brilliant mind, possessed excellent ability, and was capable of accomplishing almost any goal. He was in his early forties, his children had finished college, and his wife had an excellent job. He was able to meet his financial responsibilities at his present salary level and could cope with the demands of his job with a minimum of exertion. He missed the promotion because he lacked sufficient ambition to be entrusted with more important responsibilities. Had he been dissatisfied with his present salary, with the results in his department, and with his present level of responsibility, he would have been a more aggressive leader and a prime candidate for promotion.

Put first things first. An effective leader has to have a sense of values that may be different from that of the employee. *Hir* must be able to give top priority to the most essential matters and not get sidetracked by details that will prevent *hir* from achieving the really important goals.

Most individuals find the time and the resources for the things they consider most important—whether it be fishing, golf, or professional improvements on the job. They do not necessarily have to choose between professional responsibilities and personal interests, but in most cases they must ask themselves bluntly which one will give them the greatest reward. They should recognize that their accomplishments can be almost limitless if they are willing to establish a system of priorities in their personal and professional lives.

Develop people. It is a basic human desire to want to improve, to make more money, and to become more professional in every activity. Some people have a capacity for self-motivation and can move forward to some degree by themselves. However, leaders need to recognize that one of their responsibilities is to accelerate the development of other people through training, example, and whatever other methods can do the job. The employee will be grateful for the assistance and will respond with respect and appreciation.

Design a blueprint for growth and stick to it. A contractor does not build a house without a blueprint. However, after the blueprint has been approved, *hir* must follow it unless there is sufficient reason for change, in which case new plans must be drawn. Leadership does not suddenly emerge from nowhere; it grows step by step. The blueprint should provide for this orderly development of leadership qualities.

Leadership and Executive Growth

John A. Patton said: "Ninety-nine percent of the people in this world want to be told what to do. Be in the other one percent." For those who have what it takes to be in the 1 percent group, the rewards are great in human satisfaction and material compensation. But this exclusive club is composed only of the ambitious, the dedicated, and those who are willing to follow the roadmap that leads to effective human leadership.

The opportunity to lead, to shape the lives of others, to provide an authentic service to people and enterprises, can be an experience equal in excitement and satisfaction to that offered by any sport or hobby. Take a new look at your leadership opportunity, plot a fresh and creative approach to it, elicit the mental and physical resources of your people, and your future can be one of unlimited possibilities.

*Getting work done through others in-
volves special tools and skills that must
be understood and mastered if results
are to be achieved.*

3

Mastering the Skills of Leading People

FAILURES in human management stem principally from the failure to recognize and to master the essential tools by which people are influenced. It is in this area that the woods are full of "born experts" who find it easy to lead others. These pseudoexperts don't worry about tools or fancy guides. They close their eyes, blast away, and expect results to be harmonious and successful.

The beginning of wisdom for sincere supervisors comes with an awareness that they cannot practice their trade without having some expertise in the use of its tools. Once they realize this, they should try to identify the essential tools, and then master them. They are never satisfied, but constantly strive for greater skill.

A professional basketball player was asked why he continued to practice so long and diligently, although he was already considered the best in the game. He replied, "I practice because if I don't sooner or later I'll run up against someone who does, and then he'll beat me."

Craftsmen and Leaders Need Tools

A carpenter cannot build a house without certain tools. Hir needs a hammer, a level, a saw, a wood plane, and a variety of other implements. But the mere possession of a complete set of tools does not make a skilled carpenter. Hir must understand the exact purpose and use of each, and hir must practice using them until hir can handle them with the finesse and skill of a craftsperson. Hir learns to work with wood and other materials. Hir comes to realize that not all kinds of wood can be sawed and nailed in the same manner. Hir learns that each kind of material is best suited for a particular purpose. Hir learns when to nail and when to glue, when to brace, and how much stress each piece of lumber will take. Then hir fits each piece together in the right sequence and erects a structure, thereby confirming hirs mastery of the materials and tools of hirs trade.

The supervisor is also a craftsperson who must possess certain tools for dealing with people, and hir must develop proficiency in the use of these tools. Hir cannot hope to mesh people into a team without mastery of the skills needed to accomplish this purpose.

Key Human Factors in Supervision

The carpenter recognizes that certain factors must be dealt with during the construction process. Problems that require alteration, adjustment, and reinforcement must be faced and overcome. The supervisor, too, must be aware of the peculiarities of the problems hir will be facing. The following list constitutes some of these potential problem areas.

Individual and group differences. Just as the carpenter learns to work with each material according to its peculiar characteristics, so the supervisor must learn to work with variations in human nature that affect training, work assignments, adjustments to a given situation, and the appropriate type of supervision. There might be some variations in the way a younger or older person should be supervised, and special considerations should be made for handling the unique problems of each.

Supervisors should recognize the differences inherent in different individuals and groups and adjust their techniques accordingly. They should remember that they can operate within a certain human relations framework, but that they must develop the tools to deal with variations and still maintain the smooth functioning of the team.

Emotional behavior. This is probably the most difficult human problem the supervisor has to deal with. Fortunately, it does not occur overtly too often, but when it does, it presents a real challenge. Emotional behavior is often unpredictable, has little or no logical basis, and may be unrelated to on-the-job factors. It may stem from family-related conflicts, economic problems, or poor physical or mental health. It often builds up, unnoticed, until all at once it explodes. When the explosion or crisis is over, the individual often regrets what has happened—but by this time hir may have "told off" the supervisor and resigned.

Employee attitudes. Some people are a joy to work with; others try the souls of supervisors. The difference can usually be traced to attitudes. Some people cooperate willingly; others almost dare the supervisor to win their cooperation. Attitudes affect morale, training, group harmony, the number of supervisory problems to be solved, and the final result. The supervisor faces hirs severest test as hir attempts to change a negative attitude to one of willing cooperation.

The influences of heredity and environment. Since the time of Plato, philosophers and psychologists have argued whether heredity or environment has a greater effect on personality, ability, and behavior. No attempt is made here to answer this eternal question. Our premise is that people are what they are as a result of both heredity and acquired experience. This means that certain things can seldom be altered and that it is often a waste of effort to try. It also means that each person's knowledge, built-in reactions, and capacity for productive work or negative influence stem from hirs own experience. Since experience is composed of many environmental factors, their influence must be recognized. The supervisor logically seeks to understand those with whom hir must cope, recognizing each individual for what hir is and concentrating on influencing the areas that can be changed.

Personality influence. Personality must be defined not in isolation but rather as it touches other people's lives. It includes appearance, speech, attitudes, and total impact on others. The employee's personality has a significant effect on hirs job adjustments and on whether hir will fit harmoniously into the group. It is especially important when the job brings hir in contact with the public and when hir is being considered for supervisory responsibility. Personality is difficult to change, although some external factors can be altered.

Certainly the supervisor can gradually influence personality over a long period, but there is seldom a dramatic change.

Coping with failure and frustration. When individuals are confronted with problems to which they cannot find solutions, the result is often frustration and internal conflict. Most people keep coming back for another try, but for some, prolonged frustration often results in conflict with others. Although conflicts cannot always be resolved to the satisfaction of the employee, frustrations that interfere with job performance can often be prevented or eliminated.

Fairness and the understanding of fairness. The problem of fairness with employees can be one of the most bothersome faced by the supervisor. Simply being fair in dealing with people is not enough. The supervisor must lean over backward to demonstrate to everyone that hir is impartial.

In the bookkeeping department of a bank, three new women reported for work the same morning. Two of them caught on quickly and required only minor assistance from the male supervisor. However, the third woman was not as familiar with the procedures, and required considerable attention from the supervisor during the first few days. Because this need was not made clear to the rest of the group, it was not too surprising that on the second day, one of the older employees in the department was heard to say: "Well, it looks like the boss has a new girlfriend, but I don't understand what he sees in her."

The desire to contribute. It is generally agreed that in most instances, desire has as much influence on job results as does ability. Although this is an intangible factor, it is the responsibility of the supervisor not only to provide the work that is to be done but also to influence the employee to *want* to do it. The supervisor can supply certain guides and incentives, but the crucial factor is individual response.

Supervisor–employee relationship. What should be the personal relationship of supervisor and supervised, not only on but off the job? This problem has been the undoing of many supervisors. Some have leaned too far toward being "one of the group," while others have erred in the opposite direction of aloofness, and have lost rapport with the group.

Employees have been heard to say, "I don't want to be a supervisor and have everyone hate me." Supervisors confess, "I simply can't get them to do what I ask. I guess it's my own fault, because we've been so close." Other supervisors might try to stage a popularity contest to get employees to like them.

Supervisors should do nothing that would obligate them to any employee, nor should they permit an employee to become obligated to them. Favors on or off the job which are clearly beyond the boundaries of the employer-employee relationship may make it difficult for a supervisor to maintain the respect of an employee. Lending or borrowing money may result in a strained relationship, especially if the money is not repaid as agreed. If supervisors spend too much time with one of their employees on or off the job, they may be subject to criticism, but if they bend over backward to avoid showing favoritism, they may be unfair to this particular individual.

This is a difficult task, but one that must be mastered by every supervisor. Obviously the size of the group, its makeup (does it include both sexes?), and other environmental factors affect the handling of this particular problem.

Challenges of human efficiency. How efficient are you? How efficient are other people? "Efficiency" is the term applied to the relationship of input to output. Human efficiency cannot be measured by the same precise standards as machines, but, at the same time, the supervisor must use all available human energy in the most efficient manner.

How fast can an individual be expected to work? It is recognized that only a reasonable amount of pressure can be put on an employee to speed up the work process, but efficiency can be influenced substantially by the methods and organization of the work. Some employees seem to be busy all the time, but accomplish very little; others do not appear to give their jobs undivided attention, yet they have far more to show for their time and efforts.

Tools and Techniques for Solving Human Problems

Many of the human factors that were given special consideration in the previous section as potential human relations problems can also be approached as potential opportunities. Whether they remain problems or become effective tools depends largely on the decisive ingredient of appropriate leadership.

When a carpenter comes face to face with problems in hirs work, hir tries to understand the structure hir is building, examines the materials with which hir has to work, analyzes the problem, and then decides what goals and techniques hir can utilize most effectively. Supervisors go through essentially the same process: they identify the desired goals; evaluate the available resources of people, machines, and materials; anticipate the problems they will be facing; and then try to use the tools and techniques that offer the best potential for achieving the desired results.

It should be emphasized that the term "human resources" does not imply that the individual is a working machine who is in turn working other machines. Rather, the basic concept is always one of an individual with psychological needs to be met and a value equal to that of any other person in the company. But the company's human resources are the corporate assets which most concern the supervisor.

An employee's time is purchased at significant cost to the company. It is a precious commodity, and needs to be used profitably if the individual, the supervisor, and the company are to be rewarded fairly for their time and energy. And the individual deserves both the environment and the leadership that will enable hir to make the best possible use of hirs time and potential.

The following are some of the tools and techniques the supervisor will need to utilize in discharging hirs responsibility to both the individual and the company.

The human equation. Just as the carpenter remains constantly aware of the properties of the materials with which hir must work, so the supervisor must remain constantly aware of the special characteristics of hirs people. These give hir certain fundamental guides and a predictable framework in which to operate.

Increasing knowledge. Training by formal program or personal example enables the supervisor to increase the quantity and quality of hirs department's output. This tool can minimize the waste of time, energy, and materials, and can help the supervisor move the total enterprise forward to improved results.

Motivation. If there is a secret weapon in the supervisor's arsenal, it is that of motivation. All hirs training programs, elaborate plans, sophisticated organization, and good intentions will be worthless unless hir can use this tool effectively. It determines how much will be accomplished and how acceptable the results will be.

Emotional appeal. This tool often sets all work activities into motion. Facts and reasons can be presented, but feeling stimulates the employee to act. It moves from satisfying the employee's purely economic needs to satisfying hirs psychological, self-realization, and ego needs. This extra ingredient accounts for total job-related effort and satisfaction.

Force versus persuasion. The supervisor must be a salesperson—hir must sell hirs people on the idea that they should do certain things. One of hirs primary functions is that of getting people to see and understand what needs to be done and how it should be done. The salesperson sells a product or service by getting the customer to understand its advantages; the supervisor sells a job-related course of action, recognizing that the desired results can be achieved only if the employees apply themselves willingly.

Cause and effect. Many things do not occur on the job that should; other things do occur that should not. In either case, certain causes or influences precede the subsequent action. Control of the causative factor can make certain things happen or keep them from happening. By understanding this control factor, the supervisor can take action that makes the greatest contribution to job-related goals.

Appraisal of contribution. Every activity can be improved, but the only way to determine what needs to be changed is to appraise what is being done. The supervisor does this, not to find fault or to criticize, but to discover areas in which the employee's performance can be improved.

Correction of failures. The supervisor's greatest service to other people is in showing them how to enhance their value to themselves and to the company. In any case, it should be emphasized that correcting failures involves the *job performance* of the individuals, not the individuals themselves. This responsibility is often approached with fear and trembling by the supervisor, but, if skillfully handled, it can give hir one of hirs greatest job satisfactions.

Work-related attitudes. Much of what individuals do, how well they get along with others, and, to a considerable extent, their job-related satisfactions and their value to the company are dependent on attitudes. The attitude of the employee is a responsibility of the supervisor. Hir can mold it, but it must be part of the process of overall training on the job. It can be one of hirs most decisive tools.

Work methods. The carpenter must organize hirs work and know the appropriate sequence of steps to take. Hir cannot put on a roof until hir has erected a frame that will support it. The supervisor, too, must organize hirs tools and hirs methods of getting the work done. Some may be efficient, but others may need to be changed.

Results through communication. Most job-related problems can be solved through adequate understanding. This understanding is based on two-way communication where both supervisor and employee are kept informed of one another's problems and what is expected of each. The use of this tool must be initiated by the supervisor, and hir is accountable for its continuation. But hir must have the cooperation of the employees, who must supply the other half of the needed information

Counseling. Employees often need someone they can turn to, and the person most available is their supervisor. Although the value of counseling is often underrated, it is a tool that offers a special opportunity for the supervisor to be of service to hirs people. The extent to which employees turn to their supervisor for personal assistance is the surest test of the quality of the relationship between them. Counseling requires a highly specialized technique and requires both a delicate touch and self-discipline on the part of the supervisor if it is to serve the best interests of the employees and not interfere with their personal lives.

Organizational framework. Every job-related human activity takes place within a company framework. This framework is normally structured to give each employee the greatest opportunity to make a job contribution and assure specific results. It should constantly aim at a more streamlined and refined organizational structure in order to improve group harmony and efficiency.

Day-to-day conversations. The frequent conversations the supervisor has with each employee often provide the context for the application of the many techniques available. They are used to inform, instruct, guide, correct, and persuade employees. The other management tools lose much of their potential effectiveness in the absence of skillful on-the-job conversation.

Creativity. Humanity's growth, culture, technology, and standard of living are the result of continuing creativity. Supervisors who are themselves creative, and can encourage others to be creative, are often able to develop better work methods, new processes, and new products.

Work standards and goals. Almost every activity has stated or implied standards of quality and quantity. Since these standards comprise the criteria for judging progress and results, they should be fair and they must be thoroughly understood if they are to be achieved.

The Leader and Hirs Tools

It is inconceivable that a supervisor could achieve appropriate goals without using the tools of leadership. Without these tools hir would have almost no effective contact with people and certainly no means of influencing them. But familiarity with the tools and techniques of working with people does not in itself guarantee that an effective, productive team will be built. The tools and techniques of leadership are certainly necessary, but equally important is skill in their use. The following list provides some of the stepping stones to the most effective use of leadership tools.

Self-motivation. Athletes win only in proportion to their willingness to exert extra effort. They cannot be forced to excel; they must want to excel to such a degree that they will develop exceptional skill and performance.

It is possible to force the manual worker to engage in a certain amount and type of muscular motion. But leadership involves mental processes, rational application, and deliberate effort. The leader cannot be forced or threatened into skillful use of the tools of leadership. Just as the baseball pitcher must want to pitch a winning game, so must the leader want to lead successfully. The skills of supervision do not improve by accident. They change for the better only when the supervisor is motivated to apply hirs knowledge and refine hirs skills.

Thoroughness. This is probably the one most important skill that identifies the exceptional leader. Lack of thoroughness leaves a supervisor out on a limb, causes most of hirs errors, resultes in hirs most serious embarrassment, and leads to most of the mishandling of hirs human relations responsibilities.

Like the artist and the scientist, the leader must be concerned with every small detail. An important part of many middle-management development programs, for instance, is to have every participant undertake a research project. This is done to dramatize the process top management must go through in making decisions, including gathering and evaluating every essential detail.

The higher a person rises in management, the less margin hir has for error because the consequences of error are more expensive and affect more people. Hir learns that the best way to prevent error is to be certain that nothing is left to chance, that nothing significant is excluded from consideration, and that careful planning is the basis for all action. When top executives conduct meetings, they should seldom be surprised by any action taken. If they have sampled opinion beforehand, they can anticipate what motions are going to be made and what actions the group will take. When they plan a program, they want it timed and outlined to the last detail, they want everyone informed about what hir is expected to do and what is to be accomplished.

Most of us have worked with the young executive who comes running into our offices about once each day with a proposal for a new project. In most instances, a few questions reveal that the man or woman has not thought the idea through and analyzed the consequences of the proposed action. Truly outstanding executives are usually the most thorough. They not only determine whether the swimming pool is full of water before they jump, but they find out the depth and temperature of the water and all the other details necessary to ensure that they will enjoy the swim and come out safely.

Neophyte supervisors grow in proportion to their ability and willingness to be thorough. Their thoroughness prevents errors that would cause others to lose respect for them and would interfere with relationships. The manager who fails to use this tool consistently and skillfully may be likened to the carpenter who neglects to use a level in the construction of a house: The floor will not be level, the studs will not fit, and the result will be grotesque. The supervisor builds the same type of human relations structure when hir neglects the habitual and skillful use of the tool of thoroughness.

Before taking action, the supervisor or top executive should ask hirself the following questions.

- □ Have I considered every significant detail?
- □ Have I talked with all the people involved or affected?
- □ Has anything been left to chance?
- □ Am I positive that my information is completely correct?
- □ Am I so familiar with the facts, the people, and the consequences of contemplated action that I can predict the outcome?

Thoroughness ought to become as automatic as stopping and looking both ways before stepping into a street. The supervisor should constantly remind hirself that the absence of thoroughness can lead to disaster, but that its skillful use can become a key to leadership success.

Emotional control. Before it is possible to control others effectively and consistently, we must master our own emotions. There are, of course, strong leaders who have been emotionally unstable, but they are rare exceptions; in most instances, such leadership has eventually been disastrous.

One bright young man with two years of college education worked in the stockroom of a large Eastern manufacturer. About every three months this young man asked the personnel director when he could expect to be promoted or given more responsibility. The young man had every qualification for leadership except emotional control. About as often as he inquired about his future, he engaged in a violent argument, and many of these disagreements would have reached the fighting stage if someone else had not stepped in. Would it have been reasonable to recommend this man for supervisory responsiblity? Could he have earned and retained the respect of others? What would have happened the first time an employee crossed him in some way? The obvious answers to these questions explain why this man never became a part of management. He eventually resigned, and the company was not unhappy when he did. It is a sobering fact that a person can spend a working lifetime building a respected reputation for stability; then, with one irresponsible outburst, hir can destroy it in seconds and have to start all over again. Kipling stated it well: "If you can keep you head when all about you are losing theirs. . . ." This is a picture of a business leader—the man or woman who becomes the stabilizer, the supervisor who calms others, whose example of emotional control encourages others to get on with the job.

Emotional control does not mean curbing or eliminating strong feelings and convictions—people must be willing to take a stand and be dedicated to what they believe to be right and what they want to accomplish. It does mean, however, that judgment, facts, and logic should guide their thinking. They cannot let their emotions lead into dealing in personalities and making decisions on the basis of personal likes and dislikes. They must be willing to take and give criticism unemotionally, and they must accept the fact that some criticism of them may be unfair and tactless. But regardless of circumstances, they must have the poise to deal graciously and objectively with other people in light of the particular situation.

The skill with which the manager uses the tools of supervision is affected substantially by hirs objectivity. The energy generated by strong feelings should be directed into constructive rather than destructive channels. Outstanding leaders often have strong feelings, but their success comes only when they have learned to master this energy and guide it in the right direction.

Supervisors should recognize that emotional control is important to their success as leaders of other peoole and that setting the right example for others is half the battle. Remember that the manager who merits respect today is not one who uses a show of force, aggression, or emotional assault. Hir is a calm, persuasive, logical person who can lead others by making skillful use of the tools of leadership.

Tactful relations. Tact can become the supervisor's secret weapon for success—or the lack of it can become hirs undoing. To the casual observer, successful leaders seem to possess a sixth sense for saying and doing the right thing at the right time. They know how to make others feel important, to give them a sense of belonging to the team, and to remove sources of potential conflict before a situation gets out of control.

Supervisors who feel it unnecessary to be tactful usually find themselves in trouble because they can no longer influence other people. Tact is the lubricant that keeps the machinery of human relationships functioning smoothly.

Observing effective executives in action becomes an object lesson in tact. They instinctively use the right words and always sense what needs to be said in any situation. They are extremely sensitive to the feelings and reactions of others, and they guard against saying anything that would upset or offend.

Initiative. What contribution does a carpenter's level make if it is never taken out of the tool chest? Many potentially useful supervisory tools gather dust because the supervisor hasn't the initiative to get acquainted with them. Remember that whatever value the tools of human relations have, they can make no contribution until they are put to use.

The supervisor must have the courage to get the ball rolling. Hir must recognize the problem, decide what needs to be done, and then set about doing it. Indecisiveness or lack of courage to translate decisions into action can be the supervisor's undoing. If the tools hir is now using are not accomplishing the desired results, the supervisor should have the courage to try new ones.

Employees always have someone telling them what to do. Their need for initiative is limited, and they are not as obligated to engage in the mental gymnastics of decision making. However, the supervisor's success is dependent on hirs initiative, and the higher hir goes in management, the truer this becomes.

Mature judgment. Along with the initiative to use the tools of hirs trade, the supervisor must have the judgment to decide which tools will be most effective and to what extent they should be used. An incorrect tool can be more harmful than none at all: Also, the overuse of certain tools can be damaging.

The supervisor needs to exercise mature judgment in the use of hirs tools and understand their exact function. Hir should be aware of what each can and cannot be expected to do. No single tool supplies the productive effort needed to get the job done, and no one tool compensates for the improper use of others. Effective supervision is dependent on the exercise of judgment in using the tools needed at a particular time, with a particular person, to get a specific job done.

Attempting to understand people can be the most frustrating and, at the same time, the most satisfying human challenge.

4

Understanding Human Behavior

IN *Climbing the Executive Ladder,* Kienzle and Dare state that "few things will pay you bigger dividends than the time and trouble you take to understand people. Almost nothing will add more to your stature as an executive and a man. Nothing will give you greater satisfaction or bring you more happiness."

"Not one person in 10,000 ever really tries to understand people," says psychologist Donald Laird. For this reason anyone who does understand people has an almost limitless potential for success. For the past 50 years, top responsibility and top pay have gone to executives who have known how to mold individuals into members of strong productive teams that have helped companies achieve success. Management has recognized that no matter how many technicians and specialists it employs, the talent of greatest value is the leadership that makes everyone else productive.

It is conceivable that during the next 50 years more progress will be made in the field of human understanding than in any other. This statement becomes more reasonable when we remember that very little progress has been made to date in utilizing human potential. It has been estimated that people function at considerably below 40 percent of their mental capacity. If this were stepped up by just 10 percent, the possibilities would be fantastic. And this is precisely the opportunity facing the executive who can come to grips with the human will to produce.

Top producers and top salespeople are not necessarily promoted to positions of supervisory responsibility. Rather, demonstrated ability to get along with people, understand them, and accomplish results through them are of decisive importance.

Clarence Darrow, one of the most famous and successful trial lawyers of this century, insisted that even where laws are concerned, "the most important thing is to make the judge want to decide things your way, then give him a point of law that will give him a reason for doing what you have made him want to do."

Coping with Dramatic Human Change

Supervisors must now cope with an era characterized by rapid transition, impermanence, expanding circles of communication and influence, sudden breaks with the past, and increased government control, along with a shift from the primacy of company influences to the dominance of outside influences. Affluence and increased education have led to greater concern for personal fulfillment, increased emphasis on leisure, a more permissive morality, and a loss of supervisors' authority over employees. Once their primary economic needs have been met through the job, employees seek job satisfaction, recognition, opportunity for growth and promotion, responsibility, a sense of achievement, and use of their full potential. They have the expectation that the job will enrich and satisfy them, as well as sustain them economically.

This new era presents a complex set of challenges to supervisors. They have to understand and lead employees who have new ideas and attitudes, get results from hostile people, and tolerate lifestyles that they may find objectionable. It is in this sometimes frightening and often disconcerting human kaleidoscope that the supervisor must function and achieve results. Yet, out of this changed situation, unique opportunities have emerged for skilled supervisors to make use of the greatly increased potential of brighter, better educated employees.

Human Behavior Can Be Understood

The best way to study people is to look at people themselves. History, literature, psychology, government, industry—everything that has influenced people reveals their nature and patterns of behavior. The first step is to remember that everyone is human. This is obvious, but it needs to be repeated. As part of management, we sometimes forget that the employees think and feel, have their own needs and desires, and cope with failure and disappointment just as we do. They are concerned with the status of the job, whether they are making any progress, and what their wives or husbands and neighbors think about the place where they work.

They are closely linked to the job—often more so than the supervisor—because they may have fewer outside interests. Their job gives them a sense of importance, and through it they hope to discharge their family and community responsibilities. They do not always openly express their feelings and attitudes toward their jobs; in fact, they are often unaware of these feelings themselves. Yet, the job must meet a variety of their needs.

How difficult is it to understand human behavior? Not as difficult as it might seem. The entire history of humanity is the story of what people want and don't want, of what causes favorable and unfavorable reactions, of what elicits their will to produce and what does not. All these things have been recorded in books and in the experiences that others are willing to share with us. Our sole responsibility is to be wise enough to look, to listen, to learn, and to respond.

Find out what an individual wants; supply it, and hir will respond. Find out what things are important to an individual on the job; supply them, and you will have a productive person on your team. The key is for the supervisor and the employee to agree that the same things are important. The following table, developed by the authors of *Improving Individual Productivity* (American Management Associations), shows how foremen and workers rated the important aspects of job satisfaction. Note the disparity of opinion registered here.

The most significant fact about this table is that workers and supervisors rated the first three factors at almost opposite ends of the scale. This can lead to obvious misunderstandings. When employees do not get the type of supervision they want, they become dissatisfied with their job. When supervisors do not get the results they want from employees, they are disappointed with their own performance and with the reaction of the employees.

Experience has indicated that employees generally seek the following tangible and intangible compensations from their jobs.

Job Conditions	Worker Rating	Supervisor Rating
Appreciation for good work	1st	8th
Feeling "in" on things	2nd	10th
Help with personal problems	3rd	9th
Job security	4th	2nd
Good wages	5th	1st
Work that keeps you interested	6th	5th
Possibilities for promotion	7th	3rd
Personal loyalty to workers	8th	6th
Good working conditions	9th	4th
Tactful discipline	10th	7th

Recognition for good work. There is nothing so discouraging as not being appreciated. In the employees' eyes, the supervisor always catches the mistakes but seldom notices the things that are done well.

Recently, a management expert was asked to study morale and working conditions in a plant that produces garden tools. As one shift was changing, he asked a workman how he was getting along. The reply was unenthusiastic. Upon further inquiry, the man revealed his gripes in these words: "You know, I produced 179 hoes today. Two of them were rejected and had to have further work before they would pass inspection. Well, you know what? All I heard from the supervisor was about those measly two bad hoes. Not once did he even hint that I had had a pretty good day and made 177 perfect hoes."

According to one television commercial, we never outgrow our need for milk. The supervisor should recognize that neither do we outgrow our need for recognition. Recognition should be specific— for a particularly good piece of work, for a large sale, for better-than-average results. Don't be afraid to be generous with recognition, but be honest and sincere and give it fairly to those who merit it. Appropriately used, it results in greater production and better morale.

An interesting job. Have you ever heard an employee say that hir wanted a dull, uninteresting job? We spend a large portion of our waking time at work, and we want it to be interesting and satisfying. Many people change jobs just to get away from work that is dull and unchallenging.

Every employee needs to have the interesting aspects of hirs job pointed out. Therefore, not only should the supervisor know more about the job and its relationship to other processes, but hir should make certain the employee is aware of the significance of what hir does. This gives the employee a personal stake in the work, and will ultimately lead to better results.

Early in World War II, a number of bombers performed below standard because they were not assembled properly. Someone came up with the idea that there needed to be a closer link between the aircraft plant worker and the plane crew. In order to accomplish this, a film was made. It began by showing pilots boarding a plane and taking off for the combat zone. Then there were scenes of planes in battle and of planes disabled and returning to their base badly damaged. When this film was shown in aircraft factories, the message was obvious—every screw, every rivet, every foot of wire, every minute detail was important to ensure the safety of the crew and the success of the mission. The improvement in both quality and quantity of work was immediate and substantial.

Proper pay. What is proper pay? The answer is probably different from the point of view of the union leader, the company president, and the employee. Many old-line managers believe that pay can solve all problems connected with production. They say, "Put it in their envelope and forget all this fancy stuff about employee benefits and morale." But would this procedure be successful? Have the highest-paying companies significantly reduced their employee turn-over, guaranteed their production schedules, erased their need for real management leadership, or eliminated the need for under-standing people? The answer is an emphatic *no!*

What, then, is the role of money in increasing job satisfaction? As one manager put it, "Never pay people in money alone." The amount of pay, as well as the basis for it, should be measured against three standards: (1) the contribution value of the job performance; (2) the relationship of the particular job to other jobs in the company that have comparable duties and responsibilities; and (3) the prevailing rate being paid elsewhere in the locality for the same type of work.

The employee must understand the basis of hirs pay, and hir needs the assurance that increases are based on merit and not solely on the personal opinion or whims of the supervisor. Job information surveys often reveal that employees don't understand the basis of their pay, whether it is fair and reasonable, and what they must do to earn more money.

Proper pay represents far more than money; it is an indication of what the company thinks of an employee, the value it places on hirs service. One woman who was being considered for a key executive job said, "When I know what the company intends to pay for the position, I will know what it thinks of the job—whether it is an important job or not."

The employee wants proper pay and is entitled to it. But the successful supervisor pays the employee additional psychic wages, including recognition, praise, proper training, understanding, and respectful leadership.

A climate of understanding. Every human being wants to be understood. The employee's need to be understood is related to hirs sense of security—hirs feeling that the supervisor will at least try to understand hirs problem on and off the job. There should be no psychological barriers between the supervisor and employee; instead, there should be a climate of free and easy communication. The supervisor must be an interested listener, because listening is the most important aspect of understanding.

Opportunity for growth and promotion. The employee wants to feel that hir has the opportunity to make more money and to be promoted to a better job. Company practice with regard to internal promotions, merit increases, and programs of employee development demonstrates these opportunities.

Employees should understand that opportunity and growth can occur within their present jobs as well as through promotion and transfer. Growth on the same job can occur through increased responsibility, more difficult work requiring less supervision, increased pay, increased productivity, and increased personal qualifications for the next step up the ladder. The supervisor should make the employee aware of these growth possibilities, thus enabling hir to experience an overall sense of progress.

The supervisor has a legal responsibility to bring to the attention of the employee those factors that have a direct effect on hirs growth opportunity. Since opportunities for pay increases and promotions are related to the financial health and growth of the company as a whole, employees should be aware that they improve their own prospects by making a greater contribution to the company, thus enabling it to grow and to create greater opportunity for individual career progress.

Job security. Security has been a controversial topic in recent years. Some have accused employees of being more concerned with maintenance of the status quo than with the challenge and opportunity of growth. It is contended that modern workers have sold their birthright for government regulations, union contracts, and company policies that assure their sense of job security.

The employee wants and needs emancipation from fear, from capricious or irrational decisions, and from unjustified action. Hir wants the comfortable feeling that satisfactory work will assure hirs job and the means to provide the necessities of life for hirs family.

It is the company's responsibility to provide maximum job security, consistent with its ability to provide continuing jobs and with the merits of the individual's performance. But company managers resent any attempt by individuals or organizations to use job security as a way of avoiding work or responsibility. Managers believe that security should have a direct relation to the employee's value on the job—that the best employee ought to have the greatest security and the least satisfactory employee deserves the least security. The employee should recognize that what hir can expect from a particular job is related to hirs contribution on the job.

The need to render a service. Many decisions to accept or reject jobs, and to stay or leave, are contingent on the amount of service these jobs render to other people. Although motivation stems largely from concern for self, there is also a significant satisfaction connected with service to others. Other things being equal, the job that gives an employee more opportunity to serve others has more appeal and offers more satisfaction. Teaching, social work, church-related vocations, and many other fields offer opportunities for service to others. But these need not be the only outlets for providing service. The production worker who assembles refrigerators is contributing to the general health of many families; the textile worker provides warmth and comfort to many; the bank employee is important to our economic safety and security; the insurance salesperson affords us a measure of peace of mind. It is up to the supervisor and the company to help each employee see how hirs work benefits others.

A favorable work environment. In what type of environment would you rather spend eight hours of every working day—one that is bright and cheerful or one that is drab and tense? Employees, too, want working conditions that make them look forward to spending time on the job.

The company has the principal ethical and legal responsibility for creating and maintaining favorable working conditions, such as pleasant associates, safe machines, clean rest rooms, comfortable temperatures, appropriate equipment, and reasonable hours. It must also ensure that employees work within an efficient human organizational framework that allows them a certain amount of freedom on their jobs and does not burden them with too many bosses. The working environment is a composite of many factors, most of which are under the company's control. This requires management to pay attention to human relations within the employee group, and to be aware of the qualifications and leadership skills of the supervisor.

It is significant that the most important influence on the working environment is not the physical setting or equipment; rather, it is the type of supervision the employee receives. Surveys have shown that one of the principal reasons people give for resigning from their jobs is dissatisfaction with their supervisors. It is the supervisor who assigns work, indicates how it is to be done, and evaluates job performance. A supervisor can make the employee feel favorable or resentful toward hirs job and the company.

Respect for, and confidence in, the organization. What type of people do you like to associate with—those in whom you have confidence or those you don't trust? What type of company do you prefer to work for—one whose future, whose policies, and whose management you have doubts about, or one that merits your respect? The answers to these questions are obvious: Employees want to be able to respect and have confidence in the company they work for.

Desire to belong. Humans are social by nature. They need acceptance. They want to belong to the club, the church, or the employee group. When they are left out, they are lonely and unhappy. They look to their jobs for the opportunity to be a part of something important. They want to take pride in their jobs, their associates, their supervisors, and their companies. A wise supervisor will welcome the new employee, give hir the feeling of belonging, and then make certain that on-the-job conditions continue to give hir the same feeling.

When company executives are asked what they have done within the past six months to keep their best employees from becoming dissatisfied and leaving, they usually reply that they have given raises to these employees. But the answer should also be more personal. Has the supervisor spoken to the employee person to person, inquired sincerely about hirs family, communicated that the company is pleased to count hir part of the organization and is proud of hir? The individual who is thus recognized is less likely to slacken hirs efforts or to seek employment elsewhere.

All of these sources of satisfaction on the job can vary greatly with individuals. The young person may be more interested in opportunity; the older person, in security; the head of a large family, in money; and the working wife, in the opportunity for self-expression. The particular interest may also vary with economic conditions. During periods of economic depression, job security may be most important, when jobs are plentiful, other factors may be of more concern.

It is the supervisor's responsibility to know what each employee expects from the job. Then, through hirs leadership and hirs interpretation of the job to each individual, the supervisor attempts to make certain that these expectations are realized.

Sources of Job-Related Satisfaction

This is a free country. People are not obliged to work for a particular supervisor or company. In essence, they sell eight hours of their day to a company and expect certain things in return. Since they would most likely receive the same salary from any number of companies, why do they work for one in particular? The answer is that one company provides them with *more* of the things they want on a job.

Thus, the company that can provide its employees with the greatest number of the things they want, and to the greatest degree, will win the employees' allegiance. How are these things provided? Top management controls some of them, but the majority come from the immediate supervisor. The supervisor recognizes good work, gives understanding, influences a feeling of security, recommends pay increases, sets the human climate of the working environment, and generally functions as the link between the employee and the company. In addition, the supervisor is the employee's principal source of information about what the company thinks of the quality of hirs work.

The supervisor's primary function is to direct human energy toward achieving a specific job result. This the supervisor can do only when hir has a thorough understanding of people, their motives, and their reactions to their job environment. Therefore, hir must be accurately informed regarding the total situation and especially the factors that influence a person's contribution on the job.

Employees can be influenced by facts and reasons, but subconscious factors, based on feeling and emotions, also must be recognized and controlled. Although the salesperson sells with facts, the feelings about facts are often more important. It is essential for supervisors to realize that interpretations of facts and the emotional reactions they elicit can be vital influences on the job performance of employees.

Principles of Human Association

We are all more alike than we are different. We have individual characteristics and degrees of needs, but in the final analysis we are similar. There is a common psychological base governing our culture and our sense of values. This varies with different societies and at different times according to the mores of a particular group. However, the decisive influence of biblical teachings on Western civilization's value structure and behavior patterns has accounted for an unusually consistent pattern of thought, stable criteria for judging right from wrong, and a solid base on which to build our guides to human relations.

We make calculated predictions concerning our physical and mathematical environment on the basis of existing norms. An accurate sampling of human reaction reveals predictable patterns which, when charted, usually form a bell-shaped curve. This means that behavior patterns can be anticipated if we know the laws and the predicted reactions. The following examples of psychological laws of human contact illustrate the accuracy and importance of predictability.

Anxiety of the initial contact. In our first contact with something new—an idea, a product, a situation, or a person—we are inclined to be cautious and skeptical. When a new employee reports for work, hir regards the company, the supervisor, and the job with a considerable amount of apprehension. The supervisor can eliminate this uncertainty by making the person feel welcome. William Allen White is credited with saying, "A stranger is a friend I have yet to meet."

When the supervisor suggests a new machine or new procedure and employees are reluctant to accept it, this does not mean that they are stubborn and uncooperative; they are simply exhibiting normal anxiety. It becomes the supervisor's responsibility to eliminate this feeling by carefully explaining the change.

Strong social need and reaction. Most of us want to be with other people, and we want to belong to groups. When a sailor who had been adrift on a life raft for 38 days was finally rescued, he said that what he had missed most was human companionship, and that sheer loneliness had almost killed him.

On one particular job, secretaries seldom stayed longer than six months before resigning. Finally, it was observed that the location of the desk so isolated them that they did not have an opportunity to talk with other people in the office. When the desk was moved to bring the secretary in close contact with others, the problem was solved.

Social need can be an important factor in the productivity of the employee, since improved job performance may be the by-product of acceptance by the work group.

The need for approval. Approval can often be more important than material rewards. The strongest incentives often involve honor, prestige, titles, and other forms of approval. People may stay in jobs that pay less than they could be getting, simply because family and friends express greater approval. For example, a bank clerk's position often carries more prestige and status than that of a service station manager, but not always more money. The prudent supervisor recognizes this strong desire for approval and enables the employee to obtain it through job performance.

The will to win. Some societies are almost completely devoid of competition, and their members placidly accept certain roles in life. Not in America. Here, winning is an important part of life. We want to win at golf, at cards, and on the job. This may stem from the cave dwellers search for food in competition with other cave dwellers, but at that time, survival of the fittest was the name of the game. Today, our competitive instinct is restricted by law. Nevertheless, it is still very much in evidence in almost every phase of our lives. For example, the merchant constantly engages in the game of letting the customer win through special sales. Getting a bargain or a marked-down item makes the customer think that they have gotten more than they paid for.

The company can capitalize on this human quality through the use of incentives, contests, prizes, and activities that encourage competition. And the supervisor must use this competitiveness to stimulate interest and production. However, a word of caution is in order: Excessive competition can be harmful. When one person interferes with the rights of others, then it goes too far.

Satisfaction of physical needs. Much human energy is exerted in satisfying physical needs for food, clothing, shelter, and self-preservation. When employees earned very little, they had little time or energy left for anything except meeting their physical needs. Now, as the result of improved machines, refined techniques, and shorter working hours, other needs are becoming more important.

Resistance to change. We are creatures of habit. We like to go to work at the same time every day, eat lunch at the same time, and perform our jobs in the same way. We resist efforts to make us change. Since this reaction is predictable, the supervisor who wants to transfer an employee or change hirs working conditions must be prepared to overcome resistance.

Response to subconscious forces. Icebergs are seven-eighths submerged, and the same thing frequently seems true of the real reasons for human behavior. It is important to recognize that people often don't know why they react in a particular way. The supervisor needs to be aware that behavior is not always logically explainable. This knowledge should make hir more effective in hirs dealings with people.

No supervisor can be completely effective unless hir recognizes and responds to the basic laws controlling human response. To ignore or contradict these laws can be disastrous; to understand and conscientiously observe them can lead to more effective leadership. Those in leadership positions have the opportunity to guide both the time and the energy of their employees into mutually beneficial channels. Failure to do so results in waste. The more thoroughly the supervisor understands people, the better hirs chances of meeting the challenges of leadership will be.

Leading people is not easy. A man or woman is given a position of leadership because someone has faith in hirs ability to rise to the challenge, deal with difficult problems, and find the right answer most of the time. The exciting game of leadership reserves its greatest compensations for those who face these challenges boldly and emerge as winners.

*Attitude is the key to the employee's loy-
alty, work habits, and job results. Influence attitude and you shape job performance.*

5

Creating Positive
Job Attitudes

ATTITUDE neither causes nor cures all problems, but it does hold
the key to the success of most job-related activity. It controls to a
great extent the effort employees put forth, the care with which
their work is done, and their concern about what is accomplished.

It is doubtful if any other factor exerts as significant an influence
on the supervisor's success or failure. Favorable attitudes can make
hirs job a pleasant and satisfying human experience; unfavorable
ones can stymie supervisory activities. Positive attitudes can eliminate
problems; negative attitudes create them. Attitudes determine
whether a person is a willing, contributing member of the team or
whether hir holds back and pushes in the opposite direction.

Although some work *is* done by people who have unfavorable attitudes, such employees are extremely difficult to lead. Employees
who have negative attitudes toward their supervisors, their companies, and their jobs are curtailing both their chances for success on
their present jobs and their future opportunities for growth. Both
the company and the supervisor have a significant stake in employee
attitudes. Attitude is too critical a factor to be ignored or treated
lightly. Its development and maintenance is the responsibility of the
supervisor, who can have a substantial effect on how it will affect the
work to be done.

Understanding Attitudes

Attitude has been defined as the individual's predisposition to act in a certain way. It is a mental state affecting the employee's interpretation of surrounding stimuli and hirs response to them. It is not always based on the present situation but often on a complex set of circumstances that may have occurred over the individual's entire lifetime. The obvious danger is that attitude often does not make allowance for change. For example, one supervisor held the firm opinion that anyone who wore a bow tie was not to be trusted and that there never was a lazy redhead. Attitudes of this type are obviously going to lead to a number of wrong conclusions and decisions.

Behavior and reactions that are based on obsolete conceptions and that make no allowance for new information are very often wrong. No one can make a proper decision about today's problems without taking into consideration the facts of our present situation. Yet the individual may cling to a fixed attitude because hir finds that it satisfies hirs needs, even though it ignores logic and common sense.

Inflexibility is as foolish as aiming a hunting rifle in one direction when the deer has moved in the opposite direction. This seems ridiculous, but the attitudes of both employees and supervisors in the work environment can be equally absurd. When employees' mental postures are fixed and inflexible, they are difficult to deal with, because logic and facts have little influence on them. If employees are suspicious of their supervisor's intentions, they will probably reject whatever suggestions hir makes, no matter how much it would be to their advantage to accept them.

An attitude is learned; it is not inherited. Infants have no inborn attitudes and no preconceived opinions. It is true that children often exhibit the same attitudes as their parents, but this is the result of learning and environmental influence, not heredity. Hence, attitudes cannot be attributed solely to the circumstance of birth.

Environment is the principal source of attitudes. Parents are the principal influence during a child's formative years, and for this reason similar attitudes may continue from one generation to the next. As the child grows, playmates, teachers, and others outside the family exert an increasing influence, as do communications media such as newspapers and television.

Beginning with the individual's first work experience, hir begins to form attitudes regarding the work, the supervisors, and the company. Some attitudes are carried along to new jobs and become more and more fixed. The lazier a person is mentally, the less logical hirs thinking becomes, the more easily hir is influenced by others, and the more willing hir is to assume their views.

Individual attitudes are greatly influenced by prevailing opinions. Local customs exert a predictable influence, and tribal attitudes become part of the religion or law of the group. The same behavioral pattern can develop in a company.

Ready-made attitudes are often adopted from others. It is surprising how willingly people will accept ready-made attitudes without examining them critically to determine whether they are true. We are cautious about contamination in the food we eat, yet we are careless about our minds, and fail to guard against contamination from many opinions that come our way.

We dislike hand-me-down clothing, but we are willing to adopt worn-out attitudes. When employees base their decisions and reactions on ready-made opinions, they may be jeopardizing their future by failing to use their capacity for independent judgment. The danger is that one strong-willed person in an employee group can transfer hirs negative attitude to the entire group.

Attitudes may be based solely on one dramatic experience. The employee who is humiliated in front of others by a supervisor may assume that all supervisors are unfair. One mouthful of distasteful food doesn't make us swear off eating for the rest of our lives, but one traumatic emotional experience can establish a fixed pattern of reactions in the unthinking person.

Over a period of time, a hierarchy of attitudes develops within a company. These influence the ease with which new policies can be established, and reveal the quality of the relationship between manager and employee. Attitudes often vary from department to department and in different areas of the company.

Attitudes may prevail toward races and national groups, the opposite sex, other employees, and new people; toward company policy and benefits; and toward the supervisor. These often determine whether management's action is interpreted with understanding and cooperation or with suspicion and resistance. Therefore, attitudes have a substantial effect on climate and results.

The significant influence of attitudes on what can be accomplished offers convincing evidence that attitude development and maintenance is too important a responsibility to be ignored or left to chance. Supervisors must remember that attitudes can be influenced and controlled, and the manner in which this is handled is the very foundation on which most other management skills must be built.

Significant Facts Concerning Attitudes

Certain facts about attitudes can be of substantial value in understanding and influencing people. On the basis of this information, it is possible to predict the potential development of certain attitudes and therefore to alter conditions so that detrimental attitudes will not have room to grow.

Attitudes develop quickly. It has been said that for the new employee the first minute on the job is the most important minute and that the first day is the most important day. The new employee is usually uncertain and impressionable. If hir is ignored or left to the chance of influence of an employee who has an ax to grind, hir may quickly develop a negative attitude. Because of the importance of first impressions, every possible step should be taken to ensure that the new employee feels welcome, wanted, and convinced that the company is a good place to work. The supervisor who is warm and friendly and who demonstrates hirs helpfulness and availability will have favorable influence on the attitudes of the newcomer.

Attitudes are long-lasting. Attitudes develop quickly and, once developed, have a relatively permanent effect on patterns of behavior. Attitudes are rigid and extremely difficult to change.

Attitudes are interrelated. If an employee has a very strong attitude toward one phase of hirs job, it probably influences and determines hirs reaction to other phases. If hir considers the supervisor unfair, hir is likely to think the same way about policies, pay, working conditions, benefits, and the company as a whole. If the supervisor refuses to change an employee's vacation schedule, for example, the reaction may be that "he picks on me every opportunity he gets." This is why it is important that the supervisor explain very carefully the reasons for hirs decisions and actions—hir cannot afford to allow the development of pockets of discontent which might spread like a cancer.

Behavior stems from attitudes. Strong feelings are often associated with attitudes. A prejudice is one type of attitude, more often associated with races, religions, or groups of people than with specific individuals. Moods often cause temporary reactions which are based more on momentary emotions than on logical thinking. Although attitudes are consistent and predictable, moods may cause temporary variations in behavior and attitudes.

Individual attitudes differ. Although group attitudes are an important factor in the work environment, those of the individual are the primary concern of the supervisor. People bring with them the prejudices and opinions they developed in an earlier environment or on previous jobs. It is necessary for the supervisor to understand these attitudes in order to work more effectively with hirs group. Because people differ, and their ideas differ too, the supervisor must promote the best possible group attitude while at the same time making allowances for individual differences.

Responsibility for Attitude Development

The supervisor is in the best position to influence the employees' adjustment to the job and, in particular, the formation of their attitudes. This is a responsibility which hir cannot avoid or delegate. Moreover, hir should remember that it can't be handled successfully once a year but requires constant attention. Once supervisors recognize their responsibility for the creation and maintenance of positive attitudes, they must then develop effective practices for dealing with people's attitudes on a continuing basis.

Recognizing attitudes. How do you recognize an attitude when you see one? If we agree that negative attitudes have a significant effect on work, we must acknowledge the need to identify them in their early stages and initiate immediate corrective action where necessary.

When an individual holds a strong opinion, consistently reacts in the same manner, and refuses to change along with changing circumstances, hir is displaying a form of intellectual dishonesty—a refusal or unwillingness to recognize that the situation has changed. This is evidence that an attitude problem might exist.

Many people make no serious attempt to keep their attitudes to themselves. They quite willingly admit: "I don't like the boss and I don't care who knows it." "You can't blame me for being stubborn. I get it honestly from my dad—and he was certainly a fine man." "It's too late in life for me to change my thinking now." "I'm no eager beaver, but I once tried cooperating with the boss and it didn't get me a thing. Never again!" All a supervisor has to do to spot potential attitude problems is merely listen.

Predicting attitudes. Basic to the success of every supervisor is the ability to anticipate employee reaction and job behavior. The same holds true about attitudes. Although there are significant exceptions, the general rule is that an employee's reactions to certain aspects of the job will carry over to other areas. This principle is often applied in making decisions regarding work and benefit changes. Leadership for change is usually channeled through those who are known to be strongly cooperative, because they are likely to come through with favorable reaction to the proposed change. By the same logic, those who are not particularly cooperative will probably react negatively to the proposal, and should not be used to initiate it.

Measuring attitudes. The politician needs to know not only what opinions people have on a specific issue, but also how strongly they feel about it, because both factors affect the way they vote. Accordingly, the supervisor must be concerned with those attitudes that affect the work and morale of the group because they, in turn, affect the quantity and quality of job results. Hir needs to know not only what the attitudes are, but also their strength among employees.

Opinion and morale surveys attempt to discover the existence and strength of attitudes in the employee group. These surveys may be undertaken by company personnel or conducted by an outside firm. Attitude-rating scales can also be used. These often ask the employee to consider a given issue and, on a scale ranging from mild to strong, indicate the point that represents hirs feelings.

The alert supervisor can learn the strength of employee attitudes in yet another way—through casual conversation and interviews. And the use of a properly instituted and supervised suggestion system can also reveal a profile of employee attitudes, and the intensity of people's feelings, since suggestions may be symptoms of attitudes.

Guides for Changing Attitudes

First, we should remember that attitudes are established patterns of thinking and behavior in which individuals feel comfortable and secure. Therefore, they are not likely to change until they see that their needs can be better satisfied in a different way.

Regardless of the supervisor's elaborate care with new people and hirs attention to the present staff, unfavorable attitudes often occur on the job. It then becomes desirable for the supervisor to change them by channeling employee thinking and reaction in a more favorable direction.

Substitute a desirable attitude for an undesirable one. The small child holds tightly to a sharp instrument until a more desirable toy is offered as a substitute. Similarly, the supervisor has little success in asking an employee to give up an idea unless another is offered in its place—one that better serves the needs of the employee.

Interview and motivate. The process of substituting the more desirable attitude is usually handled through interviewing and motivating, by showing the advantage of the new attitude so that the employee will voluntarily relinquish the old one. For example, if an employee objects to having women working in the department, it is up to the supervisor to convince him that this attitude could jeopardize his chances for promotion. The employee can be told that the women's presence may represent a real opportunity for him, as an experienced employee, to assist in their training; thus, by proving that he is capable of dealing effectively with all types of people, he can increase his value to the company.

Seek only a small or gradual change at first. A major change in attitude is often more than the employee is willing to make and more than the supervisor should expect. Instead of asking a man who objects to working with women to devise and carry out an elaborate training program for all the women in his department, he should be asked to help the one woman who works next to him. It should be pointed out that this will increase his standing in the eyes of his associates. Once he experiences success, he may be willing to render the same assistance to others.

Ask for change on a trial basis. It is understandable that people may be reluctant to make permanent changes, but they may appear unreasonable if they refuse even to try something. Once they try a new idea or work method and it doesn't prove "fatal," they often find they really like the change. Although they seldom admit it, immediately, they will indicate their acceptance by their willingness to try the same thing another time.

Show the big picture. Try to understand the situation from the employee's point of view. Often hir has not had the opportunity to see the overall picture and cannot understand how the change will affect hirs job. The supervisor should explain the change and show how it fits into the total picture.

Affect a permanent substitution of the desirable attitude. The purpose of attitude change is to replace an undesirable opinion with a favorable one. When such a change has been accomplished, it should not be neglected but should be maintained. Too many supervisors make the mistake of changing an attitude and then forgetting it; later on, they're surprised when they discover that the attitude has reverted to its original state.

The Supervisor's Own Attitude

The attitude of the supervisor has a significant influence on that of the employee. Whether or not an opinion is expressed orally, it is communicated by everything the supervisor does. To build positive attitudes, supervisors must have positive attitudes themselves. The employees' opinion of the company, their confidence in it, their understanding of its policies, and their predisposition to act in a particular manner is influenced more by the supervisor than by another single factor.

The supervisor develops hirs own attitudes by recognizing what they are and then engaging in the effort necessary to make them what they should be. If hirs attitude is negative or weak in a particular area, hir should decide why, and then take steps to change. Supervisors certainly cannot afford to jeopardize their future with faulty attitudes that affect their own job performance and that of everyone they supervise.

Guides to Influencing and Changing Job Behavior

MANY supervisors who try to understand the reasons for certain reactions by people on the job often reach a state of frustration and give up, convinced that there is neither rhyme nor reason to human behavior. But before they throw in the towel, they ought to recognize that they must understand and influence human behavior on the job if they are to meet their leadership responsibilities. Supervisors will have minimum success in changing job behavior unless they discover its causes; they will have even less success if they attack the end result of the activity rather than the contributing causes.

Why People Behave the Way They Do

It has been stated that whatever an individual does, hir does it for a good reason. Every action or reaction has a cause. This principle can be an important key to success in working effectively with other people.

Consider the case of Harry Baker, bank cashier. The supervisor began to realize that Harry's attendance and job performance were slipping. She mentioned the situation casually, but no improvement resulted. Harry continued to come in late about twice a week; he was out a few days without a satisfactory explanation; he was falling behind in his work; and he was irritable with customers.

Before the supervisor called Harry into the office, she decided to investigate further. She learned that Harry had been with the company for seven years. During this time, his interest had been high, his volume of work had been consistently near the top in the department, he had been punctual and dependable, and he had worked harmoniously with other employees and customers. Additional checking revealed that it was just within the previous five weeks that Harry had changed. He had been absent and late more during these five weeks than during all the previous seven years. This sudden change was a tip-off that something was seriously wrong.

The supervisor called Harry into the office and asked how he liked the job and whether anything about it was unsatisfactory. Harry was pleasant, but insisted that nothing was wrong.

In the course of the conversation, however, he revealed that his wife had been ill for several weeks, and had not been able to get out of bed. He had to look after her and assist the children with their studies at night. Then, in the mornings, he had to prepare breakfast, get the children off to school, and try to get things into shape so that he could leave his wife for the day.

Consider what this man's reaction might have been had he been chastised without getting a chance to tell his side of the story. He might have said, "You work seven years with a good record, then something happens that you can't help and—pow! They jump on you with both feet. Maybe this isn't such a good place to work after all." This incident demonstrates that supervisors who attack the *result* without analyzing the *cause* can commit serious errors of judgment and often aggravate the situation rather than correct it.

A basic principle of causation is that behavior doesn't just happen—it is caused. When we begin looking for the causes of behavior, we approach a better understanding of why people act as they do.

It is easy to see the cause-and-effect relationship in the physical world. The laws of physics state that a body at rest tends to remain at rest, that if pressure is applied to an object it will move in the opposite direction, and that when in each instance we know the cause—the force acting on the object—we can predict the result. If we stick someone with a pin, we can anticipate the effect. Words—"Stop!" "Run!"—can stimulate a physical response. Movies move us to tears or laughter. Doctors make use of chemicals and hormones that cause a desired effect in the body. All this is based on the fundamental principle that behavior (reaction effect) is equal to the organism (human being) plus the stimulus (cause). This means that only two factors account for behavior—the individual and hirs environment. A change in either changes the individual's behavior.

The supervisor who wishes to change the job behavior of the employee, then, needs to change either the individual or the influences that act on hir.

Environmental and Cultural Influences

The factors that influence behavior are derived from two principal forces: adjustment to the physical and human environment and adjustments to contemporary culture. The culture in turn is made up of the techniques, activities, and symbols that comprise the individual's adaptation to hirs environment.

Much of our behavior is conditioned by a repetition of responses, which can develop into a pattern of habits. A woman and a young child suddenly coming upon a snake are likely to react differently. The woman will probably have a violent conditioned reaction; the child may show no fear—may even try to pick up the snake and play with it. The fear and the violent reaction of the woman are gradually transferred to the child as a result of exposure. In the same manner, the reactions of employees are conditioned over an extended period of time until eventually these responses become fixed and automatic.

We generally judge others by our own standards. This may not be sound, because we frequently do not know why we do things. Also, we tend to forget that the other person is in a different situation, comes from a different background, and has had different conditioning. It is especially difficult to discover the real causes of behavior when they are based on unconscious motivations and the individuals themselves are not aware of why they are behaving the way they are.

Since such a strong case can be made for external causation, we may tend to believe that humankind has no control over its own fate. There is no denying the substantial relationship between cause and effect, but one additional element must be taken into consideration: the individual's willpower. People can, if they wish, override environmental influences and make decisions based on their own rational conclusions.

In deciding whether to support or oppose a change of company policy, employees may not be exercising willpower; they may be weighing the relative merits of the possible courses of action. Which alternative corresponds to their own best interest? What factors cause them to lean in the direction of cooperation? What factors make them oppose the new policy? It is doubtful that their final decision will be based on careful consideration of the facts; instead, it is likely to be a response to the anticipated personal impact of the different courses of action. Modern psychologists doubt the strength of willpower. They think that whether the employee acts wisely or unwisely depends not so much on the individual's will as on which causation factors are strongest.

Physical needs influence behavior and responses, but so does the need for recognition and satisfaction, and other nonphysical drives. Among the factors influencing an employee's reactions are age, length of time on the job, health, family, temperament, education, personality, attitude, and training. These may change with time and with the changing moods of the individual. If the supervisor is to discover and influence employee behavior, hir must know hirs employees as individuals. The better hir knows them, the better hir is able to understand the influences which cause them to act as they do.

The employee is a human being constantly adjusting and reacting to hirs total environment. Lighting, noise, monotony, other people, leadership, and the efficiency of the machinery are all elements of causation. But additional factors outside the workplace must be taken into consideration. If an employee is under emotional stress at home, it may show up in hirs work. Such influences are not constant; they operate with varying degrees of force on different days.

Changing Behavior by Changing Causes

A well-known headache remedy advertises, "For frequent or recurring headaches, consult your physician." This is a recognition that aspirin can cure the symptom (headache) without affecting the cause. Supervisors who want to change job performance are wise to concentrate on the cause. They must ask *What?* and *Why?* They need to analyze both performance and job adjustment to determine where a change is needed and then bring an appropriate influence to bear on the cause in order to affect the result.

Exploring causation presents supervisors with one of their most serious challenges. They are basically engaged in the same type of pursuit as the psychiatrist. Of course, the supervisor might not be dealing with a disturbed personality, but hir has to observe, question, and analyze in order to discover the true situation. Part of the difficulty in making such an analysis lies in the fact that the individual is constantly influenced by many competing stimuli, and the supervisor needs to know which stimulus is at work at the moment. Many habits and patterned reactions go all the way back to childhood, and the current effect is but a result of the basic causal factor.

One young office worker was on the verge of being discharged because of excessive errors in her work. It was her responsibility to keep accurate records of all items sold, their size, price, and color, and the names of manufacturers. Not only did she make far too many errors, but she was so late in completing the records that the need for them had passed by the time they were available.

When the employee was called to the office, she could not explain why she made so many errors or why it took her so long to complete the work. The condition of the machines was reviewed, and she was asked whether she received the correct information on time and whether she was experiencing difficulty with anyone on the job. She was happily married, she said, and the situation away from the job presented no problems. Finally, the girl was asked if she had ever worn glasses. She replied that she had—beginning in the third grade—but she had not worn them for about five years. She had made an appointment to have her eyes checked about three months before, but had not kept the appointment. It was agreed that she could remain on the job only if she found out immediately whether she needed glasses. She did; and with the new glasses, her worked improved so much that she became an outstanding employee.

Many of the human problems facing the supervisor stem from causes rooted deep within the personality of the individual. The employee who forever complains might be exhibiting a symptom of hidden problems. Making constant excuses for failure and exhibiting apparently groundless antagonisms toward others are often outward manifestations of inner conflict. It is the supervisor's responsibility to view these complaints, maladjustments, and conflicts; ferret out their causes; and take whatever steps are necessary to eliminate the unsatisfactory job behavior. (Inappropriate supervision might, of course, be the cause, which needs to be changed.)

For example, a new employee in the shipping department was seen loafing frequently during his probationary period. He completed all his assigned jobs on time, and the results were satisfactory. But the supervisor decided not to keep him because "there was no place in the department for loafers." When the employee was confronted with the reason for his discharge, he was amazed. He stated that he had completed every assignment to the best of his ability. During his first day on the job, one of the older employees had told him that when he got through with each shipment, he was to return to the loading platform and wait there until he received another assignment. He had been doing this because he understood it to be the correct procedure.

The man was not discharged, but was instead asked to remain on the job. He was given proper instructions, and he proved to be a good employee. Had the job been explained properly in the beginning and had there been proper supervision and adequate communication between supervisor and employee, such a misunderstanding need never have developed.

It is difficult to change a person's behavior. All people tend to have fixed attitudes, to be confident of their acquired experience, and to react in a way that has proved satisfactory in the past. They have a natural tendency to resist change, and probably will not recognize that any fault or failure rests with them.

The need for change confronts the supervisor with the task of interviewing the employees, getting them to see the cause-and-effect relationship, and convincing them that the only way to correct the situation is to correct the cause. The self-interest of the employees should be used in this connection (as will be explained in Chapter 8). The supervisor must approach the problem knowing that the employees are likely to resist the change and that they may fail to recognize that the cause lies within themselves. This requires great patience, thorough planning, and careful follow-up—one attempt seldom produces a change.

In many cases, it is easier to change the environment than the individual. But this can usually be accomplished only within limits. It may not be feasible to transfer the employee to another department or even to another machine, and it is doubtful whether the workplace can be completely rearranged. However, it *is* possible to check the condition of the machine, the raw material, and the workload.

If the work environment seems to be causing trouble, ask the employees for suggestions. They may admit that nothing is really wrong with the machine but that they resent being given the most difficult assignments. This could be corrected by reminding them that they are assigned the more complicated work because of their superior skill and that they are being paid a higher rate than those doing less difficult work.

The important principle to keep in mind is that the environment may be a causative factor. If it is not possible to change the physical situation, the supervisor may be able to accomplish the same result by talking with the employees and getting them to recognize *why* it cannot be changed and why they have to adapt to conditions as they exist.

Causation and Its Effect on Supervision

If supervisors expect to change behavior on the job, then they will have to discover and change the cause of that behavior. The following guides should be helpful:

- ☐ Develop the habit of assuming that there is a cause or a combination of causes that affect the conduct of the individual on the job.
- ☐ Follow this up by conducting an open-minded search for the cause—whether on or off the job.
- ☐ Remove or alter the cause so as to bring about a more desirable result.
- ☐ Use the cause–effect principle to enhance productive behavior and to convert wasteful activities into useful achievement.
- ☐ Recognize that in some instances, even after the cause has been discovered, no constructive action can be taken.
- ☐ Avoid blaming the individual. This will prove frustrating to the supervisor and upsetting to the employee. Threats may occasionally force the employee to make certain changes, but hir will soon resume the old behavior pattern unless permanent changes are made through the alteration of causes.
- ☐ Examine closely the expected results in the light of what is necessary to bring them about.
- ☐ Be especially alert to changes in job performance or behavior. When the employee has a record of loyalty and satisfactory job results, look for an explanation if these should suddenly change.
- ☐ If causes can be discovered and changed, then the chances are that the job performance will generally return to normal.

Causes of trouble which merit the attention of the supervisor might come to hirs attention in the following ways:

- □ Personal observation.
- □ Production and attendance records.
- □ Complaints from the employee.
- □ Complaints from other people.
- □ Morale surveys revealing problems that bother employees and may be interfering with their job performance.
- □ Exit interviews.

Although exit interviews might come too late for the individuals involved, they can reveal certain changes that need to be made. When employees resign, the reasons they give the immediate supervisor for resigning are not the real causes. They may have resigned because the workload is unequal, or because others won't do their share of the work, or because the supervisor shows favoritism, or one employee runs the department and tells the supervisor what to do, or simply because "My supervisor and I just don't seem to hit it off."

Wise supervisors must take an objective look at the employee's performance as well as at hirs behavior. If they expect to change results, they must discover and change the causes. If they approach this responsibility with an open mind, they will serve the best interests of the employee, the company, and themselves.

All possible roadblocks should be eliminated and the pathway smoothed in order to speed progress toward goal achievement.

7

Minimizing Frustration for Improved Results

PATHWAYS to goals are not straight, uneventful journeys traveled with ease and surety. Rather, the journey is often thwarted, delayed, detoured, or stopped completely. When this happens for the individual employee, the goals established for the enterprise will not be met, individuals will be disappointed, and the activity will be considered a failure.

Frustration often results in abnormal behavior caused by the failure to attain a desired goal. The individual proceeds without complications until barriers are encountered over which hir is unable to move. The first few confrontations with difficult obstacles may do no harm; but when the individual begins to feel that the barrier will never be overcome, then problems often result, causing deterioration in job performance, creating additional supervisory problems, and posing a serious threat to the job security of the individual and the goals of the department.

Controlled laboratory experiments in animal psychology have proved most revealing as guides to human behavior. One such experiment is to induce frustration in a normal, healthy, growing white rat. Through careful control of food, the rat is induced to solve maze problems in order to satisfy its hunger. The decisions necessary to obtain food are quickly learned. When the maze is changed, the rat soon learns to solve the new problem. Finally, the maze is altered in such a way that no predictable pattern of action leads to the food. After a short period during which the rat tries to find some solution, there is a dramatic change in its behavior. The rat now trembles, turns in circles, loses all desire for food, bites indiscriminately at everything close by, no longer makes any effort to solve the problem, and is often willing to give up and die.

Human behavior can change almost as drastically. People start out with the confidence that they can lick the world, get the job done, win a promotion, earn an increase in pay, and experience limitless satisfaction from the terrific results they will achieve. Along the way, the timetable is thrown off schedule—they don't get the raise or the promotion expected and this causes them severe disappointment. In most cases the employees' reactions are philosophical; they vow to work harder and be more deserving at the time of the next performance review. Their energies continue to be oriented toward their jobs.

The real problems enter the picture when disappointment becomes so severe and sustained that the employee engages in abnormal problem solving and activity that is not related to goal achievement. The supervisor must now be concerned with the potential loss of production and a deliberate interference with the contributions of others, which could drastically curtail the success of the department. This situation requires quick and careful correction.

Sources of Frustration

Frustration can result any time a person expects to satisfy a desire but fails to do so. The more people are led to expect from the job, the greater their frustration if these expectations are not fulfilled. Individuals often expect too much from a job. They may have ambitions and aspirations beyond their ability. They may fail to recognize that promotions, increased compensation, prestige, and self-satisfaction only come through hard work and the type of contribution which merits these results. Too often they blame others for their failure to get what they expect.

If the supervisor has oversold an employee on the possibilities of the job, hir is asking for future disappointments. It is the supervisor who interprets and explains the company's decisions and actions.

Hir can do much to remove the sting of disappointment by learning to anticipate and forestall it.

There are many situations over which the company and those in it have little or no control, but which often affect the job-related satisfaction of the employee. Economic conditions change; the need for a particular product diminishes; old, worn-out machinery is replaced; or the company is not growing enough to make promotions available as fast as anticipated. All these factors could lead to disappointment for the employee.

For example, the company may fail to establish an expected new supervisor's job, so that one less promotion is available. It may lose an order that would have enabled it to expand. It may fail to keep the promises it made at the time of hiring the individual. It may deal too much in personalities, so that favorites receive undue consideration. Pay increases and promotions may not be handled properly.

Frustration, like any other behavior pattern, is caused—it doesn't just happen by accident. The supervisor's awareness of possible causes can aid in determining whether frustration is likely to result when certain combinations of circumstances and individuals are thrown together. The following will offer some guides.

Level of tolerance. Some people are very exacting—they are said to have a place for everything and to want everything in its place. Such individuals are likely to have definite expectations about their job, and the slightest deviation causes them severe disappointment. On the other hand, some people have a broader tolerance range. Their interpretation of what they can expect from the job is not as precise, and it takes rather severe jolts to disappoint them. Because these wide differences in reaction can be expected, it is essential for the supervisor to know hirs people extremely well as individuals and to be familiar with their expectations.

History of frustration. Employees who have a history of exhibiting frustration are likely to be disappointed at the slightest setback. Established behavior patterns are an indication of what can be expected in a given situation.

Pressures and needs of the moment. If a man has promised to buy his wife new furniture because he expects a salary increase or promotion the following week, he is going to experience great disappointment if neither is received. When a widow needs extra money to keep her son in college, failure to get a raise may cause frustration. And the man who has been bragging to everyone that he is going to get a promotion often blames the supervisor or the company if it doesn't come through.

Interpretation of the situation. People's attitudes toward the supervisor and the company may well determine how they interpret events that affect them. They may see only the most painful and disappointing aspects of every event. Some people consider each situation on its merits; others regard any unfavorable decision as proof that the supervisor is picking on them and will never let them get ahead. The amount of frustration that results from any given situation is substantially influenced by the individual's interpretation.

Seriousness of the incident and time span involved. Most people can shake off minor disappointments and can endure stress for a reasonable period of time. But serious disappointment or prolonged stress requires the supervisor's special attention lest it affect job performance.

Symptoms of Frustration

Just as certain cloud formations indicate the probability of rain, so do certain behavior patterns indicate potential frustration. When the supervisor recognizes the true nature and causes of these patterns, hir can often find solutions to the problems by rechanneling employee activities into productive job performance. The following three patterns are tip-offs that something may be wrong.

1. *Change in job performance.* When an employee has been on the job for several years and has a good overall record, something must be afoot if hirs behavior changes. Change is an indication that the employee's attitude, feeling, or overall interest has altered. Productive activity could now become meaningless or even destructive in nature.

2. *Increase in emotional behavior.* Reactions which have been rational and unemotional may suddenly become emotional and irrational. Not only does the supervisor have difficulty explaining why the employee does certain things, but the employee often seems confused as to why hir is behaving that way. This emotional reaction could show up in relationships with other people, or in job performance.

3. *Increase in non-goal-directed activity.* If employees have a clear understanding of the job to be done and the type of activity necessary to get it done, few problems will result as long as they direct their efforts toward the goal. However, when much of their activity becomes pointless, when they move in circles or start making hints about getting even with someone, then frustration is a possible cause.

Four Patterns of Frustration Behavior

The supervisor should be concerned when any of the following four behavior patterns appear on the job, since they tend to result in almost senseless behavior.

1. *Excessive aggression.* Overly aggressive individuals may attack—physically or in some other way—the object of their displeasure. Modern law and custom deter most forms of physical attack; thus, the attack may be made verbally or through negative attitudes. Often, considerable damage can be done by attacking the character, the reputation, and the job being done by the person who is the object of displeasure, especially if this is the supervisor.

Aggressive individuals have a chip on their shoulder; they throw their weight around because they have been frustrated. They exhibit such symptoms of aggression as excessive criticism, constant grievances, damaging or careless use of equipment, failure to get along with other people, and a certain belligerence in most contacts with others.

It is not the intention of this discussion to imply that all forms of aggression are harmful or undesirable. A hustling salesperson, a conscientious supervisor, and a top worker are often fairly aggressive. This sort of controlled aggressiveness should be encouraged so long as it is directed toward goal achievement and does not interfere with the rights of others.

2. *Regressive tendency.* When an adult regresses, hir goes back to childhood behavior. Take a look at these immature behavior patterns: name-calling, violent arguments, loss of emotional control, pouting, crying, blind following of a leader, refusal to accept responsibility, belief in rumors, inability to think logically and objectively. Although these are characteristic of children, they are all too often found in adults on the job. This type of job performance is harmful, rather than helpful, to the supervisor's effort to build a productive team.

3. *Abnormal fixation.* Extreme stress can cause compulsive behavior, which may continue even though it accomplishes nothing. It may go hand in hand with the employees' refusal to accept change. Frustration seems to freeze the old patterns and prevent the acceptance of new ones—often in those who have lost self-confidence.

4. *Resignation.* This negative form of behavior is most frustrating to the supervisor. It is not resigning from the job—rather, it is giving up. Frustration that results in resignation causes the individual's production to decline and has a demoralizing effect on the group as

a whole. These individuals may avoid serious trouble and escape discharge, but they are seldom good enough to deserve more money. They are the type of people who have been on the payroll for many years on the same job, often with very little change in salary or responsibility.

A woman who had been employed for many years in a major department store was quick to tell new employees that they would never get ahead with the company because the company would not promote her. However, she failed to state two important facts—first, that she had been head of the department for five years and had operated unprofitably each year; and second, that during her years with the company dozens of others had passed her on their way up the executive ladder. Here was a woman who exhibited all the symptoms of resignation to her unhappy state of affairs and blamed it all on the company. Her one aim in life seemed to be instilling in others the same unproductive resignation.

Preventing and Remedying Frustration

Although frustration can be one of the supervisor's most difficult problems and can dissipate productive potential, most frustration can be prevented at the outset or can be eliminated if it already exists. It is in this area that supervisors must know their people thoroughly and be willing to take the time to make corrections.

In their attempt to minimize potential causes of frustration, prudent supervisors recognize at all times that a major reason for frustration is the failure to achieve an expected goal. They should be constantly alert to circumstances in the department, as well as to the long- and short-range aspirations of the people who are their responsibility. They should be aware that a promotion that makes one person happy might disappoint several others who had hoped to get the same promotion. Also, changes in work schedules, machines, and systems can result in anxiety and confusion. These situations challenge the supervisor to take the necessary steps to prevent frustration before it occurs. Knowledge of the employees and the pressures under which they are working often supplies the supervisor with valuable information. Although frustration may affect a whole group, in most cases it is an individual reaction.

Problems can be detected in their early stages before they become serious and while they are still comparatively easy to handle. The battle is half-won if frustration can be detected early, so that the supervisor can consult with the individual and alter those circumstances that can be changed.

There are many approaches the supervisor can use to minimize frustration in the work environment. Among the most sensible preventive measures are the following.

Avoid unreasonable promises. Do not encourage employees to anticipate results beyond what they can reasonably expect to achieve. Serious mistakes are made in setting unrealistic goals for employees. However, it is also a mistake not to set reasonable goals for people.

Goals should not be so insignificant that they offer no challenge, but they should not be set so high that the employee cannot reasonably expect to achieve them. In either case, disappointment and potential frustration are built into the situation.

Set recognizable intermediate goals. A child does not attend school for 12 years without receiving some indications of progress. Tests, grades, report cards, and promotions mark the steps along the way. In the same way, the supervisor and the company should provide signs of progress—pay increases, added responsibility, opportunity to learn some new phase of the job, or other indicators that the company is aware of the employees' presence, wants them to grow, and believes in them.

Offer encouragement and reassurances. The individual who remains on the same job at the same pay rate for an extended period may feel that hir is making no progress—a probable source of disappointment and frustration. The supervisor can do much to prevent these reactions by helping employees understand what progress they are making while still on the same job—they learn every day, do their jobs better, merit more confidence, are closer to the next step up.

Clarify the employees' responsibility for their own goal achievement. Make certain that they have a realistic understanding of what they must contribute to the job in order to reach their goals. The company cannot assume total responsibility for seeing that every employee reaches certain levels of pay and status; it provides the opportunity, but they must contribute the work, the extra effort, and the response to job requirements if they expect to attain their goals.

Face up to realities when necessary. Although supervisors want to put their best foot forward at all times, occasionally there are situations that they should not try to ignore or hide. If they are weak, they may attempt to sweep the problems under the rug, pass the buck, or shift the responsibility to someone else. However, this only causes delays and permits the problems to become more serious.

Employees do not always get everything they expect from the

job. Not everyone can be given a promotion, and few people get as much money as they think they are worth. The supervisor's severest challenge in preventing frustration is in being honest with people when the reasons for their failure must be faced. Hir is not going to work miracles and make all hirs employees happy every time, but hir should explain hirs actions and make every reasonable effort to keep the employees informed.

When the Employee Reaches Hirs Ceiling, Then What?

A controversial question is whether to tell an employee when, in the company's judgment, hir can't go much higher. Every company needs qualified people who will stay in their present jobs and continue to get the work done year after year—those who are not ambitious and anxious to move up the ladder, as well as those who have limitations for additional growth. However, certain individuals are not going to be satisfied with limited progress, regardless of the company's judgment and their own limited contributions. They will continue to become more dissatisfied with each passing month. It seems only fair to them, as well as to the company, to inform them of this judgment. Then, with all the facts at hand, they can decide for themselves whether to remain with the company.

*The desire to contribute and the appli-
cation of effort are the two greatest determinants of on-the-job results.*

8

Motivation
for Maximum
Job Contribution

SUPERVISORS who effectively coordinate the various influences
leading to proper employee motivation will achieve the best results.
However, if they are not skilled in the use of motivation, they will be
in for a frustrating and disappointing career of trying to accomplish
results through other people.

Motivation involves the human will to work, to contribute, and to
cooperate. Motivation consists of initiating activity that will lead to
desirable results. As one psychologist has said, "The application of
psychology consists chiefly of the manipulation of stimuli so that
they will set off the desired habit patterns." This identifies the supervisor's responsibility for interacting with the employee and controlling the work environment in order to effect those job performance
patterns that will produce the required results.

In those areas of religious and civic activities where volunteers
are the major resource, leaders must rely exclusively on motivation
to get the job done. Since no salaries are involved, the volunteers
cannot be forced to participate. The total success of this type of ac-

tivity is dependent on effective motivation. In a sense, many industrial situations fall into a similar category. It is generally known that a company pays a salary and that this can be stopped. But the difference between what can be achieved merely by the employee's presence on the job and what can be accomplished by the conscientious desire to make a maximum contribution is the difference between failure and success. Therefore, no business can be satisfied with only the voluntary effort of the employee; each worker must be motivated and stimulated to full effort.

What Options Are Available

How well an employee accepts information, how much effort hir puts out, and how well hir responds to motivation are for all practical purposes at the option of the individual. From a legal standpoint, and because of the wide diversity of personal lifestyles among workers, we must accept the fact that employees cannot be coerced or forced to respond—command authority leadership influence is obsolete. Thus, the only realistic choice available to the supervisor is to recognize that the employees control the options regaring their response to motivational efforts and that they will decide, consciously or unconsciously, how much commitment they will make to overall job performance.

Once this fact is recognized, approaches to motivation take on a different type of challenge. The various options available to individuals must be examined carefully, and techniques must be developed to direct employees toward job goal achievement. Motivational constraints caused by these individual options force the supervisor to accept the reality that external influences have serious limitations. In the modern work environment, individuals must be motivated through creation of a physical and human climate that causes them to *want* to get the job done effectively. Older managers often have difficulty in adapting their management style from a pattern of "force, requirements, threats, and coercion" to one of "interaction, persuasion, involvement, and assurance of individual job satisfaction." The overall conditions of both the company and the specific job must merit a positive response, which will come about through the individual employee's interpretation of the job environment, based on hirs interests and needs. Response and full commitment to effective performance on the part of employees is the result of maximizing job opportunities.

The Leadership Skill of Motivating

Effective motivation includes discovering each individual's needs and desires; identifying how these needs can be satisfied; communicating to the employees that their desires can be achieved if they follow the recommended procedure; enhancing the desirability of the needs in order to make them more attractive; convincing the employees that their goals are worth the effort required to attain them; providing the techniques whereby the employees can attain these goals by following the advocated course; and initiating and maintaining employee activity which will ensure the accomplishment of these goals.

These steps may seem deceptively simple, but they involve critical leadership challenges. The supervisor must know hirs people and how their needs can be realized in the work environment. Hir must be able to convince the employee of the desirability of good work and full effort, and must instill good work habits by providing training, effective leadership, and other factors that will lead to increased motivation and productivity.

Today's production loss is not easily recovered tomorrow, and it is difficult to sell enough next month to compensate for this month's failures. To keep both production and sales high, motivation must be kept high. And just as the salesperson must be motivated to sell, so must the customer be motivated to buy. It isn't enough for salespeople to say they want to meet their quota for the day or to win a selling contest—these are of interest to the salesperson, but not to the potential purchaser. If a customer is to be stimulated to buy, hir must be given the answer to the question, "What's in it for me?"

Job Enrichment: The Psychic Benefits

Employees experience the "good life" away from the job: they are able to use their minds, can influence community decisions and hold significant volunteer and religious positions, and are able to experience the satisfactions of functioning as whole human beings. It should not be surprising that highly restrictive jobs that do not enable them to use their full talents and potential, and that provide very limited opportunity for a sense of achievement, will become boring and unacceptable.

Behavioral scientists have found that factors such as pay, employee benefits, company policies, physical working conditions, and supervision are at best only neutral motivators—if these factors motivate at all, it is only for a limited period of time. When an employee is dissatisfied with the job, the cause is usually one of five factors. It should be emphasized that these factors are certainly not unimportant; in fact, they are essential and are so universally expected from major corporations that the company derives very little motivational gains through providing them. Nevertheless, they are essential in order to attract and retain employees on a reasonably favorable basis.

Most positive job motivators—the nonmonetary or psychic income factors—are more connected with the conditions of the job itself. These motivators include recognition; the opportunity for growth; a sense of achievement; responsibility; job satisfaction; the opportunity to utilize one's abilities and education to reach one's full potential; the work itself; and other factors that give people a sense of well-being about themselves.

The recognition that the job itself must provide much of the motivational influence and job satisfaction has focused efforts on ways to enrich the job, redesign the work, and modify job-related acitivities. Research has shown that this psychic income or job satisfaction is most directly related to:

1. A completed unit of work—a whole unit rather than an isolated piece.
2. Decision-making and self-control—having at least limited control over one's own work activities and related decisions.
3. Reasonable innovation—the opportunity to improve methods, work flow, techniques and results.
4. Opportunity for human interaction—interacting with others on the job, not just to socialize, but also to discuss the work itself with one's fellow employees.
5. Immediate and frequent feedback—the reinforcement of correct performance and the benefits of remedial correction.

Motivating better-educated employees who have higher expectations will be accomplished only by making available to them, through the job and the company environment, the psychic compensations that they need. The company and managers are generally concerned with a return on investment in terms of resources and the purchase of human time. However, from the standpoint of employees, successful performance depends on the overall return they receive on the investment of their lives, their time, and their efforts on the job—and it is generally the degree of this response that determines the success or failure of the company.

To motivate employees to accomplish maximum results, the supervisor must take the following into account:

1. The goal and activity must be of interest to the employee.
2. Appropriate information must be presented.
3. The presentation must be convincing.
4. The process must be stimulating.

Few people are endowed with enough self-motivation to guarantee that they will give every task their full attention and effort. If employees were completely self-motivated and were performing each task to the best of their ability, there would be far less need for supervision.

Company standards are set to utilize the full potential of employees, and the supervisor's function is to see that the standards are met. If employees do not apply themselves to the job, the goals will not be met. So, in reality, we are concerned not so much with motivation itself as with the ultimate fulfillment of the goals.

How People Can Be Motivated

The foundation on which motivation can be built is not smooth-sounding platitudes or company social activities. Before the supervisor can initiate activity, institute change, or elicit extra effort on the part of the employee, a few simple questions must be answered: "How do I benefit? What do I get out of it?" Let's face facts—no employees will voluntarily change the way they perform duties until they are shown that there is a better way and that it is in their interest to follow the better way.

Several factors influence human action and reaction. People respond to the need for food, shelter, air, self-preservation, avoidance of pain, and bodily comfort; to love, parental instincts, and social drives; and to a desire for security, beauty, and happiness. They also respond to other drives and needs, including the opportunity for self-development and for promotion; financial compensation; desirable work in a pleasant environment; the opportunity to render a service; respect from others; social status; fair and helpful leadership; and an opportunity to influence their own future. These form the nucleus of job-related desires and become the means by which supervisors should direct their efforts to motivate employees.

Factors That Determine Response to Motivation

The laboratory experiments demonstrate clearly the principles of motivation. Among the factors that determine response are these four.

1. *Strength or intensity of the drive.* The degree of hunger determines whether the laboratory animal moves from the starting position, how fast it moves, and the amount of effort it exerts to find the food. Food is the incentive; hunger, the motivating factor. In employees the motives may be different, but they are certainly comparable. How badly does the employee want or need additional income? What interest does hir have in job security? How ambitious is hir? What needs can the job satisfy?

For example, some individuals demonstrate little interest in exerting extra effort to earn more money. Some working wives who expect to work temporarily may have limited motivation to work for salary increases and promotions. But the individual who is responsible for a large family often has a different response to the opportunity to earn additional income.

2. *Past experience.* Employees learn quickly whether they can count on what the supervisor says. If an employee is led to believe that a promotion will be hirs reward for exerting extra effort, and if the promotion is not forthcoming, that individual is not likely to be fooled the second time. Employees learn from every incident and their responses are influenced favorably or negatively by every experience. It follows, therefore, that the supervisor who does not play the game honestly will be bucking increased resistance.

Employees bring to the job an accumulation of experience that affects present response. The supervisor must discover the present level of response to determine the most appropriate pattern for motivation efforts. If employees fail to respond, it would be well to examine the past experience of the group: perhaps a previous supervisor made too many false promises, thereby creating a lack of trust among the employees.

3. *Amount of reward.* The amount of pay increase offered, the amount of recognition given, and the degree of satisfaction derived from a job influence workers' willingness to exert themselves. The

lure of big pay increases will not always motivate employees; but, used in conjunction with other and often equally effective forms of motivation, good responses can be achieved. Regardless of the type of incentive used, the type of reward influences the amount of extra effort exerted.

One department store had made extensive efforts to motivate its salespeople to sell more. Employees were talked to in meetings; supervisors held individual conferences; new employees were told that they could set their own salaries, since the amount they earned depended on how much they were willing to sell, but unfortunately, the campaign had little effect on sales. Closer analysis showed that the whole system was unrealistic: in several departments, not a single employee had earned any commission during the year, whereas other employees had earned insignificant amounts. When new people started, they were full of enthusiasm, believing that their earnings were unlimited; but they gave up when they learned that regardless of any effort on their part, they would not be able to earn anything extra. The commission system was unrealistic and had to be overhauled before extra effort could be stimulated. Some departments did not have appropriate merchandise; in others, the sales promotion effort needed improvement. Leadership had to be improved, and morale had to be bolstered. When these things were corrected and reasonable rewards were offered, extra effort resulted and sales improved.

4. *Time relationship of response to reward.* Experiments conducted with animals have revealed that an activity must bring forth an immediate reward if it is to stimulate learning and response. The longer the reward can be delayed and still be effective, the more intelligent the animal is thought to be. Thus, in training animals, the horse is rewarded with lumps of sugar; the dog, with tidbits; and the seal, with bits of fish. This feeding follows immediately upon each separate activity, and the animal learns to associate the reward with the action. If the reward is delayed, it loses its effectiveness.

Human beings have minds far superior to those of animals, and they respond to delayed rewards. But if a reward is delayed too long, it loses its effectiveness for human beings as well. For this reason, incentives and other forms of extra compensation are often paid as soon as possible; delay until the end of the year may well result in a slackening of effort early in the year and in extra exertion only when the time for reward nears. For some groups of employees, profit-sharing and retirement plans are far less effective than pay increases. For example, the 21-year-old will not respond to pleas to work hard, save on materials, turn off lights, and be economy-minded in order to have a bigger pension at age 65, because the reward is too remote. Some forms of compensation must be delayed, and it is not recommended that this be changed; but the fact remains that long-range promises are less effective than immediate fulfillment.

Guides for Effective Use of Motivation

The supervisor must keep in mind that employee motivation is seldom brought about by a single incident. It is developed by the total continuous atmosphere of the department, the confidence the employee has in the supervisor, and the way the tools of supervision are used. The following specific areas should be considered in seeking improvement in motivational effectiveness.

Make appeals specific. High-sounding platitudes seldom change mediocre performance into total effort. Instead, the supervisor has to get down to brass tacks. "The more specific the stimulus, the more immediate will be the response," according to one psychologist.

It is not enough to say "Work harder, produce more, and you'll get ahead around here." The job applicant wants to know what the training program contains, how long it will last, what salary will be paid, and what can be expected when the training is completed. The employee is more likely to respond if the supervisor says, "Joe, here's how you can earn 50 cents more per hour." Making appeals specific recognizes that there must be "different strokes for different folks."

Emphasize the positive. People have to believe in themselves to accomplish extraordinary feats. The supervisor can apply this principle by expressing hirs confidence in the employees, calling attention to their assets, reminding them of their successes, and then conveying the message that the goal that has been set is designed in line with their qualifications.

Make use of symbolic appeals. The salesperson cannot prove to the customer that a $10,000 automobile will provide better transportation than one costing half as much. Therefore, if hir expects to make the sale, hir must use secondary stimulators and other symbols to arouse the customer's desire—comfort, luxury, prestige, pride, and other factors that have little to do with transportation. Similarly, the supervisor must appeal to the employees' pride, to their wish to be well regarded by their associates, to their yearning for the extra security and prestige that additional money can afford, and to their desire for the satisfaction that promotions will bring them.

Make effective use of words. Joseph Conrad stated, "Give me the right word and the right accent, and I will move the world." Words can make tears flow; they can incite mobs to action; they can lift people to lofty endeavors; they can soothe injury; they can cause mayhem. Words are the principal means of influencing others. The supervisor who expects to influence employees must know how to use words skillfully.

Combine motives skillfully. A single motive, if strong enough, can provoke action, but a combination of motives elicits greater response. The supervisor needs to use motives that complement and strengthen each other. The impact of a combination of motives may be compared to the impact of a coordinated team of football players: together, they are far more effective than even the superstars can be alone.

Develop a sense of responsibility in the employee. The amount a given department can accomplish is limited if every employee must be constantly prodded. Instead, the supervisor should help each worker in hirs department to develop a sense of responsibility, because productive employees understand that good performance is in their own self-interest, and that their own efforts will affect the survival of the enterprise that provides the job and related benefits.

Early in his career, C. H. Greenewalt, chairman of E. I. du Pont de Nemours & Co., Inc. reported to work an hour early each morning and stayed an hour longer than the rest of the employees in his department. When told that Du Pont did not require such long hours, he replied: "I'm working for Du Pont from 8:30 to 5:30; the rest of the time I'm working for myself. I want my work done better than that required to just get by. I want to know that it is as perfect as I can make it." This willingness to sacrifice immediate pleasure for long-range rewards is an example of the self-motivation and sense of responsibility that can help a man or woman along the road to leadership.

Putting Motivation into Practice

Theories do not produce results until they are effectively translated into action. Thus, the principles of motivation must be put into practice by the supervisor before any improvement will be seen. The suggestions that follow can facilitate the theory-to-practice transition.

Make maximum use of the most effective tools. The mechanic has a special tool for each task and completes the job successfully by selecting the correct tool and using it skillfully to perform its unique role. In selecting the most appropriate tool for motivating employees, the supervisor must consider the personality for the individual, the goal to be reached, the timing, and long-range aims of both the individual and the company.

Resolve conflicting motives. Little can be accomplished so long as motives are in direct conflict with one another; one set of motives must dominate before decisive action can take place. Most of the decisions that employees are forced to make are not between positive and negative, but between alternatives with only shades of difference. When conflicts arise in determining a course of action, the temptation is to select the one that leads to immediate results even though the greater future gain has to be sacrificed. Impulsive decisions are usually those offering immediate satisfaction. The supervisor's responsibility is to help the employee make an honest evaluation of both sides of the question. If the supervisor can help an employee choose the right alternative and thereby work for the long-range goal, hir will have rendered a real service to the individual and to the department.

Use competition to motivate. Most people like to compete and have a strong desire to win. Winning gives them a sense of satisfaction and boosts their egos. Often the best way to stimulate a department to greater production is to show what another department is doing. Competition adds interest and zest to the job, gives the employees something to talk about and something to take pride in, and serves as a production stimulator.

The employee's response is dependent on how effectively the supervisor explains the situation and on the desirability of the reward. Competition can vary from elaborate companywide contests to one individual's effort to better hirs own record. In areas of the job that are not appealing or exciting, competition may be the best way to stimulate interest. Job-related housekeeping may be uninteresting but necessary: a clean-up campaign with prizes offered for the best department is often the most effective way to achieve results.

Use incentives to motivate. Incentive can take a variety of forms, but if structured properly and explained to employees, it can become one of the supervisor's most important motivating tools. Money may be the best all-around stimulator, but intangible incentives also produce dividends of extra effort. The most commonly used incentives are piece-rate pay and commissions on sales. In each case, employees are paid in proportion to their contributions—a form of incentive that is direct and easy to understand. However, in many areas it is difficult to pay on the basis of production. When this is the case, department incentives or some type of profit-sharing plan can be used.

One large national company employed 1,200 people in a storage and shipping warehouse where there was no reasonable way to establish incentives for individual employees. The company called in a management consultant who studied the situation, established a standard operating cost for the warehouse, and initiated a program in which a fixed percentage of any improvement in this cost figure would be shared with employees; their individual shares were payable monthly and prorated according to salary. The employees were told that this was not a scheme to get them to produce more, but simply a way for them to earn more money. Then they were shown how they could cut down on the use of supplies, avoid waste, streamline work procedures, and get the job done quicker. By the end of the third month they were making an average of $48 extra per month. And because they were proud of their accomplishment, they continued to show improvement.

Motivating Employee Cooperation

Supervisors have a clearer understanding of the importance of cooperation when they become aware of the difference between a cooperative and uncooperative employee. Among the characteristics typical of the cooperative employee are these: Hir tends to cooperate fully at every opportunity; trusts the supervisor's instructions and the company policy; has a favorable attitude; is well adjusted on the job; and generally goes along with what the supervisor and the company are trying to accomplish.

Uncooperative employees need to be sold or almost forced to cooperate. They approach most tasks negatively and discharge their responsibilities grudgingly, and the quantity and quality of their results reflect this forced effort. They do only what is required of them, and seldom put forth extra effort. They have a tendency to be suspicious of most instructions and work assignments. They constantly complain and gripe about other people and about the company in general. They are always afraid they will do more than their share of the work. And they consume a disproportionate share of the supervisor's time and emotional energy. The existence of the uncooperative employee shows that the leadership required to create and maintain a cooperative workforce is a real test to the supervisor's skill.

Cooperation requires knowledge, identification, and action on the part of employees. They must know the goals, identify themselves with them, and take action to make those goals a reality. The supervisor must not only be familiar with pertinent factors but must also make certain that employees understand these factors. Cooperation is a dynamic process, with both the supervisor and the supervised contributing their own ideas and methods to achieve an established goal. There are several techniques the supervisor can use to promote and motivate cooperation.

Provide adequate training. People are more willing to do what they do well, because it gives them a sense of accomplishment. If the employee understands how to do the job and is skillful in performing the required activities, hir is inclined to work more cooperatively.

Keep employees informed. Employees are more inclined to go along if they know where they are going. It is much easier to be a cooperating member of the team if you understand the game plan and know which signals and plays will be used.

Provide dependable leadership. Employees' experience with their supervisor determines whether they are willing to depend on what the supervisor says. If they have confidence in the supervisor, they will be motivated to cooperate rather than to question and to return in kind the degree of cooperation received.

Build positive attitudes. Attitudes set the stage for cooperation or for lack of cooperation. Employees with positive, trusting attitudes are likely to be cooperative as well.

Work for the interest of the employee. It is much easier to cooperate with someone who works for your interests and is willing to go to bat for you. Employees need someone to champion their cause. It is often difficult, despite the open-door policy stated in employee handbooks, for rank and file employees to make direct contact with top management. To the employee the supervisor is the vital link with management. Supervisors have an opportunity to win the cooperation of their people if they work consistently for the employees' best interests.

Give instructions properly. Use the "let's do it" approach instead of giving orders. Make it easy for employees to cooperate by making certain that instructions are clear, brief, and easy to understand. When asking for cooperation, be willing to explain why.

Provide safe and favorable working conditions. Avoid tensions in the work climate. The supervisor has the responsibility for ensuring that machines and procedures provide maximum safety.

Ask questions. Telling people may produce a defensive reaction, but asking their opinion can motivate cooperation. An executive of a well-known company learned that the best way to sell was to ask enough questions to find out how the product could best be used by the customer. Customers complimented him on the way he sold—he didn't use high pressure and seemed to know just what they needed. Still other successful executives and supervisors have learned the secret of asking, "Would you mind?" and "What do you think?" They always ask enough questions to make certain that all the information is presented and to assure positive interaction between supervisors and employees. Getting across information through posing the proper questions is more effective than imparting the same information with an emphatic statement.

Be a leader—not a boss. The supervisor's example is a stronger influence than hirs words. Proper leadership makes it easy for employees to cooperate—they simply follow the example of the supervisor. Employees have to work *for* a boss, but they can work *with* a leader.

It is the supervisor's responsibility to create a cooperative work environment and provide the leadership which will encourage employee cooperation. Hir should approach this area of responsibility the same way a salesperson approaches a customer—if the customer doesn't buy, the salesperson hasn't sold. If the employee is uncooperative, the supervisor must recognize that hir had failed in hirs efforts to develop a cooperative response.

Promoting Job Interest and Motivation

The activities in which we excel are those which interest us. Those which do not interest us are often performed with far less enthusiasm, with little effort for improvement, and consequently with mimimum success. Interest is the intangible quality that intensifies the desire to improve both performance and results.

Everyone wants an interesting job, but each individual has hirs own idea of what is interesting. To one person, an interesting job must present challenges to be met and problems to be solved. To others, a job is interesting if it is important but doesn't require much decision making. The real task of the supervisor is to identify the aspects that are of interest and to communicate them to the employee. The employee's degree of interest in the job, in the department, and in the total work environment has a direct bearing on turnover, grievances, and job results. Job interest might not appear on the balance sheet, but its effect is there just the same. When stimulating employees to take more of an interest in their work, the supervisor should recognize that certain job-related factors influence the degree of interest an individual is likely to have in hirs job.

Attitude toward total work environment. If the employee believes in the company, the supervisor, and the importance of the job, that job will become more interesting. Attitude is central to the formation of the other factors which determine job interest.

Progress on the job. Most employees have some degree of enthusiasm when they begin a new job, but this can wither if they make insufficient progress. Progress can be recognized by salary increases, promotions, or other rewards. It is much easier for employees to maintain interest if they feel that their day-to-day effort is moving forward.

Quality of supervision. Interest is influenced by the attitude of the supervisor—imaginative leadership eliminates frustration and maintains harmony, assuring a more congenial work environment.

Associations on the job. For many employees the associations developed on the job are the most important factor in promoting job interest. Strong social units are often developed, and the employee looks forward to being with the group. This association with the group can supply an important portion of the satisfaction and interest that the job offers the individual—especially in repetitive or routine labor, which also affords the opportunity for interaction while the work is being done. For example, in some clerical, sales, and manual jobs, the proximity of the workers and the low noise level make social exchange practical during working hours.

Challenge. For many employees challenge and interest are closely associated. College graduates often make unsatisfactory taxi drivers—because the job is not challenging, they often have too many accidents. When an employee finds no challenge in the job, it becomes boring and holds little interest.

Satisfaction. Many employees enjoy working with other people. This contact with others is the focus of interest and part of the intangible compensation the individual is seeking from the job environment. Most employee morale or job information surveys reveal that employees consider the people they work with to be the one feature they like best about their jobs.

There are many factors that tend to minimize or destroy the interest needed for maximum job performance. When the supervisor fails to recognize good work or to show appreciation for superior effort, the employee quickly loses interest. Every opportunity should be taken to say to the employee, "You handled that well. That was good work—keep it up." Mediocre workers can often be stimulated to top production if they are given appropriate appreciation.

If the supervisor loses the respect of hirs employees, they will lose interest in the job. No one likes to work for a supervisor who lacks the necessary knowledge, does not give honest answers, plays favorites, mistreats employees in any way, fails to communicate necessary information, or is unable to organize the work and provide the necessary leadership.

Often the temporary employee—or the employee who plans to resign—has little interest in the job. Since a temporary job often involves no prospect of security, increases in pay, or promotion, the employee has limited basis for job interest.

Although poor health is a factor over which the supervisor has little control, it certainly influences job interest. If the employee's physical energy is being sapped by illness, pain, or emotional strain, hir is unable to exhibit a vital and enthusiastic interest in the job. And personal peoblems that worry the employee will almost certainly result in a lack of interest.

The "bad apple" is an enemy of on-the-job interest. Workers are more easily influenced by a disgruntled employee than by a productive and interested one. Casual disparaging remarks can be especially detrimental to the newer employee who is seeking answers and who is just beginning to develop feelings about the job. If positive answers are not given by the supervisor, the employee falls under the influence of the "bad apple."

However, most jobs can be interesting if they seem important and if their relationship to other company activities is understood. Employees on identical jobs have varying degrees of interest in their work, since interest depends more on the individual's interpretation and emotional reaction than on what is actually involved in the job. The supervisor cannot depend on the job to generate its own interest, but must actively assist the employees by encouraging them to develop a more dynamic interest in the job.

Supervisors should emphasize the interesting aspects of a task. They know more about the job than the employees; hence, they should explain facets of the job that the employee might not otherwise notice. If a man or woman can see hirs job from a new perspective, what now seems dull or routine may be seen as interesting and even exciting. Operating an elevator can be viewed as excessively dull—or as an opportunity to insert a pleasant note into the lives of many people every day.

Supervisors should keep employees aware of the importance of their jobs. To a business every job is important. If it were not, no one would be paid to do their particular jobs—the services they render, the products they make. We often treasure possessions not because of their material value but because of the value we assign to them. When employees are doing work that they consider important, they will take a greater interest in the job.

Employees need to have a clear picture of the goals they are expected to meet. The establishment of quotas or goals not only stimulates interest but also serves as one of the surest ways of increasing production. Whether it is a safety standard or a production goal, employees should understand the mark they are attempting to hit. Goals should be high but not unrealistic; they should be explained clearly; employees should be kept informed of their progress toward those goals.

Job interest may be heightened by explaining one job's relationship to other jobs. A job should be viewed in its relationship to other company activity in order to make it more interesting and meaningful—and productive. Whether the job is processing papers, producing bolts, or selling insurance, employees must understand how their contribution relates to the success of the company.

Both the relationship of the supervisor to the individuals in the department and the relationships of employees with one another are crucial factors in determining job interest. This is often revealed when transfers and other changes are discussed with employees—resistance usually centers not on changes in the work but on changes in the work groups. Employees are often reluctant to leave the familiar social environment because they are uncertain how they might fit in with the new group.

Finally, employees are less likely to lose interest when the supervisor is concerned with their activities. The absence of feedback often causes the individual's own interest to die.

Motivation and Efficiency

Efficiency should be of concern to every employee in every company. Efficiency does not mean an incessant struggle to produce more at the expense of one's own health. Rather, it means the elimination of waste—wasted motion, wasted material, and wasted time.

The efficiency of an automobile is stated in miles per gallon. This efficiency is affected by the condition of the motor, the speed at which the car is driven, the terrain over which it moves, the skill of the driver, and by other variables. It is more difficult to measure human efficiency. How do we know how much effort an individual is exerting? The amount produced is not always a reliable criterion. Observation is not reliable; often the people who seem to be busiest have the least to show for their efforts at the end of the day. On the other hand, an employee who seems to be wasting time may accomplish the greatest amount.

Efficiency is concerned with human input as it relates to the quality and quantity of results. Efficient people make the best use of machines, raw materials, time, effort, and of the investments the company has made. Employees may rate their efficiency in terms of the amount they earn or on the basis of units produced in a given time. The supervisor may judge efficiency by the relationship of departmental production to the number of employees. The company and the stockholders are likely to consider return on investment the most important guide.

During the past 50 years, psychologists, efficiency engineers, and managers from first-line supervisors to company presidents have paid more and more attention to the efficiency of employees. Efforts have focused on elimination of superfluous motion, more efficient arrangements of the work area, changes in the design and speed of machines, and on more appropriate placement of individuals on the job.

Frank and Lillian Gilbreth, pioneers in time and motion studies, once made a systematic study of bricklaying and found that by eliminating unnecessary motion the number of movements could be reduced from 18 to 4, with the result that each man's output was increased from 120 to 350 bricks per hour. A great deal of research has since been concentrated on increasing efficiency, and industrial engineering and "human engineering" are the subjects of many courses now included in company training programs and college curricula.

Certain identifiable factors are obstacles to efficiency—fatigue, noise, boredom, poor lighting, inefficient supervision, lack of sleep, lack of interest, inadequate training, worry, poor health, lack of energy, and a host of others. All these factors affect efficiency in varying degrees. Studies have been conducted to measure the effect of these hindrances, and serious attention has been given to physical design, planning, and administrative organization in order to provide employees with an efficient work environment. The following steps can help promote maximum day-to-day efficiency on the job.

Make certain that the work environment promotes efficiency. Are the machines still as efficient as they were, or have they slowed down with age? What are the condition and quality of the raw material used? Are all the people in the organization making the appropriate contribution? Or are some people letting down on the job, thereby interfering with the work of others? Have the methods used in the department become obsolete? Can a more efficient method be substituted?

Many significant factors affecting quality, quantity, and efficiency of work might be beyond the control of the employee. Supervisors should identify the factors that they can influence directly and then provide, within the limits of their authority, the most efficient work environment for the people in their department. They have the further responsibility of bringing other factors—those that interfere with employee efficiency—to the attention of management. If employees are to work efficiently, they must have the most efficient machines, methods, materials, leadership, and environment.

Anticipate the employee's point of view. No matter what kind of environment the company provides, the employee will be no more efficient than hir wants to be. Some employees are merely putting in time. Some are not loafing but are just working at a leisurely pace from the beginning to the end of the work period. Their purpose seems to be to consume time rather than to complete the task. This type of performance does not meet the company's goal or improve the individual's opportunity for more pay or promotion. The following illustration shows the thought processes an employee may go through in deciding whether to respond to motivational efforts.

What's in it for me?	*What will it cost me?*
I'll make more money, since I'm on an incentive basis.	I'll have to put forth more effort.
The supervisor says it will make me more valuable to the company.	It means I'll have to get in on time, be on the job every day, and waste less time during the day.
I'll gain the approval and recognition of the supervisor.	I'll have to give up visiting other people during the day.
My name will be posted as one of the top producers in the department.	Some of the other employees may think I'm an eager beaver trying to impress the boss.

What's in it for me?	*What will it cost me?*
The other employees will think well of me if I help win the company contest.	If I work harder and produce more during the contest, the boss will expect me to do the same all the time.
I suppose the better I work, the better my chance is for promotion.	I'm not lazy, but I don't know whether I want to work that hard.
I believe I'll enjoy my work and get more satisfaction from the job if I know that I'm doing my best.	Will it be worth the price I'll have to pay?

And so it goes: employees decide, consciously or unconsciously, whether to put forth the extra effort necessary to work faster and produce more. But they don't go through this procedure all the time; they develop an attitude toward the supervisor and the job that determines their reaction to any encouragement of increased effort.

Communicate the benefits of efficiency to the employee. Efficient performance should result in benefits to the employee. Efficiency becomes desirable to the employee when it is linked to job security, more pay, promotion, profit sharing, job satisfaction, and overall value to the employee.

Keep employees busy. Efficiency can become a habit when employees work at a steady pace. It is when they stop and let their interest wander that errors occur. The myth that employees who work more slowly are more accurate and more efficient is false; generally, the rapid worker is also the more efficient. Therefore, to guarantee top performance, the supervisor needs to plan to keep the employees busy and working at a fast pace.

Continue training. A company continues to exist and grow only in proportion to its success in improving its operating efficiency. The only way this can be accomplished is through improvement in the mechanics of the operation and in the performance of the personnel. Both the supervisor and the company have a responsibility to continue training in order to achieve this improvement. Only in this way can undesirable performance be replaced with more efficient procedures.

Promote understanding of efficiency standards. Most jobs have standards of efficiency. The production operation may allow no more than 5 percent rejects, the sales operation may be permitted no more than 10 percent in returns, and the cost estimators may be limited to a 2 percent margin. Whatever the standards, employees must be familiarized with them. Standards of efficiency serve as guides as well as goals: they are meaningless unless the employee understands them and relates them to hirs own job.

Supervise closely at the beginning and end of the work period. Most errors are made and most inefficient work is performed at the beginning and end of the work period. Once supervisors recognize this, they should be able to compensate for this lack of efficiency by their presence and attention to the operation at these crucial times.

Take prompt action if work continues below standard. Supervisors must not ignore inefficient performance by assuming that it will automatically improve in time. They have a responsibility to exert every reasonable effort to encourage each employee to maintain an acceptable standard of performance. If this is not reached within a reasonable time and maintained thereafter, certain definite steps should be taken. In some instances a transfer to a more appropriate job may be advisable; in other cases, the company may not be able to justify retaining the employee in any capacity.

Encourage pride in workmanship. When an artist paints a picture or a carpenter builds a house, the finished product is a testimony of the craftsman's pride in hirs workmanship. Workers who complete an entire process and have a finished product to prove their skill usually take pride in what they do. But assembly-line workers or bank clerks may be involved with only a small phase of the overall operation, and it is easy for them to lose this pride in workmanship. Since the employee's individual effort may be difficult to determine, the importance of hirs contribution must be emphasized by the supervisor.

Expect the employee to work efficiently. Employees generally perform according to what is expected of them. If the supervisor shows that hir expects efficiency, they are likely to exert the effort necessary to justify this confidence.

Self-Motivation

Mature employees should recognize that it is in their own self-interest to meet the goals set for their jobs. Though the supervisor may have had to point this out initially, employees should supply their own motivation the second time around. Maturity of this kind is not a factor of age; rather, it is an ability and a willingness to respond to the requirements of the job.

Self-motivated employees recognize that job security is related to job performance, and that compensation must be a realistic reflection of their own contribution. They accept the fact that in order to derive satisfaction from the job—recognition, status, approval, and security—they must merit these rewards. They are aware that their own dedication, initiative, compulsion to excel, and willingness to improve will determine their progress on the job. They accept personal responsibility for their job performance and for their future role with the company. They welcome the assistance of the supervisor in clarifying and strengthening these requirements, but they are willing to work at them on their own initiative.

What has been said above about employees applies with even greater validity to the supervisor. If employees are expected to supply a sizable portion of their own motivation, the supervisor should be expected to supply an even greater portion of the motivation necessary to discharge the duties and responsibilities of hirs job. As a means of self-motivation, supervisors should identify the goals of their department; list their own personal goals; identify the ways in which their own goals can be attained through meeting the goals of the department; work out a specific program for realizing these goals; and recognize that they must supply their own initiative and motivation.

Writers and leaders throughout history have recognized the importance of self-motivation. The Roman poet Virgil put it this way: "They can because they think they can." So supervisors must recognize that it is their choice: it is up to them. Eric Hoffer put it another way in *The Passionate State of Mind:* "We are told that talent creates its own opportunities. But it seems that intense desire creates not only its own opportunities but its own talents." And in the words of one of the nation's leading businessmen: "I believe we make our own ability, talents—even genius through hard work and self-discipline." And the president of a large insurance company once said: "Determine what you are living for, what you are working for, what you are trying to accomplish, and support that philosophy with faith and energy and courage. Know where you are going, and be on your way."

*Appropriately handled employee correc-
tion can be the supervisor's unique opportunity for contributing to the
achievement of goals: the employee's,
the company's, and hirs own.*

9

Correction:
The Supervisor's
Unique Opportunity

THE football coach improves hirs team's chances of winning by correcting the techniques of the players; parents teach their children by
furnishing corrective guidance; and supervisors correct the performance of their employees to improve results. Yet many supervisors
ignore the need for correction and in so doing, they neglect a primary responsibility of their position and render a distinct disservice
to all concerned.

The need for correction is present in every leadership position,
and the skill with which it is handled can be a decisive factor in the
success of the department and in the professional progress of the
leader. Yet no other supervisory responsibility is so misunderstood.
It is neglected and delayed because supervisors do not have confidence in their skill in correction techniques and are afraid to make
someone unhappy. It is misunderstood, because many supervisors
fail to realize its purpose and the unique opportunity it presents.

We all know leaders like the mild supervisor who has been on the
job for years. They are calm, work hard themselves, and don't see
too much of what goes on in the department. They ignore most
minor incidents and laxity on the part of employees. But when a sit-

uation is brought to their attention by higher management or has become too critical to be ignored any longer, they pounce. Almost invariably, the employee is resentful and feels mistreated; the supervisor is upset; and the situation is not corrected. What could have been handled calmly if it had been dealt with skillfully before it became too serious now assumes the proportions of a major incident. Such a supervisor commits many of the errors commonly made in connection with the correction procedure.

Correction Demands Top Skills

The proper handling of correction demands mastery of the best leadership skills. There is no unique leadership involved in assigning work, prodding for more production, or discharging those who are unsatisfactory. When supervision is limited to these activities, the best interests of the employee, the company, and the department have not been met. The real test of leadership is in leading employees to improvement through correction and training.

Many leaders make the mistake of thinking they have to be "one of the boys" so they will be popular and well-liked. The fallacy of this belief is that no enterprise is created for the purpose of staging a popularity contest, and "nice guys" are not always most effective in getting the job done. Supervisors who are overly concerned about their popularity often let mistakes go unnoticed and settle for unmet production standards and half-way loyalty. The result can be a breakdown of productive activity in the department.

Still other supervisors err in the opposite direction: they think that in order to get things done, they have to be disciplinarians and let people know who is boss. They consider their main function to be enforcement of a complete set of rules and punishment of offenders. They are of the old school, which believes that it takes toughness and a show of strength to accomplish things with other people. However, the new lifestyles of human equity and dignity make this the most unacceptable style for achieving favorable employee relations and positive results.

The need for correction arises when a failure, either of omission or of commission, has occurred on the job. Employees fail to meet job standards when they neglect to do something they should have done or when they do certain things they should not have done. In either case, the supervisor has the responsibility of effecting a correction so that established standards will be met. The purpose of correction is to make the adjustments in job activity to meet these requirements. Every company sets certain policies and rules to protect the rights of everyone and to provide for orderly activity.

The need for correction may come to the attention of the supervisor in a variety of ways: Hir may observe an infraction of a departmental rule; an employee may make a complaint or request assistance; other employees may bring the need to the supervisor's attention; a check of production records may reveal that standards are not being met; or a higher executive may indicate that work or policy standards must be improved. In any case, the urgency and the seriousness of the situation that needs correction influence the way it will be handled.

Once the level of acceptable performance has been established for the department, employees are considered satisfactory so long as they meet the standard. If, through negative attitudes or faulty habits, they deviate from the norm by engaging in job performance that is less than satisfactory, it is the supervisor's responsibility to help them return to acceptable standards. It should be noted that the supervisor's concern is with correcting the *performance,* not the individual. This overall view should help the supervisor keep correction on an impersonal and objective basis.

The Unique Service of Correction

Correction is a direct and deliberate effort to bring about a change in job performance or work-related behavior so that it will more nearly meet the standards established for the job. When this is accomplished, the benefits will be felt not only by the employee but by the supervisor and the company as well.

Service to the employee. All employees who want to do a good job and increase their value should be receptive to constructive evaluation. If unsatisfactory work is ignored and permitted to continue, it will jeopardize their job security, reduce satisfaction, decrease their value, and certainly eliminate any reasonable possibility of promotion. Thus, the individual who is permitted to continue without correction is being given unfair and inappropriate leadership. When the supervisor seeks to bring about the desired correction, the employee may not agree initially that hir needs to make a change and may reject the supervisor's efforts. However, it is the supervisor's responsibility to bring about the employee's understanding of this need for change by relating it to job security, to the individual's desire to earn more, and to hirs overall growth with the company.

Service to the supervisor. Certain standards of production are expected from each department. When these are not achieved, the supervisor is not meeting the requirements of hirs job. And these standards cannot be met when employees fail to make the necessary contribution. Supervisors must therefore recognize that an inherent part of their job is to maintain appropriate work standards and behavior. Just as it is in the employee's self-interest to respond to correction, it is in the supervisor's self-interest to engage in the appropriate procedures to make the correction.

The supervisor's problems and the department's accomplishments might be directly related to the number of correction failures that occur in this area of responsibility. The time lapse before they are corrected and restored to normal standards is an indication of the supervisor's skill in handling people. The greater the time involved, and the greater the deviation from standard, the more negative reflection there will be on the supervisor, on hirs capacity to manage people, and on departmental goal achievement.

Service to the company. The company is committed to pay the salaries of its employees at an agreed rate even if a specific employee's value falls below this level. Since the company's ability to grow, expand, and provide greater job opportunities is the direct result of employee productivity, the entire organization is harmed by employee failures. And because supervisory leadership is the key to meeting standards, supervisors who do not see to it that all employees receive the necessary correction are not meeting the standards of their jobs and do not personally deserve the recognition of increased pay or responsibility.

Admittedly, correction is not the most welcome supervisory task. But the service it renders should be sufficient motivation for the supervisor to tackle it with sincerity and understanding. With this supervisory tool, the leader can do more than just correct errors: production can be increased, employee self-respect and confidence can be restored, and a loyal workforce can be built.

By discovering ways to help employees correct faults that lessen their value to the company, supervisors can lead them from failure to success. And if supervisors succeed in this effort, they will have performed their finest act of supervisory leadership.

The Appropriate Approach to Correction

The most important aspect of correction is the supervisor's own attitude and understanding of its purpose—not to punish, browbeat, embarrass, belittle, or grind an employee into the ground; not to be unduly critical of the individual personally or of what hir does apart from the job (provided it does not adversely affect either the performance of the employee or the well-being of the company); but to make an objective analysis of job standards and job performance and then to seek correction where needed.

Before proceeding with correction, the supervisor should recognize the following dangers.

Never correct in the presence of others. To do so causes embarrassment to the individual involved as well as to innocent bystanders.

A regional supervisor visited one of the company's branch units and called several things to the manager's attention which needed correcting. The manager immediately called two supervisors over and proceeded to remind them that they had been told about these things a dozen times and that there could be no excuse for their failure to correct the problems. This was done in the presence of the regional manager, a group of employees, and several customers. As a result, the manager lost the respect not only of the regional manager but also of the employees and the customers, and he failed to correct the situation.

Never correct while angry or upset. When this is done, the correction becomes personal and cannot be kept objective. To do so fails to bring about the desired results and may so upset and infuriate the other people present that their loyalty and job contribution will be lessened rather than improved.

Never correct in haste, before facts are completely verified. Wise supervisors learn quickly that things are often not what they seem. If their action is based on inadequate information, their handling of the situation will probably be wrong and unfair.

For example, a report was received late one evening that an employee was planning to take home several unauthorized company items at the end of the work period. The man was stopped as he was leaving the building, was sent to the superintendent's office, and was asked about the company property he was taking out. He explained that the items had been damaged and had been given to him by the supervisor as toys for his children. A quick check did indeed reveal that this information was correct. An apology was made to the employee for the embarrassment and delay. As a result of this incident the supervisor was reminded that a record should be made of discarded items and the employee removing them should be given a copy as his authority to take them from the building.

Recognize the purpose of the correction. The goal is not to bawl out an employee but to correct a job situation. It is to restore proper habits, confidence, and maximum contribution. Hasty and improper handling often causes just the opposite: more errors, less production, resentment, and hurt feelings.

Beware of hearsay. Every supervisor is at times bombarded with hints, gossip, and innuendoes that certain things are going on that demand immediate supervisory action. These rumors should not be ignored, but they should be kept in perspective, viewed objectively, and not be allowed to build up out of proportion. Corrective action should be based on facts that the supervisor has personally verified, not on allegations or hearsay.

Consider the case of two women who worked side by side in the personnel department. Both had been with the firm for a number of years. Margaret was friendly, talkative, and generally well-liked; Judith was efficient, hard-working, aloof, and a bit brusque in her manner. Outwardly, the two women were cordial, but in fact Margaret often complained to the supervisor that Judith antagonized people by insulting and annoying them. These complaints, which were lodged over a long period of time, eventually made such an impact on the supervisor that he reprimanded Judith for her way of handling people, and she resigned.

Only after she had left did the supervisor realize his mistake. Because he had listened to the hints and innuendoes of a talebearer, he had lost a capable and efficient employee. Had he investigated, determined Judith's need for coaching to help her learn to deal with people more tactfully, and been less receptive to Margaret's efforts to downgrade another employee in order to improve her own status, the interests of the company as well as of the supervisor himself would have been better served.

Do not delay correction unduly when it is clearly needed. The old adage about an ounce of prevention is good advice when it is applied to correction of faulty habits, work, and attitudes. The longer correction is delayed, the more entrenched a habit becomes and the more difficult it is to dislodge.

The personnel director of a large warehouse operation talked with one of the supervisors concerning the excessive amount of time involved in filling orders in his area. The supervisor indicated that some of the employees were not getting in on time and others didn't seem to have enough interest in what they were doing. He cited the case of one man who had a habit of coming in 15 to 20 minutes late every morning. When asked what he had done about the situation, the supervisor replied that he hesitated to try to correct such a good worker for fear that the man would quit. Further investigation revealed that the employee had been coming in late for so long that he now considered lateness to be his privilege. Efforts were made to correct the situation, but it had been permitted to continue for too long: the employee thought he was being picked on, and eventually resigned. It is significant that this "indispensable" employee was replaced by another man who worked faster and more efficiently.

The Correction Procedure

The correction procedure should follow a definite pattern if maximum results are to be obtained, although there will be considerable variation in its use to fit each situation. To begin with, supervisors have to take some preliminary steps before talking to an employee. First, they should try to eliminate any personal bias they may have concerning the situation and the individual so that they can be as objective as possible. Second, they should look at the incident from every angle—how it affects other employees, as well as the company and themselves, what type of employee they are dealing with, and so on. Third, they should investigate the entire situation, get all the information, be thorough in considering all the facts, check all the conditions pertaining to the specific incident, and consider the seriousness of the particular infraction. When necessary, they should consult with others, particularly their own supervisors. Their next step should be to consider the validity of all information and to check whether it is based on facts or on hearsay. Finally, they should review the case to make certain that no pertinent information has been overlooked.

In making an analysis of the problem, supervisors must consider many points and seek answers to many questions, since the cause of the incident often influences the way it should be handled, as well as its potential consequences to the employee. What were the apparent motives of the person involved? Was the incident brought about because of lack of training or of information, misunderstanding of instructions, development of poor habits, or deliberate rebellion against the stated policies of the company? Is there evidence of poor supervision, improperly planned work procedures, or off-the-job problems? Is the employee interested in the job, or does the employee feel it is one hir should not be doing? Is the job too easy or too difficult? Would a transfer to a more (or less) difficult job solve the problem?

If it is found that correction or penalties are in order, the various types need to be considered. The most common is the oral reprimand, which involves a complete discussion of the event and an admonition that it not happen again. In an increasing number of cases, a written warning is given and a copy of the information is made a part of the employee's record. This becomes especially important if recurrences might force the discharge of the individual.

A more severe form of discipline is a suspension, involving loss of both money and respect. This is seldom used because the company loses the services of the employee, and the additional workload that must be given to other employees punishes people who were not involved in the infraction.

The ultimate punishment is discharge. If the employee has a good record before the incident, this is seldom necessary; but if hir has a negative attitude after previous warnings, the best course of action may be an outright discharge.

All leaders' policies and actions regarding employee discipline, correction, and discharge must comply with various legal requirements. This means that before taking action supervisors should verify that employees were adequately informed regarding job requirements, that they were told specifically where their job behavior or performance was not meeting these requirements, and that they were given a reasonable amount of time in which to correct the problem. After these steps have been taken, decisions and actions should be equitable. All details regarding preliminary steps and subsequent action should be completely documented and should be made a part of the official employee record. This procedure protects the employee from indiscriminate treatment and the company from unjustifiable charges.

In correcting and disciplining an employee, the supervisor is in essence disciplining every employee in the company. When one person fails to meet the standards of the job, the action taken represents the policy of the company with regard to other employees as well. It is considered to be an indication of—

□ What constitutes a failure or breach of policy.
□ Whether the policy means what it says.
□ The company's attitude and policy toward violators.

□ The supervisor's ability to handle the problem.
□ What will happen to other employees if they violate the same
policies.

Correction, like every other activity, can be handled more effectively if it is done at the right time, in the right place, and with the
right approach. It is generally agreed that correction should preferably take place near the beginning of the day and certainly before the
end of the work period. This gives the employee and the supervisor
time to talk again during the day if either so desires. It also gives the
employee time to calm down or to work off any resentment before
hir leaves.

The location of the correction interview must provide privacy,
because its purpose is to restore job performance to acceptable standards, and this isn't likely to be accomplished if an individual is criticized in front of other people. Only if the employee is acting in a
dangerous manner that could cause injury to others or damage to
the company's property should the supervisor step in and take the
necessary action to avert disaster. And even in this type of situation,
the follow-up correction should be handled in private. Few
emergencies are acute enough to justify public embarrassment.

As a general rule, be as easy as possible but as firm as necessary
in order to insure appropriate corrective action. Beware of any form
of automatic approach. Companies have written penalties for infractions, but often most of these are intended as guides and not as
absolute rules. Always make certain that corrective action is legal,
nondiscriminatory, and in compliance with company policy.

Conducting the Correction Interview

After preparation and analysis of the situation, the supervisor
should be ready to handle the problem and make the correction
through an interview with the employee. It is recommended that the
interview be conducted as follows.

Arrange for the interview. Select a private place and choose a time
during which neither party will be interrupted. A correction interview that is plagued by frequent interruptions will seldom be effective for the employee, and will often be difficult to handle for the
supervisor. Take employees away from their place of work when
they can best be spared and when their absence will be least conspic-
uous.

Plan your approach. If necessary, write down the pertinent facts surrounding the situation. Don't plow into the interview unless you have a clear concept of what you believe to be the problem, as well as some alternative ways in which it might be handled. If you have notes and a carefully planned step-by-step approach, you are less likely to become emotional and lose control of the interview.

Always begin with a question. This lets employees know that you are willing to listen—it gets them involved. Never launch into a long, emotional tirade the moment the employee enters the room. Instead, proceed cautiously: there is no hurry, and it is not necessary to strike the first blow.

Listen to learn. Listening isn't just refraining from talking; it is also demonstrating that you are willing to consider seriously what the individual has to say. Get the employee's side of the story and find out hirs reasons for the action that was taken. This can often help you get to the bottom of the problem. Perhaps the employee's justification for disregarding the rules is that there is so much work to do that the only way to get it done on time is to ignore the rules.

Obtain agreement on the facts. After you have heard the employee's version of what happened, restate it and make certain hir agrees with your interpretation. Only when there is agreement can you know that you are both talking about the same set of facts and that the correction will deal with these facts.

Retain control of the interview. Although supervisors should listen to the employee's side of the story, they should not lose control of the conversation or permit the interview to be diverted from the immediate problem to be solved. The supervisor should remain calm, even if the employee reacts with an emotional outbrust. It is only normal for employees to try to justify their course of action, but remember that it takes two to argue and that the employee will not remain emotional if the supervisor's response is calm and reasonable. It is important to maintain an open-minded judicial attitude and to use a minimum of self-assertion. Get the employee to see that it is a job problem, not a personal affair, and that it must be handled because it affects the employee's on-the-job performance.

Weigh all evidence carefully. This includes any new evidence that the employee may reveal. If the individual's reasons are not justified, explain why. However, if there is a reasonable explanation for the action, then perhaps changing the work procedure, giving the employee some extra help, or bringing the rules to the individual's attention will be all the correction required.

Seek advice when needed. If the employee offers additional information, the supervisor is often well-advised to delay making a decision until there is time to evaluate the new evidence. Supervisors should seek as much help and advice as seems necessary. Consulting their superiors is not an admission that they are unable to handle the situation; rather, it is an indication of sincerity and thoroughness on their part. The supervisor's own boss will often appreciate being consulted, because what is decided could eventually affect hir as well.

Keep in mind the objective to be achieved. The purpose of correction is not to punish or to embarrass but to avoid repetition of the incident and to ensure that the rules will be followed in the future. This should obviously influence the attitude of supervisor and the techniques they use in the interview.

Consider company policy and practices. How is this type of incident generally handled? Does the company have a prescribed procedure? Is there a broad framework within which supervisors are expected to operate? Their handling of any particular matter should not be too far out of line with what is being done in other areas of the company. If the supervisor's decision sets a precedent, it could affect many other employees.

Fit the correction to the individual. The fair approach is not to use the same type of correction for every individual but to tailor the action to each person and to each situation. Consider such factors as length of service, past history of offense, seriousness of the incident, the employee's attitude, hirs willingness to make the correction, what hir has said to others about the incident, and the reasons hir gives for it. The employee may not agree with the ultimate decision, but hir is likely to understand and accept it as being fair if it takes into consideration all these factors.

However, this humanistic need to fit the correction to the individual must not run afoul of equality of treatment for individuals in different legal employee classifications. To make certain of company policy and possible consequences, supervisors will often need to consult other company executives before taking corrective action. Legal constraints often prevent supervisors from being as individualistic or responding as quickly as they might wish.

Fit the correction to the incident. The driver who overparks at a parking meter does not expect the same sentence as the drunken driver whose speeding and reckless driving result in the death of a pedestrian. By the same token, the employee does not expect severe or harsh punishment for minor infractions of the rules.

The most significant service the suprvisor can render during the whole correction procedure is to provide a specific plan of action that will lead the employee back to acceptable performance. The cardinal rule is don't just criticize—be constructive, but always keep it legal.

Make certain the employee understands. During the correction interview, make certain the employee understands your decision and the course of action hir is expected to follow. If necessary, write it down and give the employee a copy.

Close the interview pleasantly and restore self-confidence. The purpose of the interview is not accomplished if the employee leaves feeling like a whipped dog. The interview should be closed pleasantly but firmly. Don't neglect to remind the employees that their dependability and loyalty are highly regarded and that you have confidence in their ability to do the job correctly. Encourage them to ask questions if there is anything they do not understand. Invite them to talk with you in the future if they are confronted with unusual problems. When hir leaves, the employee should feel more secure in hirs job and have greater confidence that the supervisor is interested and is there to help.

Conduct a follow-up interview. The employee deserves a follow-up interview even though it may be short. If hir is now doing a good job, the supervisor should recognize the improved performance and compliment the individual on hirs response to the earlier interview. This lets the employee know that hir has not been forgotten and that hirs good work has been recognized and appreciated. If, on the other hand, it is discovered that hir has not made the correction, then a much firmer approach is in order.

After every football game, the coach views films of the game in order to learn what the players did well and where they must improve their techniques. Immediately following the handling of a correction situation, supervisors should also review their techniques to determine what went well and what needs to be improved in order to do a better job next time. Among the areas which should be reviewed are whether all pertinent information had been gathered and properly evaluated; whether the supervisor's understanding of the incident was altogether correct; whether the employee had confidence in the supervisor, an adequate understanding of the rules and policies, and a fair opportunity to express hirs point of view; what the supervisor or the employee might have done to prevent the need for correction; and what guides the supervisor can use for better handling similar situations in the future.

When corrected by the plant manager for violating the no-smoking rule in a storage area, an employee said that he fully understood this rule and admitted that he had violated it. The plant manager explained the need for the ban on smoking as a fire-prevention measure, and emphasized that if the employee smoked in the area again he would be discharged. The employee indicated that he understood. Two weeks later, when he was again observed smoking in the area, he was discharged. Failure to be firm when the situation requires firmness can weaken the whole structure of company policy and cause a general breakdown in adherence to these policies. Failure to act might also weaken the supervisor's legal right to take action in similar situations in the future.

Guides to the Effective Use of Correction

The supervisor should keep the following points in mind when attempting to correct the performance of an employee. First, do not correct too frequently. If used too often, correction is annoying and ineffective. It is generally better to handle most minor incidents as part of the continuing on-the-job training. Only the more serious incidents must be handled in correction interviews.

Second, relate the correction to employee self-interest and job security. The employee who is expected to make a change must understand how it will affect hir. The clearest way to do this is by talking in terms of self-interest.

Third, motivate employees to make the corrections. Help them work out a definite program for making the correction. Remember that individuals are more likely to make the correction if they have good reasons for doing so—reasons that are meaningful to them.

Finally, be firm. Employees respect firmness if it is fair. There is no area in which firmness is more important than in the correction of faulty habits of work performance.

Tips on Maintaining Good Discipline and a Productive Environment

The company and the supervisor can eliminate much of the need for correction by eliminating the causes for breaches of company rules and unsatisfactory work. The time and effort spent in prevention will pay rich and lasting dividends to all concerned. These guidelines will prove useful:

1. Make certain that you, as the supervisor, know and understand all policies, prescribed work methods, safety rules, and customer relations guides.

2. Make certain that your employees understand the rules, the reasons for them, and why it is in their best interest to follow them. Training, communication, and personal example are excellent guides for this purpose.
3. Instruct your employees carefully in the proper work methods. Most incorrect work is the result either of not knowing how to do the job properly or of developing incorrect habits.
4. Make certain that instructions are clear and that employees understand fully what is expected of them. The results will be no better than the instruction or the understanding employees have of what they are expected to do.
5. Take the steps necessary to prevent errors—but don't pounce on employees. They will not appreciate it, and such action will certainly not merit much respect for the supervisor, nor will it make the correction easier.
6. Ask yourself, "How could it have been prevented?" The question should be asked after every accident and after every job failure. When the cause has been determined, appropriate action should be taken to ensure that it will not happen again.

The Supervisor's Own Attitude and Correction

This chapter would not be complete without recognizing that supervisors have a stake in their own correction. They should recognize that they, too, fail to carry out their own duties and responsibilities perfectly. The degree to which they can discipline and manage themselves determines how much supervision they require.

Supervisors should constantly be aware of the production goals of the department, the company's policies, the standards of the department, and the duties and responsibilities of their jobs. They should be able to compare their own job performance with these standards and to correct unsatisfactory results. They may be resentful of any criticism about the way they are doing their jobs, but they have to recognize that their handling of such criticism—the way they accept it and act on it—will be an important factor in their future success, whether they want to admit it or not. To discharge their duties and responsibilities in the most efficient manner, they must not only seek guidance to avoid making mistakes, but they must also learn to accept correction gracefully.

The supervisor faces a severe challenge in resolving grievances and in installing change. Failure to neutralize grievances or make a change can result in the breakdown of productive job performance.

10

Guides for Handling Complaints and Changes

FROM the company standpoint, a grievance is anything the employee considers wrong, unjust, or unfair in the work situation. Employees do not have to present objective grounds for their grievances; what is important is that they react according to their feelings. Although some grievances are based on factual situations that can be determined accurately, others stem from intangible feelings and are very difficult to understand or to explain.

Two Types of Employee Complaints

A *correction interview* is usually initiated by the manager when hir has some criticism about the employee's performance or conduct on the job. On the other hand, complaints arise when the employees feel that they have grievances against the company or the work environment. Complaints, whether real or imagined, create a gulf between employee and supervisor, and so long as they remain unsettled they affect job performance.

There are two basic types of complaints—those the employees

109

talk about and those they don't talk about. When their grievances are unexpressed, the symptoms show up in their work and in their attitude. The out-in-the-open type is much easier to handle because the supervisor can talk it over with the employee, get the individual's reasons for hirs dissatisfaction, and attempt to resolve the problem. The unexplained complaint presents more of a challenge because it is difficult to pin down, identify, and root out. Whatever their form, grievances usually cause indifference, absenteeism, irritability, reduced production, and failure to get along with other people.

Approaches to Handling Grievances

The best way to handle complaints is to prevent them from arising in the first place, just as preventive maintenance is the best way to avert machine breakdown. Two prevention steps are suggested:

- Maintain an atmosphere promoting the highest morale. Watch for symptoms and danger signals, and handle complaints before they become too serious.
- Maintain open lines of communication. This allows complaints to be brought to the supervisor's attention before they become critical. If supervisors keep themselves accessible and alert to employee feeling and thinking, they will be able to handle situations on a preventive basis.

In handling real or imaginary grievances, the supervisor should follow certain patterns.

Learn the basic cause. What really caused the complaint—not just the superficial reason, but what was the real causative factor?

Try to understand all the factors involved. You may think that the employee's complaint is foolish and completely off base, but remember that if it weren't a cause of concern, the employee wouldn't come to you with it in the first place. The employee deserves your sympathetic understanding—even though your approach may have to be firm.

Assist the employee in facing the realities of the situation. The employee may be using imagined complaints or company errors simply to mask personal inadequacies. If this is the case, try to make the individual see the situation in its true light.

Attempt an explanation or settlement as soon as it is practical. The sooner a grievance is resolved, the easier it usually is to handle. Also, since it probably interferes with the employee's work, it should be resolved at the earliest reasonable moment for that person's benefit. This is not to suggest that a decision should be made before the situation has been thoroughly investigated and all the facts have been determined. But delay may cause the complaint to become more serious.

Consider the advisability of additional training. Bringing the employee to a satisfactory level of production may eliminate the basis for the complaint, since failure to meet the standards may cause the employee to look for excuses.

Use a firm or direct approach when needed. Recognize that objective firmness can be the most appropriate solution.

Replace the employee if necessary. If all reasonable effort has been made to help the employee adjust to the situation but without success, attempts should be made to transfer the individual. However, discharge may be the only permanent solution. Remember that no employee should be permitted to infect other employees with disloyalty or constant complaining.

A Four-Step Guide to Handling Grievances

The words "grievance" and "complaint" are used interchangeably here, although they do not mean the same thing to everyone. It should be noted, however, that some of what follows may not apply in instances where a grievance procedure is spelled out in a union contract. Where a contract exists, it should be studied carefully so that the supervisor's handling of grievances will conform to the contractual agreement.

Settling a grievance is not the most pleasant task a supervisor is called upon to perform; but, if it is handled correctly, if affords a real opportunity to be of service to both the employee and the company. The following four-step method is recommended.

1. *Receive the grievance properly.* The way a grievance is received is important because the way employees are treated when they make the complaint may have a significant influence on the ease of handling it, as well as on the outcome of the matter. Regardless of how angry, upset, or loud the individual may be, respond calmly and courteously. In all probability, you won't have to start the conversation. Ask the employee to tell you about the problem if hir doesn't volunteer the information. No matter what is said, let the employee have the opportunity to say it. Hir deserves a hearing. Give the indi-

vidual your entire attention and hide any irritation or impatience you may feel.

While hir is talking, take a few notes. This impresses the employee with the importance you attach to the case. After the story has been told, ask the employee to repeat it. It's surprising how much calmer and less explosive the situation appears during the second telling. Then, after hearing the story for the second time, repeat the essential parts in your own words. It is important that you get across to the individual that you understand the complaint; so check with the person to see if your interpretation is correct.

The difficulty may be one that you can resolve during the conversation; if so, handle it accordingly. If what you have heard requires further investigation and study, tell the employee why. Thank hir for bringing the matter to your attention and be sure to tell the employee when hir can expect a decision.

2. *Get all the information you need to make a decision.* It is important that you give the matter your prompt attention. Make the investigation as complete as necessary. Check every angle and talk with all the people who may be able to shed light on the situation. Make appropriate notes of your findings—this prevents forgetting or misquoting at a later time.

Check whether company policy or the union contract clearly spells out what action is to be taken. Find out if other supervisors have set a precedent in similar situations. Consult with your own supervisor, who may have some definite ideas about what should be done. Such a review of company policy, contract clauses, precedents, and upper management opinion ensures that your decision will not be reversed at a later time.

Examine the employee's record. Is the person a habitual complainer? How often has hir been absent? What is hirs record of production and cooperation? What does the job performance rating show? The answers to these questions help you interpret the complaint in the context of the individual's overall record.

3. Take appropriate action. If you have completed Steps 1 and 2 adequately, you should now be in a position to act. If the company is in the wrong, make the correction. If the complaint centers on something that cannot be changed, tell the employee why it can't be changed. If the employee is in the wrong, stick to your guns. Should you touch a sensitive nerve when you make a decision that does not agree with the employee's view of the complaint, your best position is calmness, firmness, and a shield of facts.

Above all, don't let yourself be bulldozed into a compromising position. If you have done a thorough job before making your decision, and have come across no new information that would justify changing that decision, then stick to it. It may not be to the employee's liking, but once you get the individual to agree on the facts that entered into your decision, the person's honesty will compel hir to respect that decision.

4. *Engage in follow-up action.* The initial decision is only the first step in taking action on the complaint; follow-through is necessary until the problem has been completely eliminated.

In most instances, a complaint is indicative of the company's failure to make a change or of the employee's failure to understand company procedures. The causes for most complaints can be eliminated if the atmosphere in the department is conducive to high morale and if lines of communication are kept open. Handling of complaints provides the supervisor with an opportunity to assist the employee with job adjustment, and it also provides the company with identification of needed changes.

Skillful Handling of Change

We live in a world of change. Never before in human history have so many changes taken place within so short a time. More than one-fifth of all American families move each year. Communications, transportation, new products, and new ideas are altering our total environment. Most of us take pride in our up-to-date thinking and habits. But many of us still tend to resist change in our interpersonal and job relations because in the orderly and familiar lies a feeling of security.

If a company is to survive in today's dynamic environment, not only must it be able to react to changing conditions quickly, but it should also anticipate them far enough in advance to adapt its policies, organization, personnel, and products in sufficient time to maintain a sound competitive position. The ability to introduce change with a minimum of resistance is one of the key skills of progressive management.

A new machine, technique, product, or system can make all the old ones obsolete. The growing companies, those that are offering better jobs to employees and larger returns to stockholders, are the ones that have a pattern of continuing adjustments. Their products are constantly improved through research, new uses are found for old products, and new products come from their laboratories. Not only have they changed their products, but they have altered their organizational structure and have been able to persuade their employees to accept these changes without detrimental opposition. Management foresight and adequate planning have overcome resistance and have assured the flexibility that is clearly in the best interests of these companies.

Types of Job-Related Changes

Change can take many forms, but we will deal here with the ones that affect the employees and their job environment.

Changes in tools, machines, and equipment. Almost every organization has experienced difficulty with employees who resist new tools, machines, and equipment as possible threats to their security or status. Several years ago, for example, cash registers were to be installed in a sales department. The department head was completely opposed, and no amount of reasoning about the advantages seemed to have much effect. Finally, a register was installed for a three-month trial, and the supervisor was told that if at the end of that time she still wanted it removed, consideration would be given to her request. By the time the trial period was over, however, she was so pleased with the speed, convenience, and accuracy of the cash register that its removal would have caused as much trouble as its installation had caused originally.

Changes in methods and procedures. Method and procedure changes imply that the company has learned a better, more efficient way than the old system offered. When confronted with a new method, certain employees will react almost automatically in a negative way. But the road to missed opportunity is paved with the notion that "We've always done it this way."

Changes in personnel. People are more willing to accept environmental changes than human changes. To individuals, personnel adjustments—new employees, a new supervisor, a decrease in staff—signal changes which could work to their disadvantage. People have a way of adjusting to each other, establishing rapport, and forming socially knit groups; personnel changes tend to threaten this balance.

Changes in the organizational structure. If two departments are merged into one, or a supervisor is assigned to manage an additional department, or the department is split or is shifted to a different division in the organization, the employees' reactions may be one of uncertainty about their own future. And their response may be the same if they are transferred to a different department or plant or are assigned new responsibilities.

Reasons for Resistance to Change

In an earlier chapter, it was pointed out that one of the basic human characteristics is resistance to change. When confronted with change, the individual is faced with a choice—to accept it as having a potential benefit or to resist it because of its possible uncertainties. The question is whether to disturb the comfort and security of the status quo for the uncertain possibility of greater benefit.

It should be pointed out that not all employees resist change, but management would be wise to recognize that there is a very real tendency on the part of most people to do so. Consequently, the actual installation of change should be preceded by adequate planning and communication in order to minimize resistance. Just because management can see an advantage in making a change and can even prove this to the employee, there is no automatic guarantee that the employee will leap on the bandwagon. The following are some of the more common reasons for resistance to change.

Economic considerations. Will automation replace the individual? Will new standards be set that the employee may not be able to meet? Will the economic value of hir skills be reduced? The real concern of employees is for the future of their jobs and incomes. If they have heard rumors of automation replacing hundreds of employees, they are unlikely to be enthusiastic about a machine that can perform their jobs faster and at one-tenth the cost. Since economic considerations are often the primary reason for resistance to change, this uncertainty must be met and resolved before employees will accept the change willingly.

Possible inconvenience. We tend to cling to the old ways lest we make life more difficult for ourselves. We develop a vested interest in our habits and patterns of behavior. Learning new ways requires expenditure of both mental and physical energy, as well as time. So we often reject anything that upsets our routine and causes inconvenience.

Uncertainty about the unknown. The new way is always strange, threatening, and laden with uncertainties—even when it is an improvement. Many employees have turned down promotions and opportunities for more pay because they feared the change and lacked confidence in their ability to meet the new challenge.

Threat to social relationships. The social group is an important factor in the employee's job satisfaction. The work group becomes almost a second family. If this group gives the employee identification and acceptance, change often represents a threat because it may jeopardize this important relationship.

Resistance to changes affecting status symbols. Location of desks and offices, titles, company privileges, and a host of other symbols are often attached to particular jobs. Employees are inclined to resist anything that affects these status symbols. Though a change may in fact be trifling, it looms large if it seems to infringe on one's status; if it removes any outward sign of status, no matter how small, it may—to employees—signal the undermining of their security.

Guides for Reducing Resistance to Change

The following suggestions have proved most successful in minimizing employee resistance to change.

Insure adequate understanding through effective communication. People fear the unknown; they trust and accept the things they understand. The real job of communication is to bring the employee to the point of understanding by eliminating the uncertainties, the hidden threats to job and security. The goal is to make the unknown known and thus acceptable. Research, planning, and the most effective techniques of communication should be a part of the process of providing employees with all the facts. Management and supervisors should not succumb to the temptation to slant information concerning change to the point of misleading employees.

Consider economic incentives. Money is still highly effective in gaining the attention, interest, and response of the employee. Since change may represent an economic threat, the surest way to overcome the resistance this creates is through economic incentives. Whenever possible, employees should be assured that they will continue to make at least as much money as in the past. And if the possibility of greater earnings can be offered, it will be an added inducement to accept the change without further resistance.

Promote acceptance through group decision making. It is easier for employees to accept a decision that they have had a share in making. Not all changes can hinge on employee preference or democratic vote, but practical ways can be found to involve the work group in making the final decision. For example, the matter could be brought to their attention at a group meeting or in personal letters sent to their homes, or it could be handled on a departmental level by each supervisor. This in itself becomes an effective means of communicating the necessity for the change as well as the details of the change.

Maintain an environment of continuous improvement. Supervisors are the key to making a smooth change. If they have developed a close relationship with the members of the work group, the employees will tend to trust them. And if, over a period of time, they have instituted small changes from which the employees have benefited, they will have created an environment in which change is accepted as a natural part of the work situation.

Make changes tentative. It is not always possible to make changes on a tentative basis, but the advantage is obvious. If a new product or the installation of expensive machinery is involved, permanent changes must be made. But in instances involving the transfer of an employee or a minor change in procedure, it may be possible to permit the employee to try it out on a temporary basis. Hir is usually much more willing to accept a change if there is the possibility of returning to the old and familiar way in case the new one doesn't work out.

Interview and motivate. There is no substitute for sitting down and reasoning together. The success of this device depends on the degree of skill the supervisor is able to bring to the situation. Supervisors must be fortified with facts so that they can show the employee the necessity for the change and that past changes have worked out to the workers' advantage. This method gives the supervisor the opportunity to discover the reasons for any resistance and to supply the best answers available. Even if the answers do not entirely satisfy the employees, they will at least have had an opportunity to talk about the situation and learn the truth, which is in itself reassuring.

Follow-up. It has been said that change is the only law of survival and the only constant. This is perhaps another way of saying that the company, the supervisor, and the employee should be conditioned to continuing change. The best way to accomplish change and minimize employee resistance in the future is to handle today's change effectively.

To insure a smooth transiton and continued acceptance by the employees, small adjustments should be made as needed. Bring to the employees' attention the benefits the change brings. Remind them that change is a way of life in a modern progressive company that expects to grow and offer even better jobs to its employees in the future. Gradually, employees will be conditioned to trust the supervisor and the company to make changes that will be in their best interest. But it should be remembered that resistance to change is a normal employee reaction and overcoming it requires the skillful use of human leadership tools.

Opps in mg cameras
HF 5579, M277
When giants loom
HD 58, 8 & 365 1989

the rocky mgr
HF 5579, 12, 577 2000
managmt: tasks resrcs etc
658, 4, D84

Learning draws back the curtain on a wonderful new world of knowledge and potential. Learning may well be the key to success for both the employee and the supervisor.

11

Techniques for Learning

HOW important are learning and retention to the supervisor? Should they be left to educators or training directors? If the supervisor ever expects to train new employees adequately or if hir expects to improve the quantity and quality of work now being done, hir must make efficient use of learning.

The entire process of growth is dependent on people's ability to learn and to translate what they have learned into favorable change. Unless the company and the individual are satisfied to stand still, learning must take place. The efficient application of learning techniques is the responsibility of supervisors: Their teaching ability should enable the employee to meet profitable production standards with minimum expenditures of time, energy, and money.

Learning has been described as a modification of behavior. This may be subject to debate. Perhaps learning could occur without any apparent change in behavior. But supervisors have to be practical people. For them, training time and effort are wasted until a change is effected. From the standpoint of both supervisor and company, learning is useful or purposeful only when it results in increased production, in less time required for results, or in increased overall efficiency.

The Human Learning Machinery

Many of our reactions are not the direct result of learning, but are instinctive and automatic. (For example, we don't have to learn to react to bodily discomforts.) Supervisors are not concerned with the behavior patterns and reactions that are beyond their influence. Instead, their attention is centered on those actions and reactions that respond to learning.

Single-cell animals, such as the amoeba, react to various stimuli in the environment. The amoeba possesses sensitivity and mobility, despite its lack of nervous tissue. However, because it lacks a nervous system, it cannot store up the effects of its experiences, as can higher forms of animal life, and therefore is unable to profit from learning.

Humans possess a very complicated communication system comparable to the wires of a highly complex computer. This tissue of the nervous system is both modifiable and retentive. The regions of possible change are called synapses (junction points across which nerve impulses pass). Numbering in the billions, they furnish the neurological basis for intelligence and learning. As these synapses are used, changes occur, experience is retained, and repetition of similar actions is made easier. In this manner, learning occurs. The nervous system's modifiability, sensitivity, and capacity to conduct impulses determine an individual's learning capacity. Although this feature is influenced by heredity, it is developed largely through use and acquired experience.

Basic Laws of Learning

As individuals go through life, their everyday experiences are constantly creating new tendencies. A tendency to act in a certain way because one has acted that way before is referred to as "learned behavior." This law of learning, which can also be called the *law of retention,* is applicable to the teaching of new patterns as well as to the correction of undesirable learning.

Laboratory experiments, controlled psychological tests, and experience have demonstrated that certain basic laws govern the manner in which learning takes place, the most efficient methods of learning, the amount that will be learned, and the time required for learning. This set of laws can serve as a practical guide for the supervisor as he seeks to promote learning in the employee group.

The law of frequency. Each time an activity is repeated, impulses are communicated through the nervous system, modifications are made, and the resulting changes make it easier for the same impulses to go through the system on subsequent occasions. Advertisers apply this law when they use oft-repeated slogans, and teachers apply it when they call for repeated drills, whether verbal or physical. Similarly, the supervisor who wants to implant a new skill asks the employee to repeat a job procedure many times. The more frequently the activity is performed correctly, the more likely it is to be learned and remembered.

As an activity is repeated, it moves from the conscious to the subconscious level—from the awareness that to achieve a desired result certain prescribed steps must be followed to the habit of acting automatically without thought or analysis. A baby has to learn to lift a spoon to its mouth; as an adult, he or she will go through the process without thinking. It has been estimated that more than 60 percent of our activities require no conscious thought, but occur as the result of learning which has developed into fixed patterns of behavior.

The supervisor can make good use of this law of frequency by recognizing that performing a job correctly one time does not guarantee that it has been learned. An employee may have to perform the job correctly many times. Repetition of the work cycle should therefore continue to the point where correct performance becomes a habit.

The law of intensity. We experience many things which make little or no impression on us; their influence may be so insignificant that we learn nothing and forget almost instantaneously. Other influences are so strong and so intense that they make lasting impressions and will be remembered for years. Because of this, the supervisor should attempt to make the learning experience dramatic and intense. The use of visual aids, demonstrations, and other learning gimmicks will help to make the exposure more intense and thus increase the probability of learning.

The law of recency. What has been learned most recently is most likely to be remembered, but if learning is not applied quickly, much of it will be lost. Advertisers know this. They urge us to "go to the corner drugstore right now" because the longer we put it off, the greater the chance we will forget. There is a predictable falling off of response with delay. Since supervisors can anticipate that an activity performed very recently will be easier for the employee to repeat, but that one not repeated for many months is likely to be forgotten, they should arrange for the repetition of newly learned actions to ensure that the employee retains the procedure.

Carrier-based pilots know the importance of this law of learning. So exacting is the technique of landing a plane on the deck of an aircraft carrier that training takes months of intensive practice. Yet, if a pilot makes no carrier landings for an interval of 30 days, hir is required to practice the entire procedure on land before hir is allowed to make actual landings on board ship again.

The law of duration. A short, concentrated training program usually does not result in as much permanent learning as one that can be extended over a longer time span. People reach a saturation point—they have limits on what they can absorb in a given time. Usually, more learning takes place if the same training—the same actions, and the same amount of information—can be distributed over a longer period. From a practical standpoint, supervisors need to take this into consideration in planning training. They may be more successful by separating a complex operation into various parts, teaching one part at a time, and providing for enough practice so that each part is completely learned before the next part is begun.

The law of effect. The effect that learning has on the individual will influence the amount that is learned. Experiments have demonstrated that when learning has a pleasant effect, it produces the best results. The supervisor can speed up the learning process by recognizing and praising evidence of learning, emphasizing the pleasant effect of learning—increased job security, more money, a better chance for promotion—and by making certain that the employee has a sensc of personal accomplishment.

The law of association. It is almost impossible for individuals who have just emerged from a primitive society to learn the hundreds of things necessary to meet the requirements of a white collar job. They have very little with which to compare or associate the new information. Since learning is largely a matter of associating the unknown with the known, they will be almost at a total loss. The person who knows most about a subject finds it easiest to learn and assimilate additional information. The student who has mastered two languages finds it easier to learn a third and easier still to master a fourth.

The supervisor needs to recognize that the current knowledge of employees will determine the starting point for new job training and will influence the speed with which hir can learn related information. Every effort should be made to associate new information with what the employee already knows and understands. One teacher put it this way: "In teaching literature, you have to start at the present understanding level of the student. If this happens to be the comic-book stage, then that is where you have to begin. If you start too high, you pass over the head of the student and they will never catch up. Start with what they know, and then you can bring them along to the higher ground." This applies with equal validity to the supervisor who must be concerned with training.

Methods of Learning

It is significant that people learn principally by three basic methods. Not all of them produce the same results and some are more costly than others. A careful analysis by the supervisor will determine which hir should use to promote maximum learning. Each of the following methods has a special function. If the wrong one is used, the results will be costly and disappointing.

The trial-and-error method. If a chicken is placed on one side of a wire fence and food is placed on the other side, the chicken will have difficulty getting to the food. Even if the fence is short and open at both ends, the chicken will stick its head through the fence and either try to crawl through or try to fly over. It will do these things again and again, never stopping to figure out the solution to the problem. After much trial and error, the chicken may accidentally wander around one end of the fence. A little learning has taken place and the next time, the chicken is likely to get to one end of the fence a bit sooner. The trial-and-error method of learning has its value—sometimes it's the only way to find the answers.

Consider, however, the tremendous cost, the waste of time and materials, and the number of unhappy customers there would be if all new employees had to learn their jobs through trial and error. Yet this is precisely what has to happen if the supervisor does not take the time to train new people. Too often, through neglect or lack of interest, employees are left to their own improvisations to learn the job. This obviously is too expensive to the company and too detrimental to the development of the employee. Neither can afford this type of learning, and it therefore is the responsibility of the supervisor to guarantee that employees are not left to sink or swim.

The imitation method. A dog's intelligence level is higher than that of a chicken, and it would probably solve the food-and-fence problem differently. If the dog saw people going around the end of the fence, it would be able to deduce that it could follow suit. The dog would thus have learned to solve the problem by the imitation method, and the next time it would quickly go to the end of the fence to reach its goal.

Imitation has a place in learning, and it is used successfully in apprentice programs—it is often the best method to learn manual skills. Demonstrations that can be imitated promote learning. This is the reason a new employee is often placed alongside an experienced worker and asked to imitate the work procedures of the seasoned individual.

Imitating correct procedures and techniques has a tremendous advantage over the trial-and-error method, yet it is not the most efficient way to learn because it takes excessive time and does not lend itself to all types of information.

Logical analysis, or the reasoning method. If a human being were on one side of a strip of fence and a desirable object were on the other, hir would simply look the situation over, recognize that hir was not fenced in, and figure out the best way to get to the other side before taking any specific course of action, thereby saving a tremendous amount of time over the trial-and-error method. People are able to utilize information that is stored in the brain and to deduce solutions by logical analysis. This is the most efficient learning method—it is the most direct, the least time consuming, and the most economical. To be used appropriately, this method requires preparation and the development of a definite program which can be expected to promote maximum learning.

Supervisors need to make a careful analysis of the methods used in their departments both for training new people and for teaching new techniques and improvements to more experienced employees. Supervisors cannot afford to permit the use of inefficient teaching and learning methods any more than they can justify the use of inefficient machinery.

Methods of Gaining Attention

A certain amount of learning will result from coincidental exposure or casual association, but the amount is limited and haphazard. Promoting maximum learning in minimum time demands a more deliberate approach. Learning occurs most often when the subject receives undivided attention and is approached with a deliberate intent to train. The supervisor therefore needs to devise methods that hold the attention and maximum interest of the learner.

Public speakers, sales managers, and advertisers use many methods to get people's initial attention. An almost unlimited variety of gimmicks is employed, and they all serve a useful purpose if they gain the attention of the person to whom they are directed. The *objective* determinants of attention include *change,* such as motion or relocation, *uniqueness or novelty, size,* and *color.* These are overt techniques to gain attention. The circus barker shows just enough of his unusual collection of oddities to arouse interest. Store windows feature moving displays to draw the eyes of passers-by. These techniques are valuable to supervisors, too. To gain and hold the attention of those they must train, supervisors have at their disposal many visual aids that can be used to great advantage in the learning process.

Gaining attention through *subjective* techniques involves reasoning with employees and appealing to them to meet their own needs through additional learning. People must learn the job initially and must then learn to do more difficult work in order to reach their goal. Beyond that, every person has special interests that can be satisfied only through additional learning. An individual may in fact spend more time learning about a hobby than in learning to do the job better. When these special interests relate to a person's work and when that relationship is emphasized during on-the-job training, hir will learn more and learn it faster.

A man equips his car with safety belts because he is concerned about the safety of his family. He buys insurance to help meet their need for security. And he should learn to perform his job in the best manner to meet his own need for security and for growth.

Steps in the Learning Process

Individuals go through certain steps in learning and in retaining what they have learned. The supervisor needs to make a close study of these steps and use them in order to promote learning. The first step is *set,* or *adjustment.* This refers to the degree to which individuals want to learn: their attitude must be receptive. The second step is *selection of contributing factors,* such as motions or procedures essential to adequate performance. A clear understanding of what is to be learned enables people to include those factors that contribute to the final goal. These are then made a part of their knowledge and skills.

The third step is *discarding noncontributing factors,* such as wasteful procedures. Certain factors are negative and actually interfere with the learning process. These need to be identified and discarded. Improvement requires gradually focusing on correct techniques. *Fixation of learning* is the final step in the learning process. Learning has not become permanent until it can be repeated and becomes fixed in the response pattern; but even at this point, attention must continue to insure that negative habits do not inadvertently set in.

It is within the framework of these four steps that supervisors must plan and execute training so that they can bring their employees to the point of satisfactory retention of the knowledge and skills required by the job.

Influences on Learning Achievement

How much learning will employees achieve? The answer is significant to their success as well as to the achievement of the department as a whole. The following factors should be considered in predicting the probable amount of learning.

The influence of motivation. The amount of learning a person achieves is determined by ability plus motivation. Motivation, then, is one of the two necessary ingredients. If the desire to achieve a goal is increased, the determination to learn becomes greater and learning is increased.

A bright and capable young man was coasting along, making no effort to expand his knowledge because he believed that he was doing his job successfully and that there was no point in exerting himself. The supervisor pointed out that some changes were contemplated, that additional supervisors would be needed, and that these positions would be filled by promotions from within the company. This was motivation enough: the young man asked the supervisor's advice about what training would best prepare him. He then took company-sponsored courses and was ready when there was a new opening for a supervisory job.

The effect of age. "You can't teach an old dog new tricks" is an oft-repeated cliché that has caused both supervisors and employees to miss tremendous potential improvements. Facts simply do not support the theory that older adults cannot learn. An objective evaluation shows that the ability to learn increases through the early twenties, levels off through the early fifties, and shows an almost insignificant decline thereafter unless senility sets in. Our ability to develop new physical skills that require strength, quick reaction, and muscular coordination does decrease as we grow older; the best years for the athlete are his twenties and thirties. But the ability to acquire knowledge does not decline as rapidly as is popularly believed.

Often, what seems to be a limited ability to learn may instead be a lower energy supply or lessened motivation. Older people might cling to the status quo and resist learning new techniques if they begin to feel less secure and less confident in their ability to cope with new experiences. This seemingly lowered ability to learn is a defense mechanism that may stem from a fear of failure, since age might make it more difficult to get a new job. This often creates a tendency on the part of older people to hang on to the security of their existing knowledge, status, and skills.

When the supervisor who works with older people understands that much of their resistance stems from insecurity and that they are able to learn—even though they may be reluctant to do so—hir will encourage them and instill in them the self-confidence that will promote learning. Where possible, hir should modify training procedures to suit an individual's pace.

The impact of education. The more education a person has, the more hir can acquire. This is based on two facts: Educational achievement is in itself an indication of learning ability, and acquired knowledge is a foundation for additional knowledge. Innate intelligence, acquired knowledge, and vocabulary are significant factors in learning. For instance, 14-year-old children may be handicapped in competing with adults by the very fact that their vocabulary and understanding of word symbols are limited.

Often, employees already know a considerable portion of what they need to know to do a new job. If they are new in the company, they must learn new procedures and perhaps also learn to operate a machine that varies somewhat from the one they might have used on the last job. If they are transferred within the company, they must learn the routines of the new department and perhaps also the operation of a new machine. But in neither case do they have to learn everything about the job from scratch. In each case they bring to the job what they already know, and adapt this knowledge to the needs of the new situation. The same is true when a football player takes up baseball—the speed, coordination, timing, and other factors used in one sport are also useful in the other.

The influence of conditioning. Learning can be stimulated by subconscious association. Ivan Pavlov's experiments on conditioned reflexes are a case in point. Pavlov, a Russian physiologist, knew that when food was presented to a dog, its saliva would flow. To test his theory that reflexes could be conditioned, he presented dogs with two stimulators at the same time—food and the sound of a bell. Eventually, as a result of conditioning, the reaction was transferred to the bell, and the dogs' saliva flowed when the bell was sounded even though no food was offered at the time.

The supervisor can make use of the principle of conditioning by presenting more than one phase of a job at the same time. If, for example, the more unpleasant aspects of a job are presented along with the pleasant ones, the employee may be conditioned to cope with the unpleasant factors and to consider them acceptable. Thus, the presentation of related aspects of the job in conjunction with each other may speed the learning of both.

The pace of presentation. People learn at different rates, depending on their ability and their experience. If the supervisor attempts to present too much new information to the learner at one time, considerable waste or spillover will result. The situation may be compared to the attempt to pour liquid into the mouth of a jug too quickly: only so much can pass through the neck at once, and the excess is spilled or wasted. The supervisor's training methods should be adapted to the employee's learning pace in order to minimize wasted effort.

Changing Incorrect Learning

The supervisor is often faced with the need to change the incorrect habits employees bring either to the job or have acquired on the job. This can often be more difficult than teaching them something from the beginning. The elimination of old patterns delays acceptance of the new, because each time the individuals follow a new technique they have to overcome their old habits. The best course for the supervisor is to substitute a stronger and more desirable learning pattern. Once the new pattern has been acquired, it should be used frequently.

An efficient method of study and the learning environment are of utmost importance. The amount of time the individual devotes to learning is one of the least significant factors affecting the amount learned. Of greater importance are motivation, interest in learning, and the efficiency of study techniques. The more systematically a learner tests or reviews new information, the faster learning will be achieved. Of course, if an employee has only half a day to learn to operate a machine, the process must be speeded up to meet the demands of the situation. Generally, the less time available, the more testing and repetition are required for satisfactory learning.

When information must be memorized, experimental data show that, instead of focusing on small units, the information should be read through from start to finish and studied as a whole so that attention is divided uniformly throughout. Similarly, when an employee is learning to operate a machine or to perform a job activity, seeing the overall operation promotes learning and retention. When isolated bits are learned separately, they must eventually be fitted into their appropriate slots: this requires additional learning even after the various parts have been mastered.

The operator of a bakery machine had difficulty remembering to activate the salting button at the right time. The resultant waste of dough was irritating to the supervisor and expensive to the company. In analyzing the situation, the supervisor discovered that the lady had not been taught the operation as a whole; instead, several people had taught her isolated parts of the process. The supervisor decided to retrain the woman, and this time the process was outlined, a checklist was made, and the activation of the salting mechanism was included at the proper point in the sequence. The job now became a logical series of activities, and the omission of one step was corrected.

In another instance, a department store in Boston decided to take a new approach to training salespeople in the techniques of completing sales. The normal procedure had been to spend about two days teaching new employees how to write out sales tickets, ring the cash register, and handle the other written and mechanical routines. When this had been completed, the salesperson then had to learn how to sell.

The new procedure was to set up a counter with merchandise and let one salesperson take the role of the customer and have another assume the role of the clerk. Now the new employee learned the selling technique as a logical first step, and the completion of the sales transaction became more meaningful when it followed the customer's decision to buy. Learning improved, and the salespeople were able to handle the complete operation more efficiently when they finally arrived on the selling floor.

Sometimes, trying to learn too many unrelated activities at one time results in confusion and a minimum amount of learning. Most jobs involve many different skills and activities, but it is usually unwise to try to introduce them to a new employee all at once. Instead, all the steps of one activity should be learned thoroughly before learning the next one. For instance, if all the steps in a bookeeper's job were presented to a new employee at once, the total operation would seem so complex as to be impossible to understand. But if the procedure for receiving and verifying invoices is the new book-keeper's introduction to the job, and if, after this step is mastered, the process of posting to the proper department is well learned, and so on, then the entire training process can be speeded up.

Most people find that a certain amount of pressure speeds up the learning process. The student who simply reads casually will probably learn a minimum amount, but the more active approach of out-lining, writing down key points, repeating special passages, and working with a degree of urgency will speed both learning and re-tention. Supervisors need to recognize that they can substantially increase learning if they bring in the more active factors—visual aids, discussion, and participation by the learner—while at the same time eliminating distractions of all types, which are deterrents to learning.

Learning and Supervision

No one can have more interest in results than the people who are delegated the responsibility for those results. In the case of a com-pany, these are the supervisors, who must train new people and improve the performance of the present employees.

Work results will remain static unless knowledge is increased and skills are improved. These are the direct result of learning. If super-visors are to discharge their responsibilities, they should keep the following facts in mind:

1. They need to know the principles involved in learning.
2. They must be convinced of the importance of learning.
3. They should be aware of the reasons why learning does or does not occur.
4. They should be able to select the most efficient learning meth-ods.
5. They should make adequate provision for interest and mo-tivation.

6. They should evaluate progress and make appropriate adjustments along the way to ensure that learning continues.

Supervisors must remember that there is no rigid pattern that will guarantee training results. This chapter has emphasized that a wide variety of techniques should be utilized, as dictated by circumstances.

Training is the process by which the ability to perform specific jobs is acquired and increased.

12

Improving Performance and Results Through Training

TRAINING is an expensive activity. One utility company has set the cost of executive training at $14,000 per trainee. The training of a single production, office, or sales employee usually costs hundreds of dollars. Yet a company can justify the expense by comparing it with what an untrained employee wastes in payroll dollars, resources, lost customers, and jeopardized competitive position. The financial burden of an untrained worker can be far greater than the cost of training. Consider, for example, what an untrained shoe salesperson can cost the company. There will be lost sales because the salesperson may not know how to fit shoes, may not be able to find the merchandise, may be ignorant of the unique properties of leather or the construction of shoes, and may be unaware of how to sell accessory items. Inefficiency irritates some customers so much that they never return to the store. Extra work is created for the bookkeeping department when transactions are written improperly. And because of fumbling and bumbling, the employee feels a sense of inadequacy and failure, so that the likelihood that hir will ever become a competent and productive employee is diminished.

A company is committed to paying each employee for every hour spent on the job. To receive an appropriate return on its investment, it must make certain that each employee reaches and maintains a profitable level of production. This can be done only through an effective training program.

The Objectives of Training

The general objectives of training are to:

- ☐ Increase the quantity and quality of output by improving employee skills.
- ☐ Reduce accidents.
- ☐ Increase the return to the employee in personal rewards—that is, more pay, recognition, and other benefits which the employee wants from the job.
- ☐ Make the operation more profitable by reducing the amount of equipment and material required to produce or sell a given unit.
- ☐ Make it possible for the supervisor to spend less time in correcting mistakes and to spend more in overall supervision.
- ☐ Minimize discharges because of inadequate skills.
- ☐ Improve morale and achieve a more satisfactory working environment.
- ☐ Enable new employees to meet the job requirements and enable experienced employees to accept transfers, operate new machines, adapt to new methods, increase efficiency, and adjust to changing needs.
- ☐ Encourage willingness, loyalty, interest, and the desire to excel.

Training is a deliberate effort by the company to supply employees with the skills and information that will enable them to perform the job satisfactorily. The starting point for this important management activity is the determination of need. The first step in determining training needs is to identify the skills required on the job. The second is to find out how much of those skills the employee already possesses, and the third is to decide what must be learned to bridge the gap. The need for training is revealed in many ways: poor production results; incorrect or inefficient procedures; low merit ratings of job performance; adverse employee attitudes; poor quality; high wastage; antiquated work methods; or unachieved goals.

Supervisors have the primary responsibility for training. Some companies have a central training department; in others there is no formal training facility. In either case, the ultimate responsibility for training rests with supervisors. They know the job better than anyone else and have the opportunity to conduct the training in a realistic rather than an artificial environment, as well as being more vitally concerned with the worker's adjustment and production. Supervisors are also in the best position to observe, evaluate, and follow up the results of the training.

Centralized training is especially useful for indoctrinating new employees—informing them about company history, policies, and benefits—and for teaching general information that is necessary for all employees. For example, all department store salespeople must know how to make out a sales ticket and handle a cash register, whether they will sell bath soap or bridge tables. These procedures can be taught in a central training facility in which an expert with a specialized training background can teach employees what they need to know without distraction and without interfering in the operations of any department.

But centralized training cannot supplant the training each supervisor must provide for employees in the department. Each department has special needs and unique problems for which special instruction must be given. And the social relationships within each department are unique and must be adapted to within the department. Since supervisors are rated on the basis of departmental accomplishment, their own personal interest in results is often greater than that of a central training director. The final training and follow-up must therefore be done in the department by the supervisor.

It is evident that centralized and departmental training each have unique advantages—they complement each other in the well-planned program. The company, however, should not provide so much of the training that the supervisor feels no responsibility for training or for the results of training.

The preparation of a training program must be based on the goals to be reached and the performance necessary to reach these goals. Planning should include the following considerations:

Type of training needed.
Most effective methods of presenting each type.
Time and place for conducting the training.

Preparation of the outlines, visual aids, props, and other items.
Selection and indoctrination of the instructors.
Administration and scheduling of the program.
Employee notification.
Evaluation of the results.

One of the most serious challenges faced by the training function is the difficulty of measuring results. Many company activities can be measured and evaluated precisely, but that is not true of training. Perhaps, in a sense, training ought to be considered in the same light as advertising; although the exact value of advertising may be difficult to measure, its overall value is nonetheless evident.

An evaluation of training can be made by before-and-after comparisons of job performance and production through the use of questionnaires and rating forms to check results and through interviews with individual employees to determine their reactions. Or a more scientific method of evaluation may be used by dividing the employees into two groups before the program is begun—having one (the test group) take the training and the other (the control group) continue working as usual—and comparing the before-and-after performance of both groups. This method is especially good for testing new training techniques—programmed instruction, for example—to determine whether they are suitable for use throughout the company. The key test is whether production increases, costs, and waste are reduced, and whether customer relations and profits are improved.

Special attention must be given to welcoming, inducting, and training new employees. Since supervisors become the symbol of management, what they do during the early stages can have a decisive effect on the employee's future work results and length of employment.

New employees should be assisted in forming a favorable attitude toward the firm. They should understand fully their conditions of employment. By exhibiting friendliness toward them and by supplying them with all the necessary information, the supervisor can help eliminate their anxieties and uncertainties. The supervisor should take time to get acquainted with them. The few minutes taken for a get-acquainted interview can set the stage for employees' better understanding their new environment. Since the supervisor cannot cover adequately all the information the employee may want, the best thing hir can do is to create an atmosphere in which the employee will feel free to talk and ask questions.

The company receives no actual benefit from the employee's

presence on the job until a profitable contribution is being made. Training is preparation; good job performance is the end result. The supervisor should have available a specific plan for teaching each job so that training will be accomplished as quickly and economically as possible. The four steps in this type of instruction normally include a complete introduction to the operation; a supervisor's or instructor's performance of the operation; the employee's performance of the operation; and correct continuing practice to ensure that the training will not be forgotten.

Effective Training Techniques

An almost endless number of training techniques have come to the fore in recent years. The techniques discussed in this chapter are those found to be most effective in producing results and those that are practical for use by individual supervisors as well as in company training programs.

Individualized training is perhaps the most commonly used and the most effective technique. It consists of a supervisor training one person at a time through the process of explaining and showing how the job should be done. The first step in this technique is to recognize what the job requires, learn what knowledge the employee already possesses, and decide what the individual still needs to learn to meet the requirements of the job. This can be one of the most effective types of training, because it can be designed to meet very specific needs.

Department meetings are ideally suited for communicating changes in work schedules or in departmental operation and for uniformly disseminating other information to entire groups. These meetings should be announced in advance, and the materials needed should be in readiness. Every meeting should start and end on time. Employees should have a clear understanding of the purpose of the meeting, and should have an opportunity to ask questions and to participate fully. Appropriate visual aids should be used to help make the meeting stimulating and interesting, and every meeting should end on an enthusiastic note.

The real success of the group approach to training depends on the leader's ability to involve the entire group. It has been clearly established that employee involvement in the training process, whether through discussion or role playing, leads to greatly improved response. The extent to which the supervisor can involve the employees often determines the effectiveness of the training.

The incident technique uses one or more occurrences as a basis for discussion and as a means of making specific points—without, however, singling out any one employee for criticism. Errors that are common to the group should be discussed, not one individual's mistakes. After describing an incident, the supervisor asks for suggestions as to how it should be handled. Incidents can be taken from the department, borrowed from other departments, or structured to emphasize the point that the supervisor wishes to cover. This technique is simple and interesting, it does not require much time, gets the point across effectively, and involves employees in the discussion.

Role playing is one of the most flexible training techniques, and it almost always gets the employees' interest. As the name implies, one person assumes the role of another—supervisor, employee, or customer, for example. Each person playing a role is asked to improvise and use hirs imagination in supplying the information necessary to move the interview to a successful conclusion. To make the situation more realistic, the two should have a specific job or job setting in mind. It is sometimes helpful if the individuals playing the roles get together beforehand to compare notes and decide how the situation should be handled. The basic facts should be given to the group before the two individuals begin role playing. Then, after 10 to 20 minutes of role playing, the entire group should be asked to comment on what was discussed and how the matter could have been handled more effectively. Role playing gives the participants the feel of handling the problem and involves everyone in the discussion of the particular situation. It can be one of the supervisor's most effective training techniques.

The case method is usually a longer and more involved version of the incident technique. It may cover a chapter in the life of the company and of the employees concerned with the case. Information on the case for discussion is given to the participants in advance to enable them to study it thoroughly. They are asked to give their opinions on what went wrong in the first place, how the problem could have been prevented, how the same sort of situation could be avoided in the future, and how the matter should be handled at this point.

When the employees assemble for the discussion, they should be seated around a table. The leader's function is to initiate the discussion, keep on the subject, see that all essential points are covered, and act as a referee. The group should be led to develop ideas and solve the problems by recognizing the differences between problems that must be solved immediately and those that can be dealt with over a longer period—and by realizing that problems usually have several correct as well as several incorrect solutions and that each individual's way of solving them reflects hirs own ability and personal characteristics.

To be effective, these discussions should involve everyone in the group and should express opposing points of view so that there will be a thorough analysis of the case. Sometimes, impromptu role playing is useful in clarifying the issues. When the case has been discussed thoroughly, the supervisor should pull together the thinking of the group and restate the conclusions. The case method is most commonly used for training supervisors and higher levels of management in the skill of problem-solving.

The conference method generally has a leader or chairperson and one or more subjects to be discussed. There are no prescribed rules for this type of training meeting. The group usually functions in an informal way with almost complete freedom of discussion. The leader or chairperson should exercise some direction, or there is a danger that the group will stray too far afield and fail to cover the assigned task.

Demonstrations use visual aids or pieces of equipment to illustrate and supplement verbal instruction. Employees like demonstrations because they can actually see what is being done, thus making the training more interesting and easier to remember. Learning and retention are improved even more if the employee takes part in the demonstration technique.

The following are visual aids commonly used in training: chalkboards, closed-circuit television, models, teaching machines, maps, manuals, transparencies, movies, charts and graphs, actual objects, posters, opaque projectors, mockups of actual machines, specimens, bulletin boards, photographs, and film strips.

Apprentice training is still used for many jobs. A skilled worker performs an operation repeatedly and the trainee gradually learns through imitation. It was through this method that skilled craftsmen learned their trades in the past. Although the principle of imitation is still used, the techniques have been refined and made more sophisticated through the use of visual aids designed to speed up the learning process.

Important Training Guides

The trainer or supervisor should review the training plan to make certain that hir knows thoroughly every aspect of the job that is to be imparted to the learner. The trainer's ability commands the confidence of the learner and leads to fast and efficient mastery of the activity.

Determine how much the newcomer needs to learn. The supervisor should prepare a complete job description for training purposes and then compare the job requirements with the qualifications of the new employee. The job requirements minus what the employee already knows should equal the training needed. The supervisor should not assume that because the employee performed a similar operation elsewhere, hir is qualified to perform the job now involved.

Prepare a training plan. This should include a breakdown of the job into its logical steps, with special notation of key points. In making the training plans, supervisors should ask themselves these questions:

- □ What do I want to teach?
- □ Why should the employees learn? What are the advantages of training for them?
- □ How can I show them these advantages?
- □ What do they already know that is similar?
- □ What method is best to use in teaching the unknown in terms of the known?
- □ What is the best follow-up, to make certain that the information is understood and used correctly?

Consider individual differences. People come to the job with differing ability to learn and vastly different degrees of acquired skills. Some learn slowly at first; others learn quickly. As much as possible, all employees should be considered individually, and the training should be adapted to their individual needs.

Build motivation and interest. The supervisor creates interest in training by showing the importance of the information and of the skill that is being taught and by showing the necessity for the mastery if the employee expects to meet the requirements of the job.

Maintain a sense of humor. A sense of humor creates a closer and friendlier relationship with the employee and lessens tension.

Ensure clarity of expression and explanation. The presentation of information should be understandable. The supervisor should use only those terms and symbols with which the learner is familiar.

Build self-confidence in the learner. The learner needs to know how hir is getting along. Recognition of progress gives the individual the confidence to move forward to additional learning.

Evaluate progress. Many companies have check sheets to gauge the amount of learning that has taken place. These sheets may be used at the end of the first day, at the end of the training program, or as a follow-up check after the employee has spent some time on the job. Evaluation of learning identifies incorrect habits and techniques and indicates what additional training is still needed. Remember that practice does not necessarily make perfect. For practice to contribute to improvement, a deliberate effort must be made to eliminate errors and to benefit through repetition.

Selecting and Training an Assistant Supervisor

In selecting an assistant, certain qualifications appear to be of prime importance: seniority, production, ambition, interest in promotion, intelligence, aggressiveness, dependability, ability to get along with others, leadership qualities, and cooperation. Due consideration should be given to all these traits, but each must be evaluated in relation to the requirements of the specific position. The individual finally selected must be the one who has demonstrated leadership qualities more clearly than anyone else. Hir should have maintained harmonious working relationships with others, as well as being an excellent producer; hir should have shown willingness to assist others in the department, although this may not have been required; and should have displayed leadership during the supervisor's absence, even though hir did not have the title or official responsibility of the supervisory position.

The training program should bring the assistant from hirs present level to the point where hir is able to handle all the duties and responsibilities of the supervisor's job. Since the supervisor will probably be promoted or transferred (or may take another job or retire), hir should regard the assistant as an eventual replacement.

Let hir know everything that you do. Explain the responsibilities of the job and how it fits into the organizational structure of the company. In short, transfer your understanding of the job to the assistant. Remember the effectiveness of coaching as a training technique. The development of your assistant is important to your own future.

Ask hirs opinion. Before telling the assistant how to do something, ask for hirs opinion. Hir will appreciate the opportunity to make a contribution, and it will give the assistant a good opportunity to develop judgment. Always ask the assistant to give reasons for the opinion. Rather than supplying answers yourself, encourage the assistant to make decisions.

Build a feeling of responsibility and self-confidence. Make the assistant responsible for part of the work, and follow up to see that the work is done properly. Try to move gradually into the background, and let the assistant move to the forefront. You must retain general responsibility and, if a few mistakes are made, supply the needed encouragement.

Support the assistant. Explain to the employees in the department that the assistant's instructions are to be followed in the same way as those issued directly by you. If an employee does something wrong because of the assistant's instructions, don't correct the employee. Instead, talk with the assistant and explain the correct procedure. Let hir correct the employee. Never criticize the assistant in the presence of others. Public criticism is the surest way to destroy employee confidence in your assistant—and in you. Refrain from making remarks that show disapproval of your assistant's handling of a situation.

Be straightforward and frank in dealing with the assistant. The assistant usually needs plenty of constructive criticism as hir learns and develops, to know what mistakes are being made and how they can be corrected. Probably the most unfair thing you could do would be to keep the assistant in the dark concerning hirs shortcomings. Your job is to train the assistant, so make the training straightforward and constructive. Your experienced judgment and direction can be of the greatest benefit to hirs development.

Recognize and commend progress. If the assistant makes a suggestion and it is adopted, give hir credit for it. If hir finds better ways of doing certain things, don't take it as a reflection on the way things have been done, but as an indication of the assistant's development and good judgment. Demonstrate that you appreciate the progress being made.

Gradually put the assistant on hirs own. The pilot instructor teaches a student to fly by instructing, demonstrating, and letting the learner get the feel of things. Then the instructor rides along as a passenger, and the student handles the plane. The last step is a solo flight, with the student in full control.

The supervisor–assistant relationship should be much the same. If the supervisor has done the proper job of training, hir should gradually let the assistant get the feel of things until hir is ready to take charge. But even then, it is not enough to let the assistant just get by. Hir must learn to refine and perfect hirs technique. The supervisor should keep in touch with the assistant in order to build hirs self-confidence, improved hirs skills, and give hir the needed support.

The primary purpose of training is creating a skill that in turn produces job results. But skill training is the simplest part; the necessity to train the employee's attitudes, loyalty, willingness, and desire to excell are more difficult. Before results are achieved, the whole person must be trained. Thus, training that limits itself to skills falls far short of fulfilling its potential. As supervisors approach their training task, they should recognize the types of skills and traits necessary to produce the required results. The supervisor must also remember that training must be continuous. So long as there is a need to learn new jobs, improve performance on the present job, learn new machines, and move to higher levels of responsibility, training will be a significant supervisory responsibility.

*Knowledge forgotten is like the tide that
has lapped on the beach and departed,
leaving no trace; it must be acquired all
over again.*

13

Improving Memory and Retention

MEMORY is generally understood to be the capacity to retain or revive impressions or to recreate previous experience. No one associated with an activity can have more direct concern with the retention of information and training than the supervisor who is charged with getting results. An accurate measure of net gain is not what has been taught but what has been learned and retained. In fact, training that is forgotten may do more harm than good, because the supervisor may be depending on a level of knowledge and skill that the employee does not have. The result is a waste of time and resources.

Training is costly, and training that must be repeated is costlier still; it wastes time, money, and equipment. Every effort must therefore be made to minimize waste by ensuring maximum retention.

Memory is a marvelous instrument but, like all complex instruments, it must be used properly. Many job failures have been summed up in the words, "I just forgot." Employees forget to wear safety equipment; they forget essential techniques of the job and company policies; they forget to be courteous to customers. Experts agree that memory can be significantly improved through deliberate effort. But first, we must realize that a poor memory is not an inherited trait like the shape of our bodies—we have simply not been trained to remember. Actually, a normal brain has stored within it

143

every impulse and experience to which it has been adequately exposed. The real challenge is to stimulate the conscious recall of these elements.

Why We Can't Remember

The first step toward improving memory is to recognize the reasons for insufficient retention and to eliminate these stumbling blocks. Perhaps the most significant cause of poor memory is an inadequate original impression. Memory can be compared to a camera. The snap of the shutter stores "information" on the film. But this information will be no better than the exposure. Memory can also be compared to a computer. Vast amounts of information can be inserted, stored, and recalled by the machine. However, nothing can be reproduced if it was not inserted, and correct answers will not be forthcoming if incorrect information is fed into the computer. The machine's capacity for retention and reproduction is based on the accuracy and adequacy of the original information.

Except for the adequacy of the initial impression, the most significant influence on the amount retained is motivation. People must have a reason for remembering; they must be able to see the benefit to themselves before they will put forth the effort necessary for maximum retention.

Our civil laws operate on the basis that "ignorance of the law is no excuse." It is the citizen's responsibility to understand and follow the law—the penalties provide the motivation for remembering and obeying them. For employees, the relationship between remembering and better pay should provide the motivation. They should understand that the things they want from their jobs are more likely to come their way if they remember how to do the job properly, meet the standards of job performance, and comply with company policy.

Many teenagers get good grades in driver education courses because they are approaching driving age and they know that the course is a prerequisite for a driver's license. However, their motivation to do well in Latin and other subjects will be less if they don't understand the need for these courses and don't have as much interest in them. Accordingly, employees must understand the need for the information they are being asked to master.

One famous political figure supposedly knew 20,000 people by name! This won him many friends and gained many votes for his side. Similarly, a well-known general of World War II was regarded as a walking file cabinet. While others were scurrying around to check the location of a division or the accuracy of a detail, he could produce the information from his seemingly limitless memory. To him, having the facts meant being able to make quick, correct decisions. A salesman who sold equipment on a commission basis could remember every customer who had ever bought from him. When customers called years later, he greeted them by name, asked about the performance of the equipment they had bought from him, and advised them of improvements made on newer machines.

In each of these examples, there were strong motives for remembering, because the retention of information served personal as well as professional interests. For employees, remembering must be related to job security, satisfactory job performance, supervisory approval, and personal satisfaction if they are to be motivated to exert the effort not only to learn but to remember what they have learned.

In addition to an inadequate original impression and inadequate motivation, another cause of poor memory is lack of effort. Let's suppose that you go to a party and are introduced to 30 people. If you were to meet these same people the following night, how many names would you remember? Probably very few. But suppose you go to another party where 30 people are present and just before you enter the room someone tells you that you will be paid $1,000 for every name you remember for a 24-hour period. Now how many names will you remember the following night? Probably most of them, becauuse you will have an interest in listening carefully to each name, hearing it adequately, repeating it to fix it in your memory, and associating it so that it will be easier to recall. You are still working with the same memory and the same basic information, but the difference is one of interest and motivation for remembering.

When a personnel department employee who was writing out records by hand remarked to her supervisor that she wished she could type, she was advised that typing courses were available. The same conversation was repeated six months later and then again a year after that. When she brought up the subject the fourth time, she was told: "You will never learn to type because you simply aren't willing to put forth the necessary effort." Few people are willing to put forth the effort required for efficient remembering.

John Kieran, famed memory expert, has said, "Everyone remembers what he is interested in. The more I learn about a person or subject, the more I become interested; and the more I become interested, the better I remember." It doesn't take much analysis of our own personal experience to realize that this is true. We remember vast amounts of information about our hobbies and special interests, but we sometimes have difficulty remembering elementary facts about our jobs.

If supervisors are not to be disappointed in the amount of learning employees retain, they must be as concerned with the influence of interest and motivation as they are with the content of the training program. Unless these factors are embodied in the learning process, time and effort are largely wasted because the process has to be repeated.

How Ideas and Events Can Be Recalled

It has been demonstrated that forgetting occurs very rapidly at first and then tends to level off with time. An activity can be learned completely and repeated without error, but a week later a certain amount will have been forgotten unless the activity has been repeated often enough. Supervisors who recognize the initial rapid rate of forgetting do not assume that just because information has been learned one day it will be remembered the following day or at the end of 30 days. Instead, they make follow-up checks to determine the amount forgotten, and plan additional training to refresh the employees' memories.

Like learning, memory can be improved by applying the following five laws as the occasion demands:

1. *The law of association.* If different things are experienced or heard together frequently enough, the presence of one will elicit the recall of the other. Just as we learn by association, so do we remember by association. We recall the things that are easier to remember and then make the transfer to the more difficult. Things that are to be remembered and used together should therefore be learned together.

2. *The law of succession.* If two things are frequently experienced in immediate succession, the presence of the first one tends to produce the recall of the other. For instance, it is sometimes difficult to remember what letter comes before another in the alphabet—until they are recited in sequence. The advantage of learning in succession is that when you remember one item in a list, you recall the next, and so on.

3. *The law of similarity.* If two things are similar, the recall of one causes the recall of the other.

4. *The law of contrast.* Extremes or opposites serve as reminders of each other. When you think of the biggest person you have ever seen, you may also think of the smallest. If you think of the brightest room you ever saw, you also probably remember the dullest. The use of contrast improves the vividness of the impression and the ability to recall.

5. *The law of visualization.* Being able to visualize the object you want to recall can be an aid to memory. Sight and sound together represent 95 percent of memory and recall influence.

Techniques for Remembering Names

It has been estimated that every time you call a person by name you have hirs undivided attention for the next eight seconds. We make friends and create business by remembering customers' names. Why? Simply because a person's own name is the sweetest and most important sound to that individual. If we expect to influence people, we need to master the technique of remembering both their names and the things that are of most interest to them. The first step in remembering names is to recognize that there is a technique involved and to follow a few simple steps. In fact, these steps apply with equal validity to remembering in general, not only to recalling names.

Be interested. You will not remember people's names if you are not interested in people. The first step, then, must be to develop or increase your interest in people. We must recognize the decisive role others play in our lives and the vital influence they have on our future success. This insight can help stimulate our interest in other people.

Pay attention—listen. If you don't hear or understand a name correctly to begin with, you certainly won't be able to remember it correctly. Concentrate on the name. Give its enunciation your undivided attention, and listen intently to the sound. If you did not understand it clearly, don't hesitate to ask it to be repeated. It flatters individuals that you think them important enough to want to know their names.

Repeat the name. Repeat it immediately and often. As soon as you understand the name, say: "I'm glad to meet you, Mr. Berryhill," rather than just "I'm glad to meet you." When you speak a name you do two things: You get the feeling of the word and you hear it once again. This repetition—which is often possible during the conversation and when you take your leave—helps fix the name in your memory.

Observe the person. You don't remember people by noting the shape of their feet. Instead, notice any distinguishing facial features, the shape of their faces and the color of their hair, and other physical characteristics. These are trail blazers—special markings that will help you remember people's names when you come their way again.

Associate the name. Some names can be associated with familiar objects or ideas or with famous persons. Names such as Black, Frost, and Forest offer natural associations. Hoover and Kennedy, Washington and Hamilton can be easily associated with historical figures. Other names can be associated with places, objects, or symbols that are comparatively easy to call to mind.

Think about the name and the person. Repeat the name and think about the person as you do so. If you have observed the person intently, you probably have a mental picture that you can associate with the name. Focus particular attention on the distinguishing features or on the famous person or idea with which you are associating the name. This intensive thought process will be of great assistance in fixing an image of the individual and hirs name in your mind.

Write the name down. Writing the name helps you to get the feel of it; of course, you must understand it correctly in order to be able to write it in the first place. Develop the "write down" habit for lists and names that you will need in the future.

Supervision and Memory

Supervisors' jobs can be frustrating if employees are forgetful. The supervisor's time and effort are wasted if employees do not remember the company orientation and job training. Many unnecessary conflicts are created if they forget safety rules, company policies, and othr requirements of the job. Supervisors need to be concerned with how retention and memory affect their employees, and how they affect the discharge of their own responsibilities. The basic principles are the same in both cases, but supervisors must provide the methods and motivation for their employees, as well as the stimulation for their own remembering.

Several points should be kept in mind about memory. First, memory is not inherited; it is an acquired skill that can be improved. Second, memory is no better than the initial impression—the seeing, the hearing, and the understanding must be sufficient in the beginning. Third, interest is indispensable to good memory, because we remember most about those things that interest us most. Fourth, there must be a reason for remembering, since motivation is a reasonably accurate measure of the amount of information that will be retained. Fifth, memory can be compared to a muscle: the more it is used, the more skillful it becomes. Sixth, exceptional retention is dependent on deliberate effort—not just once, but continually.

Many people put up with unsatisfactory retention because they are not willing to exert the mental effort to master the techniques that lead to improved memories. Work, effort, interest, concentration, motivation, tenacity, and practice are necessary. A good memory is worth money, friends, influence, prestige, promotions, customers, and tremendous personal satisfaction and enjoyment. There are no secrets involved—merely the willingness to exert effort and to practice effective techniques.

A serviceable memory is essential for effective leadership; an exceptional memory can provide the competitive edge. It adds significantly to self-confidence, can help a person gain greater respect from colleagues, and often gives an individual actual advantages in decision making and achieving results.

14

Harmonious Results in Working with Women

THE basis for getting harmonious performance results through working women begins with the right attitude, acceptance of certain realities, and following some fundamental good human relations guidelines. This applies equally to male and female supervisors, who should consider the following statement about women's status in the business world today.

> Shattered and destroyed forever are the traditional concepts that a woman's place is in the home, that her role is limited to serving the pleasures and needs of man as sex mate, field hand, household servant, cook, and bearer and keeper of children. She is no longer satisfied to remain placidly at home—no longer content with limited education and unimportant jobs. She has arrived on the business and industrial scene in quantity, and is committed to co-starring roles with men in every phase of enterprise. The transition has moved her into the factory, the office, the laboratory, and the executive suite as a participant and contributor equal to her male counterpart. Although business has yet to recognize her as man's equal, she insists on two things: a challenge and a chance—a responsible job to be done and an opportunity to do it.

She has come to stay and to produce. She expects opportunities and compensation comparable to a man's. She intends to be heard. She anticipates recognition and personal fulfillment. She expects to work in comfortable and pleasant surroundings. She insists on personal and courteous treatment from her associates and supervisors. She demands facilities appropriate to her special physical and emotional needs. She wants to prove herself as a human being who is able to do a job. And she doesn't care that her presence causes changes in traditional practices.

What does she plan to contribute in return? She intends to be dependable, to produce, to make a profitable contribution to the company in line with the proper matching of her capabilities to her job responsibilities. And she is willing to be judged by the contribution she makes to the goals of the organization. She knows that there is a critical need for capable management with trainable potential in every area of the business. She is also painfully aware that the greatest available leadership resource—namely, qualified women, has been virtually untapped.*

Differences and Likenesses

Men and women are more alike than different with regard to the work environment. The same human relations rules should be used to supervise both. However, in supervising women, it may be important to follow the rule book of good human relations even more strictly, because women seem to have a greater sensitivity to other people than do men and are therefore quicker to detect unfairness. Women have a stronger "feeling relationship" about the job and associates on the job, especially the supervisor.

An excellent starting point in working with women might be to recognize that nothing should be expected of women—either more or less—than is expected of men. Women expect basically the same things from the job environment as men do, and should not be expected to contribute differently just because they are women.

Traditional myths and misconceptions about women in general, or as employees, should be identified and eliminated. Generalizations about "all women" are no more accurate than generalizations about all men. It should be remembered that both men and women represent the entire spectrum of age, education, job interest,

* Killian, Ray A. *The Working Woman,* New York: American Management Associations, 1971.

emotion, ability, prejudice, and performance potential. Special surveys and interviews I have conducted have given one loud and clear
message: all that women are asking for is equal opportunity in hiring, promotion, pay, and other job considerations. They want to be
treated and judged on their individual merits, not as stereotyped
females. The only valid and legal supervisory relationship with
women is to treat them as individuals in every job-related area.

Her Expanding Impact and Influence

Ingredients for job performance and achievement have become less
a test of physical strength and more a matter of technique, dexterity,
and mental skills and their application. Criteria for job success have
begun to favor women's special talents and interests, and women
have moved into the job market in increasing numbers. Almost
every valid statistical report shows evidence of women's changing
roles. Consider the following information reported by the U.S. Department of Labor and other sources:

- Approximately 38 million women are now gainfully employed.
- Almost 40 percent of the workforce—or more than one out of
  every three people employed—are women. This percentage
  will continue to increase.
- Almost one-half of all women of working age are working outside the home.
- More than one-half of all employed women are married and
  have a husband who is present in the home.
- In 1920 the average working women was age 28 and single;
  today the average has changed to a married woman aged 41.
- Women are now employed in every one of the more than 400
  job categories listed by the U.S. Census Bureau.
- Life expectancy for women has increased from 48 years in
  1900 to 76 years today.
- In 1920 only 20 percent of women graduated from high
  school, and today this has increased to almost 80 percent. In
  1920 only 2 percent graduated from college; today, this has
  increased to over 20 percent.

This dramatic statistical change has occurred principally since
World War II. Women are beginning to exert a decisive impact not

only on the social and cultural world in which we live but also on the total environment of the business enterprise, especially on the roles of supervisors. As this change occurs, the real challenge to both men and women is to preserve traditional values that are worthwhile, to discard those that are antiquated, and to move boldly to meet the new challenge posed by these changes and opportunities.

Women have made their presence felt in a variety of ways. Work benches have been adjusted in height, and have been designed to correspond to a woman's size and contours. Safety rules and equipment have been redesigned as required for accident prevention. Rest rooms, lounges, machinery, and a host of other facilities have undergone changes that reflect the particular preferences and requirements of women. Benefits such as hospitalization, vacations, sick leave, maternity leave, and retirement have been restructured in ways that take into account their special concerns.

Legal Considerations in Supervising Women

Although there are many local and state laws affecting the employment and supervision of women, the most significant regulations are those passed by Congress. These laws establish requirements for all employees, but they also have special provisions regarding women and other minorities. The following are the laws with which supervisors must be most concerned.

Fair Labor Standards Act and Amendments—This law was originally passed in 1938, but has been amended many times since. Its provisions include minimum hourly rates of pay, age requirements, overtime payments, and special restrictions for minors under age eighteen. Additional regulations in the form of presidential directives have established requirements, especially for those companies doing business with the government.

Equal Pay for Equal Work—This requirement became effective in 1964 and requires that women be paid on the same basis as men with regard to hourly rates, piece rates, commission rates, and all other forms of compensation. The equal pay requirement was intended to include jobs that were basically equivalent. For purposes of comparison under the equal pay provision, jobs need only be substantially equal—not identical. This equal payment includes employee benefits and all other forms of compensation. Simply stated, the law requires that where women are doing essentially the same type of work as men, they must be compensated and treated in every way on an equal basis.

Title VII of the Civil Rights Act—This law prohibits discrimination on the basis of race, creed, color, national origin, and sex with regard to compensation, opportunity, conditions of employment, or for any other reason. In addition to the equal pay requirement of the Fair Labor Standards Act, this law guarantees equal opportunity in employment, upgrading and promotion, and in all other job-related areas. Together, the two laws require companies and supervisors to provide equal opportunity for women on a nondiscriminatory basis.

Although there are many other legal ramifications regarding the employment of women, these are of most concern to the supervisor. Every employer is required to know and abide by all federal, state, and local regulations pertaining to the employment or conditions of employment of women. In some instances, the regulations do not cover very small businesses; but the exemptions and noncoercion requirements are largely illusory, since employees and the public expect all employers to follow the laws as they are generally understood. Supervisors should be aware that employees often have only a vague understanding of various laws and often believe that the law entitles them to certain benefits, considerations, and protections that it does not in fact include. For example, white males under age 40 are covered by Title VII, and the law does not require employers to provide vacation or holiday pay. Most benefits are voluntary (except as provided for by union contract or competitive practices), and are regulated by law only in that benefits provided for one class of employee must be provided to employees of other classes on an equal basis.

These laws have required companies to establish policies and operating guidelines designed to ensure compliance. Supervisors act as legal agents for their companies and must make decisions and take action regarding all areas of these legal requirements. Therefore, all supervisors must be completely familiar with all company policies and procedures relating to these laws.

In day-to-day supervision and activities, supervisors must be aware of the legal consequences of everything they do. Noncompliance can result in complaints by employees to outside government agencies, time-consuming investigations, and costly back payments and fines. In addition to the actual cost, the impact on other employees and on public relations can be negative.

Employers are also required to display government-provided posters that keep employees informed of their rights and protections under the law. The laws also provide that no punitive action can be taken against an employee who makes a complaint either to the employer or to a government agency.

For the individual supervisor, the impact of government regulations is that to achieve harmonious relationships and effective results in working with women on the job all of these laws must be fully known and observed. Both male and female supervisors should be thorough in ensuring that employees understand these laws and that all company decisions and activities are in compliance with them.

Understanding Her Differences, Roles, and Expectations

Psychologists and educators contend that there is very little difference between men and women, but even the acceptance of this factual information doesn't erase the feminine mystique. The legitimate right to supervise and to exercise their authority over women, and the necessity of coping with women's job-related concerns, present some special challenges to both male and female supervisors. For example, both men and women have generally indicated a preference to be supervised by men; home and family responsibilies still fall most heavily on the woman; and it is still a little less acceptable for the women to be away from the family and to travel out of town for extended periods of time.

In attempting to work effectively with women on the job, it should be remembered that much of our current thinking is based on traditions, myths, mores, and entrenched prejudices. Nevertheless, supervisors must always bear in mind that the only realistic and legal approach to working with women is one based on equity and merit—all other considerations are irrelevant. In attempting to do this, it might be helpful to remember that recent changes in the status of women are among the fastest and most dramatic shifts ever to occur in human history. Both men and women are still learning to cope successfully with these changes. The following considerations might be helpful in assessing the status of women in the job environment today:

□ In many instances, women are new arrivals in certain jobs and at certain levels of management.

□ Women often feel that they are being judged; therefore, their defensiveness sometimes causes them to make a special effort to prove themselves.

□ Women are more people-oriented, more sensitive and intuitive, need more reassurance, are quicker to resent favoritism, and often have need for more assistance in adjusting to job requirements.

□ Working women generally have more demands on their time at home because of their special roles as wife, mother, cook, housekeeper, purchaser, and family coordinator.

□ Work is more optional for certain women than it is for men, and they often face a conflict between their jobs and their family responsibilities.

Thus, although women should be treated exactly like men on the job, it would help to have some understanding of their current attempts to prove themselves, the many roles they have, the extra demands on their time, and their special job-related needs.

Although some women might be working to meet "Mr. Right" or to prove to the world that they are as good as men, most women are working for exactly the same reasons as men—for the money, benefits, security, career opportunities, and satisfactions they can derive from the job.

Employing and Making Full Use of Potential

Women should be employed, placed on the job, paid, promoted, and supervised based on their merit, just as men should be. However, those who make decisions regarding the employment and job utilization of women should be aware of the need to be legal and fair in the decisions they make.

Guides to Recruitment, Employment, and Placement

In its recruitment and employment practices, the company should seek qualified women. This means making overt efforts in advertising, recruiting, and employment to attract qualified women applicants. Women should be encouraged to work for the company. The employment office should be pleasant and businesslike in appearance and the interviewer (both those in the employment office and interviewing supervisors) should be skilled in appropriate interviewing techniques. Interviewers should be cautioned against asking questions or establishing employment requirements that are not part of the employment process for men.

The details and requirements of the job should be carefully explained. Women should be told what they can expect from the company in terms of pay, benefits, working conditions, work schedules, and dress regulations. Adequate information should be provided by both the company and the woman applicant so that each will be in a position to make the best decision as to whether this particular woman belongs in this particular job.

Induction and Training

Although each man and woman should be viewed on an individual basis, many new women employees may be less familiar with general company policies and job requirements. It is possible that a woman may be entering the job market for the first time at age 40 or for the first time since part-time employment during her school days. For these women especially, a first job requires them to make drastic changes in their patterns of living. The woman who has never held a full-time job may be uncertain about her responsibilities. She needs reassurance, patience, understanding, and encouragement from her supervisor. This is especially true in the beginning, when the newcomer meets the other employees, learns the details of the job and the physical layout of the workplace, and receives the training she needs in order to do her work properly.

Special attention should be given to training women in the skills needed for the job. Both the company and the individual should be concerned with successful job performance, and this is not likely to occur unless proper training, coaching, and supervision are provided on a continuing basis. Many of the traditional disappointments regarding women's job performance have been due to the women's lack of training. Women expect to be paid and promoted on an equal basis. Therefore, management should make special efforts to ensure that they are qualified to produce results and to merit upward mobility.

Results Through Appropriate Supervision

Women are often easier to supervise than men. This opportunity for effective supervision occurs because women are generally more overt in their responses and statements of their preferences. It is easier for the supervisor to discern what is acceptable and unacceptable because women are more communicative. The supervisor who has difficulty in supervising women generally is not paying enough attention to what they are saying. Ironically, female supervisors often experience more difficulty in supervising women than do men because some female employees seem to prefer male supervisors and find their leadership more acceptable. Women who have been brought up in traditional surroundings tend to be skeptical of other women, especially those who are in a position to tell them what to do.

During the initial contact, supervisors should be especially careful to establish rapport with women employees who may be new to the workforce and to create a climate of mutual credibility. Be businesslike, but friendly. Openly demonstrate your confidence and your readiness to cooperate and be helpful. Be courteous and considerate. Be willing to listen. One can be firm, but also fair and predictable. Clarify and enforce policies consistently. Don't grant special favors, put women on the spot, cause them to suffer loss of face, or make unkind generalizations about all women. Be flexible. Don't take any female employee for granted or become involved in her personal problems, or underestimate her capacity to make a significant contribution to the success of the department and the company.

In supervising women, apply the same rules and guidelines used in supervising men. Supervisors who ignore the rule book for good human relations, give the appearance of favoritism, withhold recognition and praise, and fail to be consistent may experience serious difficulty with female employees, because many women have experienced some forms of discrimination in the past and are quick to detect signs of it. It is important to develop a comfortable but businesslike climate—one in which women feel secure and reassured, and experience personal satisfaction.

Effective Leadership Skills and Techniques

Effectiveness in providing leadership to women is dependent on the degree of skill used. Women perform best if leadership provides the appropriate input, which will in turn elicit their maximum understanding and effort.

Communicating Effectively

Regardless of their initial understanding and ability, women must achieve acceptable competency levels required by the job. This is done principally through communication. Initial and continuing communications should clarify what the company expects by way of attendance, performance on the job, response to training, and relationships to supervisors and others. Women should understand what they can expect in terms of job security, pay and advancement, supervisory cooperation, training, and employee benefits.

Although the same things should be expected of all employees, it is especially important for women to have a thorough understanding of them to avoid breakdowns in communication, hurt feelings, unsatisfactory results, and job failures. In communicating with women, the following observations should be considered:

- Women often reject a message when they are suspicious of the motives of the supervisor.
- Their current emotional state or mood influence their receptivity and responses.
- They are inclined to interpret information in ways that fulfill their desires and expectations.
- If the information is technical, mechanical, or uniquely different, women might require more detailed explanations.
- Frequent feedback should be used to test understanding.
- Alternative methods of communication should often be used.
- Women must be given time to accept changes or new ideas.
- Direct, comprehensible language should be used, and the message should be repeated as often as necessary.

Communication is the supervisor's best method of informing women about the job and for eliciting successful job adjustment and performance.

Motivating for Maximum Effort

A good starting point is to identify and clearly explain expected performance results. The supervisor's motivational responsibility is to bring about this type of performance. This can be done by first ensuring that the physical and human environment of the job provides the opportunity for expected response and performance. The next step is to determine what the individual wants from the job and to communicate how the job can make this available through certain types of behavior and results. Women should understand that they will get what they want from their jobs in direct proportion to their overall job contribution.

Once job expectations have been clarified, the supervisor must provide all the assistance, training, coaching, encouragement, and direction necessary for achievement of the goal. Special attention should be given to enhancing female employees' self-confidence, elevating their expectations and competency, making their work interesting and stimulating, and recognizing and reenforcing the progress and results they achieve. Supervisors should make use of intermediate goals and team and group stimulation, provide frequent feedback, and ensure a full measure of expected job satisfaction through job achievement. Women must be shown how they can meet their needs through job performance, and once they have this understanding, the supervisor should help them implement it. The physical job environment and the human factors are especially important to women and should be favorably utilized to enhance motivational efforts.

Evaluation and Improvement of Job Performance

There is a special need—due to legal requirements and company policy—to pay, promote, and treat women fairly based on job performance. Since most companies pay employees on the basis of merit, the supervisor has a significant challenge in evaluating the job performance and future potential of women.

From the outset, the supervisor must be thorough in ensuring that women understand how the job is to be done, what are the required results, and what constitutes satisfactory or unsatisfactory work. Female employees should get frequent feedback on their performance, giving them the opportunity to make corrections and adjustments along the way. This will avoid surprises when job performance is evaluated and will also make it easier for supervisors to justify their evaluations.

Every effort should be made to base the evaluation on quantitative criteria and to avoid subjective judgments. Remember that job performance results, and not the personal feeling, is the purpose of the evaluation. Emphasis should be put on the number of items produced, the amounts sold, the employee's attendance record, the number of customer complaints, and other factual items on which both the supervisor and the woman employee can agree.

Caution should be exercised to minimize criticism of past performance or job behavior. Nothing can be done to change this, but the real opportunity for both the employee and the company is in the change that *can* occur and that will benefit both in the future. Past performance is best used as a basis for jointly developing a program to achieve this future improvement. Agreement should be reached as to time, methods, what the improvement will consist of, and how it will occur.

Coping with Attitudes and Correction

The subject of attitudes and job correction is always delicate, regardless of the sex of the employee, but it is especially delicate where it involves women. The attitudes women bring to the job, and those they develop after they have started working, are based on all their previous influences. Male supervisors might have some existing attitudes about women, and women employees might have some existing attitudes about supervisors, companies, jobs, pay, opportunity, and the entire question of working or not working. The wise supervisor—male or female—looks only at the job and its requirements and becomes concerned only with those attitudes that have a valid relation to performance and job behavior.

Supervisors should recognize the significant impact attitudes have on job performance and human relationships. Attitudes develop quickly and, once formed, are often difficult to change. Therefore, the supervisor should make an overt effort initially to develop a positive attitude on the part of women, and should constantly try to maintain those favorable attitudes and improve them.

All supervisors and employees should accept the fact that changes will be necessary in the way the job is being done. This might occur when the employee fails to meet the requirements of the job or does something unacceptable. The supervisor's role is limited to correcting the job performance—not the individual. It should be made clear to the woman that the correction is strictly related to the requirements of the job and is not a reflection on her personally.

The supervisor should view the correction role as an opportunity to improve the job security, the earnings opportunity, and the promotional potential of the individual. Failure to make the correcton jeopardizes job-related benefits to the individual. Correction should be carefully related both to ways in which the individual benefits and to the requirements of the job.

The Delicate Area of Counseling Women

Women often have personal problems, which may or may not be job-related. These problems might interfere with job performance, and sometimes the employee will want to discuss them with her supervisor. The supervisor should listen attentively and sympathetically, but then guide the individual toward making her own decision. Supervisors do not have the right to get involved in employees' personal affairs, nor do they have the specialized training required. The supervisor can be helpful by referring the employee to available company or community resources. The woman needs an understanding ear, but the supervisor should not attempt to exercise a value judgment by deciding what the best solution is to an employee's personal problem.

Women as Leaders and Supervisors

Women make excellent supervisors and executives. The number of women moving up to higher levels of leadership is increasing, and they are handling the responsibilities very effectively. Women possess characteristics and qualifications that give them unique advantages over men as supervisors. These include their understanding of people, empathy, ability to communicate, compassion, and attention to detail.

Women who expect to be successful leaders must be willing to meet the demands of leadership, such as long hours, continuing professional development, travel, acceptance of criticism, objectivity, acceptance of responsibility for results, and a willingness to compete and be judged by results. Some of the criticisms encountered by women as supervisors includes:

□ Lack of confidence on the part of male executives: The common employee preference for male supervisors.
□ That women are too subjective, take things too personally, and do not give proper credit to people they supervise.
□ That they are too skeptical of other women.
□ That they cannot stand the pressures of leadership.
□ That they do not delegate responsibility effectively.

These statements are not necessarily true, but if male and female leaders think that they have validity, then both should make every effort to eliminate their attitudes.

Accelerating Her Upward Mobility

Special attention should be given to encouraging the promotion of women. For women to be promoted and to perform successfully after they are given leadership opportunity, the following must occur:

- □ Only those women who are best qualified and who possess the potential for success should be selected.
- □ They must be given access to the type of information and training that will make them able to perform effectively.
- □ They must be ambitious enough to want the promotion, and must be willing to meet the demands of the job.
- □ They must be willing to exercise initiative in developing qualifications for leadership, both educationally and through job results.
- □ They must be willing to accept increased responsibility.

A woman's upward mobility should be viewed as a cooperative effort on the part of both the company and the woman herself. All companies should prefer a competent woman supervisor to an incompetent male. Results-oriented leaders should seek to identify and promote the most competent individuals. Women have demonstrated that they can measure up to the requirements of leadership, and they deserve every opportunity to be judged strictly on merit. Women who want promotions should make their desires known, and they should accept promotions offered to them.

Conclusions about Supervising Working Women

Perhaps the single most significant error committed by male and female supervisors is the tendency to assume that all women are the same and that they can be judged on a group basis. When supervisors make this error, they yield to the temptation of making decisions based on assumptions about groups rather than on the merits of each individual. This has too often resulted in inaccurate bench marks for decision-making concerning women. This approach penalizes the woman involved, the supervisors, their departments, and the company.

Supervisors should evaluate working women on the basis of the following facts:

☐ Women are capable of making an outstanding contribution to the productive goals of the department and the profit goals of the company.

☐ Although some women might have different reasons for working, this does not necessarily have any influence on their job performance or on how they should be supervised.

☐ In many companies and departments, they are an underutilized resource—capable of making a greater contribution if given the opportunity, and trained and supervised properly.

☐ The full potential of women will be realized only when they are dealt with objectively and realistically, abandoning all myths and using facts and experience as the only criteria.

☐ Women have demonstrated outstanding potential and competence for leadership at all levels, and deserve equal opportunity for promotion.

☐ It can be recognized that some women have greater home responsibilities, that they might be subject to absenteeism and resignation due to their husbands' relocation, that ambition and self-image might vary from individual to individual, and that often supervisors feel less competent to manage them. However, these facts also apply to some men, and should not adversely affect women's opportunity or potential.

☐ Women can be easier to supervise because they are quicker to express their preferences and to communicate with supervisors. When supervisors experience difficulty, it is because they fail to hear, to understand, and to respond promptly.

When all the numbers, percentages, prejudices, myths, facts, experience, and results are considered, companies and supervisors have but one course of action: to utilize to the maximum extent the potential that women can offer the company. A wise supervisor will seek to recruit, train, promote, utilize, pay, and supervise women in ways that will make this tremendous resource and potential available to benefit the supervisor's own area of responsibility and the company.*

*For additional information regarding the leadership of women, the book *The Working Woman—A Male Manager's View,* written by Ray A. Killian and published by AMACOM, is recommended. It can be obtained from the same source as this book. Every concerned supervisor who works with women in any way will find this book most informative.

15

There are moments in the life of every individual when hirs greatest need is for a friend. The supervisor who gives sympathetic friendship through counseling renders a genuine service and earns the employee's gratitude.

Counseling: Helpful Understanding

COUNSELING allows employees to talk about emotional problems and to seek a satisfactory solution. Most companies have found that counseling is good business as well as good human relations. The employee with personal or job-related problems may be inefficient and unproductive and may create problems for other employees, for supervisors, and for the company. Both the supervisor and the company have an interest in correcting this job intereference. An important aim of counseling is to help employees develop the ability to solve their own problems by examining them in a new perspective and by selecting the best of available alternate solutions. When employees are relieved of their worries and frustrations, they are in a position to make a more harmonious and productive job contribution.

Physical proximity and the organizational relationship of supervisor and employee thrust the role of counselor on the supervisor. Since the supervisor must handle counseling as the need arises, hir should familiarize hirself with this highly specialized technique. In hirs relationships with people, especially in the counseling area, the supervisor must be constantly aware that people want to be understood more than they want to understand.

A need for counseling may be indicated when employees exhibit radical changes in behavior, attitude, or job performance. Sometimes employees recognize that they have a problem they have not been able to solve satisfactorily. When this is the case, the employee may take the initiative and seek the supervisor's assistance. Sometimes it is the supervisor who recognizes the employee's need for help in solving a problem. In this case, it is the supervisor who takes the initiative and suggests a counseling interview. A need for counseling may be indicated by any of the following situations.

The employee's mood and manner change.
The employee's job performance changes from satisfactory to unsatisfactory.
The employee becomes irritable, and is at odds with everyone.
The employee's energy level takes a sharp dip.
There is a sudden rash of seemingly unjustified accidents.
There is an increase in careless mistakes.
The employee resents suggestions and correction.
The employee becomes a troublemaker.

These are only a few of the symptoms of problems that affect job performance or harmony in the department and require supervisory action. Situations that require counseling are difficult to handle because they are usually of a personal or emotional nature. Some are job-related, but a significant number concern family and other off-the-job matters. Even when the root of a problem lies in areas over which supervisors have little or no influence, it can still be as damaging to job achievement as the factors that they can control.

The Goal of Counseling

The goal of counseling is to minimize or eliminate problems that interfere with morale, productivity, acceptance of change, or harmony. This goal can be reached through several channels.

Communication. Inadequate or inaccurate communication can create problems and build barriers between the supervisor and the employee. The counselor has the opportunity to uncover and correct areas of poor communication which may be causing misunderstandings. And the knowledge that they are free to communicate with the supervisor often helps lessen the pressure of the job-related aspects of their problem.

Guidance. Although the supervisor must serve in an advisory capacity, hir should not give advice that hir is not qualified to give, or try to force advice on employees who do not want it. Instead, the supervisor should refer troubled employees to specialists, inside or outside the company, who are qualified to give advice about special problems. Hir may suggest the possibility of seeking guidance from a minister or professional counseling agency in the community.

Release of emotional tension. A problem often approaches an explosive stage before the individual is willing to discuss a subject that may be a source of personal embarrassment. Yet talking with someone about it tends to release some of the pent-up tension—a step in the right direction. The elimination of emotional pressure often makes the problem less overwhelming and frightening, and the employee is then able to find a satisfactory solution.

Reassurance. Many emotional problems are created by insecurity. For instance, rumors may lead employees to think that their jobs are about to be eliminated. As their insecurity grows, they start resenting authority, losing interest in their work, and becoming unsatisfactory employees. Counseling gives the supervisor an opportunity to reassure the employees that there is no truth to rumors of this sort, thus restoring the employees' sense of security.

Reorientation. An employee may be disturbed because of failure to achieve a promotion. Perhaps there is a need for additional formal education or specialized training. Counseling can help reorient thinking so that employees will have a more realistic understanding of the necessary qualifications for promotion.

The Counseling Technique

Counseling is distinctly different from other types of interviews. If it is not conducted skillfully, the result can be to destroy the employee's confidence in the supervisor, thereby making the problem worse. There are five basic guides for the counseling interview:

1. *Method.* In the correction interview, the supervisor directs the course of the conversation. The counseling interview, however, is nondirective, and almost the entire course of the interview is left to the discretion of the employee. Supervisors must resist the temptation to take charge, express their own opinions, and give advice.
2. *Responsibility.* Employees must be made aware that they are responsible for solving their own problems. The supervisor

may help them work toward a solution but must not take responsibility for making the decision.

3. *Status.* The employee is equal to the supervisor in authority
   and function during the counseling interview.
4. *Role.* Employees must be given the independence to choose
   their own solutions. The employee and supervisor have special roles in the counseling interview, and should not assume
   each other's function.
5. *Emphasis.* The emphasis in counseling is on feelings and problems deeper than those that appear on the surface. The supervisor should encourage employees to discuss their hidden
   feelings and emotions and to focus on self-expression, insight,
   and recognition of the potential solutions.

Many supervisors do not have the temperament and patience
required for counseling. When this is the case, the employee should
be referred to someone better qualified in counseling. However, the
supervisor who is not willing to handle simple counseling problems
is denying hirs staff one of the things they have a right to expect
from leadership—sympathetic understanding. The chance to talk
out a problem is itself of considerable therapeutic value. In order to
put thoughts into words, employees are compelled to think their
problem through completely, perhaps for the first time. And sometimes, by the end of the discussion, a satisfactory solution will have
been found.

The supervisor should conduct the counseling interview in private. No employees should be expected to discuss their problems in
the presence of others. Uninterrupted privacy is essential for counseling interviews. Since employees are likely to be in a state of emotional anxiety, they should be put at ease. The supervisor's ability to
do this and to minimize barriers to free and frank discussion have a
decisive influence on the success of the interview.

Communicate a feeling of interest and understanding. Convince
the person that you are interested in hir as an individual. As their
trust and confidence are bolstered, employees will be more willing to
discuss their problems. When an employee is reluctant to discuss the
problem, the supervisor should open the conversation, always keeping in mind that hirs role is that of listener and not talker. Some
ways to break the ice are commenting on the length of time the employee has been with the company, complimenting hir on favorable
job performance, or talking about other neutral subjects. The employee can then turn the conversation in any direction hir wishes. If

the employee still avoids the issue, the supervisor can probe gently into pertinent areas.

The employee should be encouraged to talk, and the supervisor should listen in a friendly, patient, and sympathetic manner. Listening is an active process that requires more than merely being in the presence of someone who is talking. This is especially true of the counseling interview, since the primary role of the supervisor is that of serious and understanding listener. Supervisors must not disagree or argue with what the employee says. Hir has a right to call the shots as hir sees them. Disagreement almost invariably jeopardizes the chances of resolving the issue successfully. The supervisor should avoid showing surprise, amazement, or critical response to what the employee says. If employees feel that they have startled the supervisor, they may back off completely.

At times, it will be evident what employees are trying to say and what they are trying to avoid. But the supervisor should not try to put words in employees' mouths. Let them choose their own way of revealing the problem. Encourage them to keep talking until the complete story has been told. Often they get halfway through what they want to say and then stop. It is then up to the supervisor to keep the conversation going without seeming to force the issue. Try to grasp what the employee is omitting from the conversation. Often what is avoided is the focal point of the problem.

When the employee needs to know where to get the help of a professional counselor, the supervisor should be able to supply this and other special information required.

Areas of Employee Counseling

Employees' personal problems, whether job-related or not, fall into several categories.

Vocational and educational. Many employees, especially younger ones, have problems concerning their vocational goals. If they do not receive guidance, they often become frustrated and disgruntled with their jobs. If employees do not have a realistic approach to their goals, the supervisor should help them adopt a planned and practical approach to their objectives.

Relationships with other employees. The source of many problems is human relations on the job—personality conflicts, jealousies, resentment of authority, and conflict of interest among employees. Counseling can help resolve such conflicts.

Family. These problems are the most difficult because they are beyond the control of the supervisor. Yet the opportunity to talk about them may make such problems more tolerable. Or the supervisor may be able to refer the employee to a family counseling agency.

Health. Many people worry about their health. Their symptoms, real or imagined, often cause feelings of anxiety. If this nagging worry continues because employees have neglected to seek medical attention, the supervisor can encourage them to see a doctor. And if the employee has been procrastinating because hir is worried about the expense of medical care, the supervisor may be able to aid with financial guidance.

Financial. Worry over money or inability to meet the family's financial obligations can keep an employee from doing a satisfactory job. There is a limit to what supervisors can or should do in this area. But they can certainly tell the employee about any financial assistance—such as a credit union—available through the company. Or they might refer the employee to someone who can help them plan a family budget.

Job-related situations. Employees may feel that their progress is too slow or that they have no chance for further advancement. Others may expect transfers and feel threatened by the prospect of taking on a new job. Still others may have been offered a higher-paying job elsewhere, but can't decide whether to accept it. Whatever the problem, the supervisor can use the counseling session to offer reassurance and to help the employee work out the best way to deal with the situation.

One day an employee came into the personnel office to resign, saying that he planned to work elsewhere because he was not making enough money to pay his bills. Further questioning revealed that he had not yet looked for another job because he thought that it would be unfair to do so while he was still employed.

During the conversation, the personnel director pointed out that because of the man's limited skill he would probably be paid about the same by other companies, that he would certainly lose his seniority and accumulated employee benefits, and that he might lose income during the period when he was between jobs. After additional consideration, the employee was able to see that he was not likely to make any more money elsewhere and that his real problem was one of better financial management.

Developing Counseling Skills

Certain counseling techniques and skills are very helpful to the supervisor. The supervisor should be familiar with personnel policies and procedures, educational and financial resources, promotion policy, grievance procedure, specialized counseling, legal requirements, and other information that may help employees resolve their problems. The supervisor should also be familiar with services available through community- or government-sponsored agencies and ways in which the employee can obtain their assistance. If the employee recognizes a need for such assistance, but is reluctant to make the initial contact, the supervisor should consult with the personnel department. In some special situations hir may be advised to arrange an appointment between the employee and an outside agency if the employee asks for this assistance.

The most important counseling skills are those of interviewing and listening. Supervisors must gain the confidence of employees. They should be able to conduct interviews in such a manner as to encourage employees to discuss their problems openly. To do this, supervisors must learn to stay in the background, yet encourage employees to talk about their problems, recognize the possible solutions, and make their own decisions.

Emotional maturity and stability are marks of well-adjusted counselors. They should be interested in understanding all types of people and problems; they should respect the rights and dignity of the individual; and they should be objective, trustworthy, and sufficiently flexible to adjust to all types of people and problems without undue strain. Employees never lose sight of the fact that the supervisor is important to their future, and they want their supervisor's approval and respect. They are, therefore, often reluctant to discuss anything that may reflect unfavorably on their ability to handle their own problems.

Supervisors must develop a climate in which employees feel free to talk, knowing that the information they reveal will not affect them adversely and that it will be kept confidential. This reassurance is communicated by the relationships supervisors maintain with employees on a day-to-day basis, by the way they convey concern and sympathy, and by their constant availability.

Today, large companies have professional counselors as full-time staff members. These counselors are professionally trained, have no line authority, cannot influence the future of the employee's job, and do not reveal what they are told in counseling interviews. In this environment, employees know that they will obtain professional assistance in complete privacy. Since it is almost impossible for the supervisor to remain completely neutral about factors that can influence the work in the department, hir should refer employees to these qualified counselors whenever hir is confronted with problems hir cannot handle.

When employees who have a problem seek the supervisor's help in finding a solution, this expression of confidence is a sincere compliment. But supervisors must not yield to the temptation of playing the role of big brother or try to take charge and solve the problem. Instead, they must play the more difficult role of impartial observer, willing listener, and sounding board. They must not pry, must not get involved in employees' personal affairs, must be discreet, and must keep confidences. Above all, supervisors must respect employees' rights to make their own decisions. Skillfully handled, counseling can establish a bond of mutual trust and confidence between employee and supervisor.

16

Evaluating and Improving Job Performance

DURING recent years, I have conducted numerous top management seminars for company presidents. At these seminars I have often asked the question, "What is your toughest and most challenging problem as a chief executive officer?" Almost invariably, the answers have been: how to judge people, evaluate job performance, and especially how to rate the raters—that is, knowing how accurate raters are in judging others.

The survival and growth of a business enterprise depend on evaluation—evaluation of the raw materials it buys, of the finished products it sells, of production standards, marketing techniques, manufacturing methods, and other factors that affect its profitability. Since payroll expenses constitute more than half the expense dollar in most companies, efficient management of the employee's time on the job is essential. Evaluation of employee job performance is the process used to gauge whether employee time is being used efficiently. It is the basis for determining how to improve performance. It keeps the supervisor informed about how each employee is doing. And it gives employees the opportunity to learn how well they are doing and how they can do their jobs better.

The armed forces pioneered in the development of evaluation procedures as a means of making a systematic comparison of large numbers of officers. Since there was frequently the need to promote one person out of ten candidates, and since the ten were often scattered around the world, a technique had to be devised for determining each individual's qualifications so that promotions could be made on the basis of merit. The solution was to rate all employees regularly, thereby providing a record of their qualifications and the way they discharged their duties and responsibilities. Today, performance rating programs have become very popular and are being used widely, not only in the military and in government, but also in business and industry.

If a rating is informal and unreliable, it is often unfair to both the employee and the company because it does not identify the performance areas that deserve commendation or those that require correction. Until these are identified, the supervisor cannot construct a specific improvement program.

The real value of evaluating job contribution becomes clear when it is recognized that the company pays more to buy the time of its employees than for all other expenses combined. This time is purchased for one reason—to make a productive contribution to the goals of the company. Job performance evaluation is an attempt to measure how much of a contribution is being made, its value, and where it can be improved.

Every company has some basis for determining who gets a promotion, who is to be granted a raise, and how big that raise should be, who is to be released in the event of a general layoff, and who is to be given additional training. If the measuring instrument is unreliable or inadequate, the results can be no better.

A job performance evaluation program is the company's best method of helping the employee do a better job. The evaluation program aids employees in reaching their maximum potential and helps the company make profitable use of the employee's time. If there is not a company-sponsored evaluation program, the supervisor is still responsible for determining the contribution made by each employee.

The information that follows should enable the supervisor to do a more reliable and objective job of evaluation, regardless of the type of program used by the company. The evaluation also becomes part of the legal record and can serve to justify pay changes and promotions.

The Purpose of a Rating Program

Most employees are conscientious and want to do a good job. If they have the ability and receive proper training, they usually do well. However, employees should be told how they are getting along, and they should receive constructive coaching for improvement. The purpose of a rating program is to analyze the strong and weak elements of the employee's job performance in order to:

- Set performance standards for everyone in the department.
- Improve the efficiency of the individual and the total work group.
- Recommend pay increases, promotions, transfers, or dismissals.
- Identify serious deficiencies so that they can be corrected.
- Determine individual and group training needs.
- Determine the relative value of each employee's service to the company.
- Avoid overlooking employees who merit increases as well as those who are slipping in their performance.
- Tell employees how they are getting along and how the company regards their work.

An evaluation program helps supervisors spot problems in their departments and identify specific areas where employees need assistance. It opens pipelines of communication, thus enabling the supervisor to get the ideas and suggestions of the employees. It also presents the supervisor with an opportunity to make suggestions to employees regarding work improvement, as well as to talk with them about employee benefits, future company plans, and continuing company goals. It develops leadership and supervisory qualities and reduces bias in evaluating others.

Advantages to the Company and the Department

Some of the benefits of job performance evaluation are these:

- It provides criteria for measuring performance and determining the assets and liabilities of each employee.
- It assists the supervisor in setting standards and quotas for each individual in relation to the overall department goals.

- ◻ It gives the supervisor an opportunity to evaluate the effects of training and supervisory leadership.
- ◻ It should result in increased individual and collective achievement.
- ◻ It should result in better employee and supervisory morale, because it demonstrates the company's interest in employees and their development. It assures that if any aspect of an employee's performance is unsatisfactory, that individual will be given an opportunity to improve.
- ◻ It should reduce employee turnover, because it assures recognition of outstanding performance and provides a systematic way for improving the productivity of those who might otherwise have to be discharged.
- ◻ It should reduce payroll cost through better utilization of every employee's potential. If every employee learns to work more efficiently, a more profitable operation results. The program also motivates the employee to work harder in order to receive a favorable rating and its benefits.
- ◻ It facilitates long-range personnel planning, since the promising employee can be spotted and given special attention. The program also provides an inventory of the individual's potential and qualifications for promotion.
- ◻ It has the major advantage of indicating how well a department is being operated. It reveals what kind of relationship exists between supervisor and employees, whether employees have had appropriate training, whether leadership or motivation is lacking, what procedures and arrangements in the department need to be reappraised, and what areas need improvement.

A performance appraisal program, however, is not intended to be a panacea. It should not be expected to correct problems that crop up every day, although many of these might eventually be eliminated through the improvement of overall performance and attitude. The correction of these problems should not be delayed until a job performance review. The rating should not be used as the sole determinant in making decisions on promotions, discharges, transfers, and pay increases. Since it may represent only a part of the employee's value to the company, it should be used in conjunction with all other relevant information. It can serve as an effective means of individual training, but it should not replace any other training presently in use. It cannot and should not be expected to substitute for top quality day-to-day leadership and supervision. A rating program can, however, make the use of all leadership tools more successful.

Methods of Rating

Personal opinion is the best-known rating method. This serves a purpose, but certainly in a very unsystematic way. The lack of effective results reflects the unreliability of this method.

The checklist method consists of rating various characteristics on a scale from zero to five. The higher the number, the better the rating. The sum of the weighted points is the employee's score.

The profile method rates a number of traits that are itemized and described. When the employee is assigned a rating from excellent to unsatisfactory on each of the traits, a line can be drawn between the marks to produce a "profile" of the individual's job performance.

The cluster method groups related traits into categories. The number of traits rated is thus reduced to such areas as leadership, ability to plan and organize, emotional stability, and judgment. The employee is then rated from superior to unsatisfactory in each category.

The descriptive method consists of a written description of general characteristics and job performance. Certain crucial areas such as human relations, initiative, and judgment are among those covered, but more attention is given to whatever characteristics are most meaningful to the evaluation of each person. This method has the advantage of comparing the person's performance with a pre-established standard. Its main disadvantage is that it is difficult for a new supervisor, or one who does not have writing skill, to do an adequate job of rating.

The fitness report is used by the Navy for its officer group. It consists of rating certain factors at given intervals or when an officer or hirs commanding officer is transferred. The rating ranks each individual on a scale compared with others in the group.

The group rating method is used in a few instances. This requires a group of people, possibly several supervisors who are familiar with the employee's job performance, to make the rating. Sometimes *seniority* becomes a prime factor and, in rare instances, the need of the individual is considered in placing a value on hirs job performance.

Most large companies use several types of rating forms, each of which reflects those elements considered to be of greatest importance on each individual job. For instance, the form used for an employee who works in the production department should be different from the one used for a salesperson who represents the company to the public.

Regardless of the methods used, the supervisor plays the key role in any rating program. In the absence of a company-initiated program, supervisors may wish to install and follow through with their own informal programs as a means of assisting employees and improving the results in their departments.

Successful Performance Appraisal

Top executives must believe in the program and actively support it. Supervisors should understand and approve the plan to be used, since they are the key to its effectiveness. Rating others is not an easy task, and unless supervisors believe in the program, they will not put enough effort into it to guarantee its success. If this role is mishandled, no amount of care and doctoring of the results can make the program effective.

The rating form must include provisions for rating all the factors important on each job. It should include all standards which are important on the job, such as quality of work, volume of work, knowledge of the job, initiative, work attitude, dependability, and cooperation with others.

Clear, specific, and detailed instruction should be given to the raters. Many experts feel that the supervisors should play an important part in writing the descriptions of the various characteristics, so that these descriptions will then be in terms that will be understood by other supervisors and employees, and the statements will probably be more realistic and specific.

The rating must be done by the immediate supervisor who assigns work, reviews it, knows the attitudes and feelings of the employee, and is familiar with the employee's job performance. He has the following duties in the rating program:

Communicating information about the program to the employees.
Completing the rating forms.
Conducting rating interviews.
Engaging in follow-up action.

The Training of Raters

Most companies recognize the importance of the rating program and train their supervisors to rate accurately and fairly. Supervisers are told why the program is being used, what its advantages and disadvantages are, and what it can do for them, their departments, and their people. The rating forms are thoroughly explained, and appraisal factors are defined. Common rating errors and ways to minimize them are brought to the attention of supervisors. The technique of the interview is emphasized and perhaps demonstrated by having supervisors act out the roles of participants in an interview. They are encouraged to consult with their own supervisors or the person responsible for the rating program in order to check their judgment and thus benefit by another's experience.

During training, the following guides for effective and reliable ratings should be emphasized:

- The rater must be familiar with the job behavior and performance of the employee.
- An adequate amount of time must be spent on the rating.
- The rater must be able to evaluate objectively and make use of factual information.
- The rater should be willing to seek and follow advice pertaining to the rating.

Common Rating Errors

When one phase of an employee's work is outstanding, or when that individual has some personality trait or characteristic that impresses the supervisor favorably, the rating on *all* characteristics may be higher than it should be because the supervisor's judgment on all points is colored by hirs reaction to this one factor. This is known as the "halo effect."

The most common cause for a negative halo is the occasional run-in between an employee and the supervisor. If the employee has done something to cause the supervisor to be criticized, for example, this may influence the level of the whole rating.

The low-tolerance error occurs when everyone in a department is rated low compared with other departments. This generally results when supervisors are particularly demanding of their employees and when their standards are excessively high.

The central tendency is probably the most common error. The novice rater who is not certain of the facts and who has difficulty in making decisions may follow the line of least resistance. The average or central rating is a way of avoiding conflict with the employee or the company.

Another error is the high or lenient tendency. This results when supervisors avoid the hard decisions of rating according to merit, or are trying not to hurt anyone's feelings, or want all their employees to be happy or to like them. In this case, all are rated too highly.

Another error is the "no fault in friend—no virtue in enemy" evaluation. Other common errors include inadequate observation of work performance, failure to evaluate facts properly, and lumping unrelated traits together.

To avoid such errors, raters should be familiar with each trait being rated. They should know the definition of each trait and how it differs from other traits, its relative importance to the job, and how it can best be evaluated. They should rate every employee on the same trait at the same time. This will help raters focus on the trait and its relationship to the job rather than on their feelings toward any particular individual.

Raters should make maximum use of production records, statistical information, and other objective data not based on personal opinion, and they should rate as though their own future as well as that of the employee and the company depended on the accuracy of the rating.

One further caution is that in evaluating employee performance the standards against which performance is to be judged must be realistic. For example, when an employee's production record is low, his work would ordinarily be classified as less than satisfactory. If the fault is the employee's, the rating is justified. But if the employee works at a machine that is old and slow and subject to frequent breakdowns, the cause of the poor production record is beyond the employee's control. In such a case, judging performance against a standard that can be met only by new, fast machines is unrealistic and unfair.

Characteristics of Good Raters

There can be little doubt that job performance evaluation is greatly influenced by the personalities of the raters. Their physical condition influences their reaction to other people. Their skill, past experience, and education are also reflected. There are, however, general characteristics which are common to all efficient raters.

Sincere interest in the rating. Supervisors should see performance evaluation as a useful tool which serves the best interests of the employee, the department, and the company. They should also be willing to participate in training in the rating procedure.

Willingness to make the necessary time available. Most rating programs stipulate that evaluations must be completed by a certain date. If supervisors wait until the last possible moment and then complete the form in great haste, the evaluation will have little value. Supervisors must recognize that it takes time, study, and careful consideration to fill out the rating form properly.

Well-adjusted personality. Quirks of personality may show up in the rating and cause distortion. If, for example, supervisors who are overly enthusiastic about certain things demand the same response from others, they may underrate qualified employees who do not share their enthusiasm.

Sympathy and understanding. Raters should not expect perfection; they must instead be understanding of the weaknesses as well as the strengths of employees.

Flexibility and objectivity. An employee may deserve "excellent" on dependability and "unsatisfactory" on quantity of production. This demands flexibility on the part of raters so that they can go up and down the scale objectively in accordance with the actual job performance they are judging.

Willingness to recognize their own limitations. Self-examination often reveals many traits in supervisors that may influence their evaluation of the performance of employees. These should be identified, and every effort should be made to counteract any tendency to let them influence judgment. Raters should recognize the wisdom of seeking assistance from others when it will result in a more accurate rating.

The Rating Procedure

When evaluating job performance, raters should:

- □ Read carefully all instructions and information about the rating and ask for assistance if there is anything they do not understand completely.
- □ Base the rating on employees' actual performance, not on their potential ability. It is often difficult to separate what em-

ployees have done on the job from what the rater thinks they are capable of doing.

☐ Avoid letting temporary ups and downs in performance alter the rating. Employees may make sudden improvements as a means of raising their ratings. By the same token, temporary illness or problems on the job may throw them off their normal levels of productivity. Performance for the entire period should be considered in determining the rating.

☐ Keep isolated instances in perspective. One customer complaint or letter of praise should not in itself make for a good or bad rating. Think of isolated instances as part of the overall picture.

☐ Never discuss the rating of one employee with other employees.

☐ Remember that employees should be rated unsatisfactory only if their performance is below the standard established for the department. Employees who are rated excellent or exceptional should be making contributions above and beyond their department standard. Each rating should be a reflection of actual performance in comparison with the measuring criteria. And the collective rating of the employees in a department should be reflected in overall department results. For instance, if all the department's employees are rated high on productivity but the department's production is below standard, something is obviously wrong with the individual ratings.

The Evaluation Interview

A major goal of evaluation is the improvement of job performance. If the rating form is completed and then hidden in a file, then no progress has been made in reaching this goal. It is during the evaluation interview that the supervisor has an opportunity to give recognition for good work and make effective use of the rating as a basis for improving performance.

Supervisors who come to a performance appraisal interview unprepared may be letting themselves in for a hard time. If they consider the work of an employee unsatisfactory, they should be ready to back up this opinion with evidence. If a bank teller's tactlessness and brusque manner have antagonized customers, the supervisor should have the details of these incidents so that hirs comments can be specific. Generalizations may be rejected by the employee in such a situation.

No employees like to be reminded of the shortcomings of their job performance, but employees who really want to get ahead recognize the need to know where they stand. The degree of acceptance of the rating depends largely on the manner in which the interview is handled. The interview must therefore be planned so that the employee receives recognition for outstanding work and guidance both in improving job performance and in building a closer relationship with the supervisor. The employee should leave the interview self-confident, in high spirits, and determined to improve. In preparing for the interview, the rater should:

□ Review the factors that affected the evaluation.
□ Have on hand records and other pertinent information.
□ Organize a simple, straightforward plan for conducting the interview.
□ Review the possible problem areas or uncertain ratings with other key persons before setting up the interview.
□ Conduct the interview when neither supervisor nor employee is pressed for time.

Conducting the Interview

Put the employee at ease. This is not difficult if the relationship is already cordial. In any case, the supervisor should make a point of being friendly, sincere, and solicitous.

Restate the purpose of the interview. Stress its benefit to the employee.

Go over the evaluation. Explain the reasons for the rating of each factor, beginning and ending with the favorable factors. Remember throughout the interview that you are discussing not the individual but the performance on the job. It is easier for employees to accept criticism about their work than about themselves. Keep in mind that some of their shortcomings may have resulted from your failure to guide, instruct, and motivate.

Encourage employees to speak freely. Let them ask questions, make suggestions, and offer ways to improve their own performance, as well as the operations in the department.

Avoid putting employees on the defensive. Supervisors should not conduct the interview as though it were a trial, with themselves as prosecuting attorneys and the employees as defendants. The objective is to reach agreement on past job performance compared with a satisfactory standard and on opportunities for improvement.

Be specific. Whether you are complimentary or critical, refer to specific instances. And clear up any misconceptions or misunderstandings that employees may express about any phase of their jobs.

Give credit where credit is due, and set goals for job improvement. Remember that once good work has been adequately recognized, the most important responsibility of the supervisor is to offer—and ask for—constructive suggestions for job improvement.

Let employees explain the obstacles they consider detrimental to better job performance. They may bring out some very real problems which prevent them from performing at their maximum level. If they reveal a situation that needs correction, the supervisor should investigate the matter and talk with the employee again in the near future about what has been done to improve it. If the employee's points are not valid, the supervisor should explain why they are not sufficient justification for poor job performance.

Welcome objections from employees. The most difficult interviews are with employees who say nothing. It's like trying to make a sale to a man who shows no response. You don't know whether he agrees or disagrees with what you say. You don't know his reasons for not buying, so you have no opportunity to answer objections. It is much easier to conduct an effective interview if employees are willing to talk freely about any objections they may have to the rating. This gives the supervisor something to work with and is an indication of the employees' interest.

Concluding the Interview

In job performance evaluation interviews supervisors and employees may talk about many things, but when it is all over and the employees go back to their jobs, what is their frame of mind? Are they enthusiastic? Do they feel that the company and the supervisor have been fair? Will this be reflected in better job performance? To ensure that the interview achieves its purpose, supervisors should do the following.

Work out a definite plan for achieving improvement. Don't be content to talk in generalities: Identify specific areas for improvement, consider each one separately, and work out a program.

Make a record of the key points for follow-up and see that the employees also have records of the program that has been agreed on. This should make clear to employees what specific action they will be expected to take to improve their performance.

Bring employees back to a high level of self-confidence before ending the interview. Communicate your full confidence in their ability to make the changes that have been agreed on.

End the interview on the highest possible note. Again thank the employees for their contributions and their good work. If there is to be a follow-up interview, give them the approximate date. Thank them for their suggestions. Assure them of your continuing interest and of your availability at all times to answer questions and be of assistance.

The Uses of Evaluation Results

After the rating and interview have been completed, the supervisor and the company can use the individual and collective results of the rating program as guides for management decisions and follow-up action. Many companies use the rating for the following purposes:

- As a measure of improvement in individual job performance. It is useful to compare the most recent rating with previous ratings to determine what changes have been made.
- As a basis for determining training needs. If the ratings reflect a lack of information or skills in some area, management can provide corrective training.
- As a basis for promotions, pay increases, and transfers. Decisions concerning these factors are more objective if they are based on a merit rating program.
- As a follow-up check on company employment and placement procedures.
- As an aid in standardizing interdepartmental evaluation, thereby ensuring that the same duties, responsibilities, and overall job contribution will receive the same compensation throughout the company.

Follow-up

If the rating has identified some areas that need immediate attention, and if the supervisor has worked out with the employee what corrective action should be made within a specified period of time, a follow-up interview should be arranged to check progress. In addition, supervisors should follow through promptly on any action they have promised to take, and talk with the employee about the results of this action.

The follow-up interview should be recorded and made a part of the employee's personnel file. Because of current wage–hour laws and other government regulations, this record is necessary to protect the company because of the rating's influence on employee-related action.

Supervisors should not feel that the absence of a formal evaluation program relieves them of responsibility for evaluating employee performance.

Performance appraisal and appraisal interviewing offer both a critical challenge and a unique opportunity to supervisors. To develop the high degree of critical judgment and finesse required, they should obtain as much training and assistance as possible. Supervisors who handle rating programs successfully are well on their way to effective leadership.

17

Techniques for Improving Work Methods

WILLA Cather once remarked that "man is the only animal that fights to stay in a rut." Today, growing numbers of companies want to get their employees out of the rut of obsolete work methods and procedures. Company survival is dependent on improvement—on finding a better way, on speeding up the process of change, on leading the field with changes that mean a competitive advantage. The emphasis is on work simplification, operation improvement, job enlargement—all aimed at increasing the operating efficiency of the organization by improving its working methods and procedures.

Many large companies use the services of specialists, such as time-and-motion-study experts, to improve methods and procedures. But these efforts are doomed if the supervisor is not involved in the development and application of the new improvements. Too often the analysis and improvement of work methods are considered to be the responsibility solely of the specialist. Supervisors should recognize that this is an important part of their jobs. The specialist brings a scientific and systematic approach to the problem and has specialized training and experience, but lacks the supervisor's daily exposure to employees and work methods. Supervisors must guard against the natural tendency of letting their closeness to the job and the habits of years blind them to possible improvements. Instead, supervisors should cultivate an objective approach, question everything, and recognize that no one method is the best way just because it is the one now in use.

In its simplest form, improvement consists of examining how a job is being done; eliminating any nonessential step, movement, or phase of the operation; and developing improved procedures for doing the job. Today's most efficient technique may be obsolete tomorrow. It is essential to remember that the improvement of work methods is not a one-shot effort but should be a continuing part of the supervisor's responsibility.

Approaches to Methods Improvement

Scientific investigation. The supervisor who seeks to bring about improvement in work methods can profit from the techniques used by scientists in tackling problems. Scientists go through the process of:

- Stating the problem to be solved.
- Recognizing the materials and resources with which they have to work.
- Being thorough and systematic.
- Investigating previous work in the same field.
- Discussing the problem with others and learning from them.
- Assuming that the problem has at least one solution and possibly several.
- Remaining objective and being guided only by facts and results.
- Recording every activity. As much may be learned from failure as from success.
- Testing every theory, principle, and conclusion.
- Looking for similarities with other problems and studying their solutions.

Like scientists, supervisors should never assume they have found *the* solution to a problem. Instead, they should continue to look for improvements and refinements.

Improvement of equipment. Many companies have made dramatic changes and improvements in the design and function of tools and equipment, thus enabling employees to produce more with less effort. Yet many others still use the wrong size and type of wrench (or other basic tool), thus slowing down production.

Many improvements that should be made are so simple that they are overlooked. For example, in one firm, large cardboard cartons were opened by tearing up the flaps. Some were glued; others were secured with sharp staples that were dangerous when they were pulled loose. Yet, inexpensive knives with safety guards had been in existence for many years, especially for this purpose; when they were finally obtained, cartons were opened faster and more safely.

Alert supervisors have made significant improvements in their operations by introducing more appropriate tools or by altering the equipment being used. The supervisor should detect instances where equipment can be changed or improved, even when procedures appear to be going smoothly.

Improving the training program. Most of the methods and procedures used by employees are those they have been trained to use. Perhaps the quickest and easiest way to bring about an improvement in work procedure is to retrain present employees and change the program for new employees.

One hardware store had had difficulty in getting employees to engage in suggestion selling. Both initial and follow-up training stressed that whenever a sale was made, the salesperson should suggest an additional item in order to increase total sales. This program, however, was only about 15 percent effective. The situation was analyzed and the training procedure was changed. The new program incorporated the complete process of selling from the time customers were approached until they were handed their purchase, thanked, and invited to return. There was only one important change: after customers said, "I'll take it," the next step was to show them a second item. This was always a companion item or one which was appropriate to the customer's needs or to the season. The salesperson now learned this step in logical sequence, and the selling procedure was incomplete without it. As a result of this change in training—which made suggestion selling an integral part of the procedure rather than an incidental addition—the number of salespeople engaging in suggestion selling increased to 60 percent.

Analysis of Work Methods

Performance of the operation. The best way for supervisors to learn the details of an operation is by actually doing it. In this way, they will get the feel of each step—its difficulty, exactly how it is being done, and how it can be improved.

Observation of the worker. By observing the employee who does the work, the discerning supervisor will detect areas of difficulty and should be able to devise ways in which the procedure can be improved.

Employee questionnaires. Having employees answer questions about their work encourages them to think about the routine they follow and may result in constructive suggestions for improvement. When the questionnaires are considered collectively, overall patterns of improvement are often evident.

Employee interview. Talking with employees about how their jobs are being done and how they could be improved should encourage new ideas and ways to perform their jobs more easily and efficiently.

Charts and manuals. A great many industrial operations and business procedures have been studied minutely by industrial engineers and efficiency specialists. Their findings have been published in book, chart, and manual form, and are available to supervisors who seek to improve the operation in their departments.

Work flowcharts. Highway engineers determine the location of two cities on the map and then lay out routes and specify a road surface best suited for carrying traffic between these two cities. As they plan the road, they consider ways to eliminate curves, fill in valleys, grade down peaks, bridge rivers, avoid dangerous intersections, and place essential signs along the way. Each of these steps is considered with one end in view—a smooth, quick, safe, and economical trip for the motorist who will travel between the two cities.

When the plan has been spelled out, the highway engineer develops a chart to establish the sequence of steps that must be taken to build the road and to assure that both employees and materials will be where they are needed when they are needed. This is a flowchart—a detailed record of every step that must be followed to complete an operation, showing not only what must be done, but also when and in what sequence.

Supervisors can also use the flowchart to advantage. By detailing the steps in each operation performed in their departments, they can visually portray which steps are done simultaneously and which are done in sequence from initiation to completion of an operation. The flowchart can be helpful to supervisors who need to determine whether greater efficiency can be achieved by rearranging the order of the steps or by adjusting the flow of materials needed for specific steps.

Study of unrelated activities. Many dramatic improvements have been made in industrial work procedures by alert supervisors whose observations of seemingly unrelated activity have offered clues to more effective ways of working in their own departments. It was the smooth coordination of a line of chorus girls that gave Knute Rockne the idea for the four-horsemen shift for the backfield of his football team at Notre Dame. And it was a random apple falling from a tree that led Sir Isaac Newton to formulate the law of gravity.

Progress in related areas. Business and industry have continued to benefit from advances in education by applying these advances to company training. The competitive pressures of free enterprise force the constant search for better and more efficient methods. This search leads to any area which offers possibilities for improved operation.

Guides for Improving Work Procedures

The first step in improving work procedures is to describe completely how the job is now being done. This should be a complete audit—a word picture of the work flow process and a diagram showing the step-by-step procedure and the overall picture. Identify the necessary action. The description must be complete enough to show each step of the operation clearly. For example, a list of the steps in answering the telephone might read: (1) Reach for the receiver with left hand; (2) lift receiver; (3) bring receiver in contact with ear; (4) talk into mouthpiece; (5) reach for pencil and message pad with right hand; (6) write message; (7) finish talking; (8) replace receiver with left hand; (9) replace pencil and message pad with right hand.

When the steps in an operation have been itemized, the next requirement is to study every step, movement, and detail, and then to ask questions: Why is the job being done this way? Is what it accomplishes necessary? Are we trying to improve an operation that is not necessary in the first place? Can this task be accomplished better some other way? Is the work being done in the right location? Why is it being done where it is now? Could it fit better into the work flow at some other point? Who should do this part of the job? Is the job being done by the person best suited to do it? Is a worker's skill being wasted on tasks that are too simple?

What follows is a motion economy checklist for a manual operation developed by a well-known company to train supervisors and employees in improved manual work methods.

1. Does each element begin simultaneously with both hands?
2. Does each element end simultaneously with both hands?
3. Are simultaneous arm motions in opposite and symmetrical directions used?
4. Are hand motions of the lowest classification for satisfactory operations?
5. Does the motion path stay within the normal working area?
6. Can sharp changes of direction be avoided by using a continuous curved motion path?
7. Are small objects slid instead of being picked up and carried?
8. Are materials and tools located in proper sequence at definite work stations?
9. Is maximum use made of rhythm and automaticity?
10. Can pieces be pre-positioned for the next operation?
11. Is proper-height chair with comfortable seat and back rest provided?

Remember that any changes that make the job easier, faster, more accurate, or less expensive should be made. These principles can be applied to the job of the secretary, the bank teller, or the assembly line worker. The goal is always the same—the reduction of unnecessary activity and effort.

When the proper questions have been asked, the correct answers have been found, and a direction for improvement has been determined, the next step is to develop a new plan incorporating all the desired changes and improvements. The best plan is one that eliminates the greatest amount of waste, effort, and nonessential motion.

When the plan has been developed and management approval has been obtained, it's time to explain the details to the employees, emphasize the advantages of the plan, and answer their questions. Once the plan has been put into operation, the supervisor should keep a close check on it so that adjustments can be made as soon as they are needed—and then it's time to start looking for ways to make further improvement.

Dr. James L. Williams, former director of industrial relations for Burlington Industries, said: "The most important factor in production is 'people' in industry. Two factories can be just alike in layout and manufcturing, yet one will succeed while the other may go out of business. Two banks can have the same advantages, yet customers flock to one and avoid the other." The difference lies in the willingness of people to increase their own skills and improve the

---

PRINCIPLES OF MOTION ECONOMY

Eliminate idleness. Never use the
hands as a holding device.

Avoid unnecessary motions.

Smallest body member should move
the shortest distance.

**FOR
THE HANDS**

Improve workplace with bins, lip
trays, and workplace appliances.
Pre-position tools and materials.

Employ fixtures, clamps, and guides
for productive work.

Relieve hands with foot controls,
ejectors, chutes, and drop delivery.

**FOR THE
WORKPLACE**

---

methods by which they work. The improvement of people's skills
through training means improvement in overall results. Many companies seek to upgrade job techniques through better placement,
maximum utilization of employee skills, proper delegation of the
workload, and individual supervisory attention to employees who
need help in making these improvements.

18

Appropriate delegation is a means to growth, expanded influence, and increased results through people. It is doubtful if any other leadership skill affords as much opportunity for increasing managerial effectiveness and achievement.

Effective Delegation of Responsibility

STATED simply, delegation is sharing the load. A single employee working alone carries the full burden. When the workload increases significantly, a second employee must be hired. Eventually someone is needed to supervise the group and, as the burden of leadership increases beyond one person's capacity, the supervisor must share a portion of the load to get work done quickly and allow time for decision making. The following statements are symptoms of the need for delegation:

- "I wish someone else around here would start worrying about getting the work done."
- "I know I have too much to do, but no one else wants any responsibility."
- "The delegation stuff sounds good, but it takes longer to tell other people what to do and then have to check on them all the time than it does to do it myself."
- "I don't want any more responsibility. There aren't enough hours in the day to do everything I've got to do now."

One of the most important ways for increasing results is to give more people a measure of responsibility for achieving those results. By sharing a portion of the supervision with an assistant and a portion of the responsibility with each employee, overall results can be improved, the supervisor can devote more time to work that cannot be delegated, and this in turn leads to still further departmental improvement.

The only business that can be successful without delegation is the one-person operation. Wise executives learn early in their careers that to advance, they must expand their leadership by means of delegation. They recognize that failure to delegate stifles the growth of the business, and this in turn limits their opportunities for personal growth.

A study of the top business leaders of America reveals a significant relationship between successful delegation of responsibility, the growth of the company, and the growth of the executive. One of this country's greatest business executives was prouder of having delegated responsibility than he was of the size of his mills. He said, "Take away our factories, but leave me my organization and in four years I will have reestablished myself."

A company consisting of small factories in the Midwest failed because the president insisted on personally approving the purchase of every office machine, and deciding which lines of supplies should be dropped or added and how much money should be spent on advertising—in short, he insisted on making both major and minor decisions regarding the operation of more than 50 units. Failure was inevitable because the job was too big for one man.

The need for delegation of responsibility began a long time before the increased complexities and demands of modern business. One of the earliest references to delegation occurs in *Genesis,* where Jethro tells Moses,

> Choose able men from all the people . . . and place such men over the people as rulers of thousands, of hundreds, of fifties, and of tens. And let them judge the people at all times; every great matter they shall bring to you, but any small matter they shall decide themselves; so it will be easier for you, and they will bear the burden with you.

It is noteworthy that "Moses gave heed to the voice of his father-in-law and did all that he had said."

Managers cannot keep track of every detail of every job for which they are responsible. The more nearly they try to do this, the more they limit their span of leadership, stifle the growth of the enterprise, and defer the development of leadership in other people. Too little delegation is typical of leaders who believe that to get a thing done right they must do it themselves. It is also true of energetic executives who pile one responsibility on another until they succumb to the pressure of "executive overload." At the opposite extreme is the supervisor who delegates responsibility but forgets that authority must also be delegated before results can be achieved.

Responsibility is a duty or an obligation to act. With it must go the *right* to act—that is, the *authority*. And to ensure that the responsibility has been fulfilled, a third ingredient—*accountability*—must be included; that is, the person who has been given a job to do must account to the supervisor for actions taken in carrying out the assignment. For example, when a supervisor delegates responsibility for the department's stock of supplies, hir must also delegate the authority to reorder, and can then hold the employee accountable for keeping enough stock on hand. If the supervisor were to withhold the authority to reorder, then the delegation of responsibility for stock maintenance would be meaningless.

How Well Do You Delegate?

Most supervisors think they do a pretty good job of delegating. They realize that it is a reflection on their overall leadership and faith in other people if they fail to delegate—so many cover up, even to themselves. Delegation actually begins with the ability to analyze and categorize problems, divide big problems into manageable units, size up the capabilities of subordinates, communicate clearly, develop controls, and follow up on the activities of the group. These are the building blocks of realistic delegation.

What would happen if you were suddenly taken from the job? How well would the work go on without you? Are you constantly tied up with giving employees instructions? Are you spending too much time checking details that could just as well be left to the employees?

Are you up to date with your work? Is your desk loaded with reports, forms, and other memos which must have your personal approval? How much has the work of other people been delayed because you haven't had time to approve this material? How much work do you have to carry home? How much of this work can be channeled to someone else?

Are your employees afraid to make decisions because of past reprimands or because you have asked them not to decide things on their own? Do you lack confidence in other people's ability to follow through successfully on their own? Are you afraid to risk letting them take the initiative?

Are you willing to seek the advice of others, especially the employee group, or are you afraid that asking for their suggestions would be an admission that you don't know all the answers? Are you reluctant to admit to your group that you need help to get the job done?

If your answer to too many of these questions is "yes," then you need to give serious attention to improving your delegation practices.

The Need to Delegate

The failure to delegate can be damaging in many ways. It causes a shortage of people who are trained and ready to assume greater responsibility. It causes key supervisors to be so overburdened with routine that they cannot plan or supervise properly or meet other important leadership responsibilities. It limits decision making to only a few individuals, and fails to develop the capability in others.

Failure to delegate makes it necessary to promote employees before they have had adequate training—or to have to go outside the company to obtain the skills and leadership needed for executive jobs. This often causes employees to leave their jobs because they believe they are getting nowhere, and it can also result in general apathy among employees.

A reasonable first step in delegation is to analyze and categorize activities that must take place in a department. When considering whether to delegate, ask yourself these questions.

Can someone else do it? Even though you are the individual best trained for the job, can you do everything? Can you be everywhere? Perhaps someone else can do some of the work—possibly not as well, but well enough.

Can anyone else do it better? Many companies employ experts and then do not make full use of their specialized skills. Are you now spending time doing jobs that could be done better by others in the organization? Do you seek—and follow—the advice of specialists? Do you determine who is best qualified to get the job accomplished and then allow that person to do the work?

Can anyone else do it at less expense? In many companies, $10 hour supervisors do $6-an-hour work. How many jobs are being performed in your company by employees who should be spending their time doing more highly skilled work?

Can someone else do it at a more opportune time? Why cause unnecessary delay just so you can put your stamp of approval on an activity? Delays can be costly to the firm and frustrating to the people who are kept waiting.

Will delegation to employees contribute to their development? It may be worthwhile to map out portions of the work for the year ahead and plan to have key personnel participate more fully in handling certain responsibilities. If the work can be done satisfactorily and the delegation results in employee growth and development, the effort is justified.

Does the work need to be reorganized? Should certain duties which you are now handling completely be given to an assistant or a lead employee? Supervisors should identify those things which they must do themselves and delegate as much of the remaining work as possible. For example, in a purchasing operation, the department head could maintain contact with important suppliers and make decisions on matters outside the company, while an assistant could handle those matters that pertain solely to internal company activities.

Many experts believe that failure to delegate responsibility to others is a psychological problem. Although there is no clear-cut profile of leaders who fail to delegate, it is likely that they feel insecure, lack confidence in the ability of others, are reluctant to admit that someone else can handle the job, fear that they won't get complete credit for what is done in their departments, are afraid that others may move ahead too fast, or simply do not want it known that they are not well informed about what is happening in their departments.

One of the most dangerous conditions that can affect a plane in flight is the formation of ice on the leading surface of the wings and other lift areas. When this happens, the wings become blunt and lose their sleekness, lift is lost, forward speed is slowed, and the plane begins to lose altitude. Modern planes are equipped with various forms of deicers in order to avert this danger. Executives who gradually assume too many responsibilities often take on the characteristics of the plane on which ice has formed. The only way they can maintain speed and efficiency is to delegate. Sharing the load enables them to spread the executive leadership over a much larger area, thus multiplying both influence and accomplishments. It usually results in a quicker and more economical handling of the work, and it develops self-confidence in people.

The executive head of a $30-million business had learned the art of delegation well. He had confidence in his managers' ability to make the right decisions and in their strong desire to succeed, and he backed them up fully, even when they were wrong. When he was away for long periods of time, the ongoing operation of the business did not suffer. All key employees knew their jobs and knew that they were expected to make decisions and to carry out the necessary duties and responsibilities. This executive made the major policy decisions, coordinated leadership, and spent considerable time analyzing ways to improve the business, but he had organized and delegated to the point that he didn't have to be concerned with a multitude of details and decisions. His time and energy were therefore free to actually "manage" the business.

Delegation creates mutual trust and confidence. The teenager who is entrusted with the family car or is asked to take charge of the house in time of crisis feels an enriching sense of self-confidence and trust. The opportunity to assume responsibility is necessary to help adolescents develop into mature and responsible adults. Likewise, employees develop a sense of enrichment when the supervisor is willing to trust them with additional responsibility. It is doubtful if anything else will develop their potential as quickly as the challenge to live up to a new responsibility. However, the supervisor should be cautioned against delegating too much too quickly: Too much responsibility may leave employees feeling overburdened and unable to cope with their new roles.

When a supervisor shares the work, the department will grow faster because more people are given the opportunity to use their full potential. At the same time, employees who have leadership qualities can be trained to replace the supervisor, who can then be freed for further promotion.

Selective Delegation of Authority

Not all authority can be delegated. In some instances, it would not be legal to do so; in others, the supervisor is specifically required to make certain decisions. Some matters that should not be delegated are disciplinary power, long-range planning, and policy making. When authority is delegated, the nature and bounds of that authority and the effective date when it will begin should be spelled out, and a notice should be given to all interested parties to ensure their cooperation. Furthermore, those who are to assume the authority should be given freedom of action. But sufficient controls must be established to monitor the results. Accountability must be a part of the understanding.

An appropriate time to delegate or change responsibility is when other changes are taking place—in personnel, in machines, or in the layout of the work area. But whenever the change is made, the delegation of authority must be as clear and precise as possible. Failure to do so can cause conflict and frustration for employees who are trying to fulfill their new responsibilities, and can create resentment and confusion throughout the department. If the supervisor expects the affairs of the department to proceed smoothly and efficiently, the authority of each person must be clearly understood by everyone in the department.

Avoid delegating authority until there has been an opportunity to make certain that the recipient knows how to use it. Delegation of authority should not be attempted until supervisors are sufficiently acquainted with their personnel to know what each person is able to accept and discharge successfully. Delegation of authority to someone who cannot handle it can be damaging to both the individual's job performance and the department's goals.

If practical, start delegating authority gradually and check with the employee frequently to answer questions and build self-confidence. Be tolerant of mistakes, but when mistakes are made, they should be corrected without sarcastic criticism. Instead, coaching will promote an understanding of what corrections are necessary.

Mastering the Skill of Delegating

Supervisors can profit from occasional objective assessments of the degree of success they are having in delegating work and responsibility. There can be no better way of doing this than by actually checking the results in the department or by an outside appraisal. In pinpointing results and needs, it will also help if the supervisor asks: Are my people properly challenged, and do they have sufficient goals to work toward? Are they constantly growing in their willingness and ability to accept additional responsibility? What additional work or responsibility can be delegated to them? Do I have enough time to do the things that cannot be assigned to others? Is there sufficient evidence of growth in all areas because of the steadily increased delegation?

The ability and willingness to delegate are trademarks of mature executives who are confident of their own ability, have confidence in other people, and are willing to build leadership in their subordinates. Failure to delegate stifles the growth of the business and of every individual associated with it.

The goals of a business enterprise are shaped, clarified, and achieved through effective communication—understanding and response are its ultimate purpose.

19

Goal Achievement Through Two-Way Communication

THE story is told of a visual signal sent from a hilltop immediately following the battle of Waterloo. "British defeated. . . ." This news spread throughout England, and the country went into mourning. Not until later was the full message received: "British defeated Napoleon at Waterloo."

Communication breaks down when the message sent and the message received do not jibe. Not all breakdowns in communications are as spectacular as the one about the defeat at Waterloo, but they can have serious and widespread repercussions. Remarks made in jest but taken seriously can lead to major grievances. Chance comments by an executive can result in a change in company policy. Misunderstood instructions can cause a whole department to fall behind in its production schedule.

Effective communication is the key to successful group dynamics. To succeed as leaders, supervisors must be able to communicate—to express their ideas accurately and precisely—since this is the first step in the process of getting things done through people. The following statements are symptomatic of the communications gap:

- □ "I didn't know you wanted me to check every item."
- □ "Nobody told me it was a dismissal offense not to put a receipt in packages."
- □ "Why is it that the employees in your department never seem to get the word?"
- □ "You can't trust management to give you the facts around here."
- □ "I heard that the company is losing money and may close at the end of the year."

It has been said that nine-tenths of the people don't know what the other tenth are talking about. People in general and companies in particular fail to develop a common language of words, symbols, and methods for understanding.

Neither our complex business structure nor our culture could exist without reliable systems of communication. In *Exploring the Ways of Mankind,* Dr. Walter Goldschmidt refers to language as humankind's peculiar gift and adds: "Without the human capacity to communicate intricate patterns of thought—to recreate experience in words—culture could not exist. . . . Language, then, is an elaborate structure of vocal symbolization, capable of infinite variation, through which ideas, understanding, and feelings are communicated and through which we tend to perceive the events of the world." In animals, the knowledge one generation acquires cannot be passed on to the next generation. Each generation must learn from the beginning everything it needs to know. Through language, the human race is able to both store and transfer its knowledge from generation to generation and from person to person. Within the company framework, this is precisely the job of communication—the transfer of knowledge, skills, and understanding to influence the employeee group.

Words are the supervisor's best tool for selling concepts, expressing ideas, and explaining plans. But supervisors must also recognize that communication goes beyond verbal expression—it includes action, example, and attitude. They can communicate with a look, a changed tone of voice, a shrug of the shoulder, or a silence. Supervisors communicate even when they have no intention of doing so. When they storm into their offices after a bad weekend, they are communicating. When they give orders like tyrannical overlords, they are communicating much more than just the words they are using. And what they communicate by action, example, and attitude—as well as by words—will influence the employees' total job performance.

Communication activates. As a management tool, its purpose is not only to inform employees of plans and goals, but also to show that the movement from plan to achievement is beneficial to both employees and management. The belief that major company decisions are not an appropriate concern of the employee has been abandoned, and management now recognizes the essential need for favorable employee reaction and opinion. Management is serving its own best interest when it maintains effective two-way communication with its total personnel group.

What Communication Really Is

Communication is the exchange of information, ideas, and even attitudes among employees and management. Failure to communicate can lead to administrative errors, lowered production, increased costs, excessive turnover, negative public relations, and blighted individual development—in short, to a less efficient operation. Communication involves two distinct processes—sending and receiving. But the mere fact of sending a message does not ensure that it will be received or understood, as the sender intended it to be. The person initiating a communication must be concerned not only with the organization and effectiveness of the presentation, but also with the condition and receptiveness of those to whom the message is directed.

The limited concept of communication is that it consists of capsule doses of imformation—letters to the employees, memos on the bulletin board, a company newspaper, a departmental meeting. In reality, these are but the veneer of the communications process. The real job of communication is to accurately convey understanding and objective facts to both parties involved; to influence thinking, feelings, and attitudes; and to encourage active mental involvement of both employees and management.

If six men were separated from their supervisor by a soundproof wall, hir could not influence the group, and it would in effect function without leadership. If the members of the work group were also isolated from each other, each would be limited still further. When the walls are removed, the situation is completely changed. The supervisor now shares hirs experience, knowledge, skills, and enthusiasm with the group. Hir learns from them, and they learn from each other. As a team, the group can accomplish far more than it did when the walls were up and each employee worked alone. But the removal of walls is not in itself enough; for maximum benefit, word barriers must also come down. Communication must actively take place.

The Supervisor's Role

Supervisors are the most decisive links in the communications lifeline. They are the bridge between top management and employees. They are the only people who are in constant contact with these two groups that must understand each other if the purposes of both are to be realized.

The importance of supervisors in the communications mainstream cannot be overemphasized. Supervisors are not only the principal instruments of communication but, even more decisively, they are the primary interpreters of messages. By their past relationships and attitudes they determine to a large extent the receptiveness of the employees. Supervisors also influence management's action and reaction toward the employee group by integrating employees' responses. For example, if they report that employees are bitter and hostile toward a proposed change in policy or that the employees feel they need additional information and assistance in making a more effective presentation, the company's attitude toward employees and its method of handling a change will be affected.

A problem department is often in that situation because of faulty understanding. Unsatisfactory work is often traceable to inadequate understanding—or misunderstanding—of how to do the job. Most grievances, too, stem from a lack of understanding. And failure to understand is the result of failure to communicate effectively.

What to Communicate

Employees should receive all the information necessary to maintain their job interest and to increase their job contribution. The specific types of information conveyed vary among companies and among units and levels in each company. There are, however, areas of communication common to virtually all businesses and situations:

☐ Production schedules and quotas.

☐ Health and safety information.

☐ Product changes, sales campaigns, special promotions, and contests which will affect employees or in which they are expected to participate.

☐ Information designed to build favorable attitudes and improve cooperation.

☐ Recognition of outstanding service and accomplishment.

Communications Media

In *Personnel Policies and Practices Report,* Prentice-Hall lists the most common communication tools: employee handbooks; contests; bulletin boards; information and reading racks; meetings, conferences, and individual interviews; company magazines and newspapers; letters, leaflets, and pamphlets; movies, filmstrips, video tapes, closed circuit TV, computer printouts, and slide presentations; visual aids and posters, such as safety and production charts; company reports to employees; telephones; suggestion systems; and public address systems.

The variety of communications media is almost unlimited. Many firms use only a few of these because of their limited size or need. Others, usually larger companies, engage in a variety of activities, utilizing most of them. The choice should be dictated by the needs of the particular situation.

Improving the Downward Flow of Information

The downward flow of communication enables management to tell its side of the story—the "why" and "why not" of company activity. It presents essential information about products, policies, and plans; and it also helps the employee understand, accept, and cooperate with the management's decisions and proposed changes. An adequate flow of information to employees tends to diminish their fears and suspicions, which may result from misinformation or no information. It can also make the company's side of the story available; build pride in employees and *esprit de corps* in the company; improve morale and team feeling; and help the employee to understand, accept, and cooperate in moving toward company goals.

When a specific department—personnel, public relations, or

communications, for example—is charged with the communications responsibility, much of the downward communication is planned, prepared, and initiated by this department. But regardless of the method used, supervisors cannot depend on others at higher levels to furnish all the information the employees need. Supervisors must remember that general information prepared for all other departments is available, and they must follow up with meetings within the department and personal contact to make the information more relevant and specific.

Increasing the Upward Flow

By opening the channels of communication upward, management can increase employee acceptance of its communications. The upward flow of communication is one of the most neglected areas in management. The need for downward communication is readily apparent—as are the attendant problems—but the potential and advantages of upward communication are less obvious.

An upward flow of information reveals the attitudes and feelings of employees and their reactions to downward communication. Knowing that management will listen encourages employees to use their minds as well as their muscles in achieving better job results. If they are encouraged to express their ideas, employees are more likely to make suggestions for improving the efficiency and economy of the operation. Also, if they have the "ear" of management, they are more likely to report potentially troublesome situations that could get out of hand. A textile worker once remarked, "It says in the employee handbook that this company has an open-door policy. But just try getting into the boss's office. It might as well be in China for all the good it does me. Either he isn't in, or he's too busy, or he's hurrying to a meeting. I've given up. I'll never try to see him again." Unfortunately, this situation is all too common.

What can management do to eliminate barriers to the upward flow of information? What steps can be taken to make the open-door policy a reality? Employees must feel that what they have to say will be welcomed and taken into consideration. The supervisor should not display impatience or lack of interest in what the employee is saying.

Often the physical distance separating employee and supervisor is itself a barrier. In large organizations, the office of the supervisor may not be easily accessible to the employees. Although supervisors are not always able to change the location of their offices, they can compensate for physical separation through written communications and more effective personal contact.

If an employee's suggestion is not responded to promptly—or remains unanswered—that person may well be discouraged from making any further suggestions. And one of the strongest deterrents to upward communication is the company's failure to act on undesirable conditions—when management fails to act, the employee loses faith in its sincerity. If there is good reason for leaving things as they are, then employees should be told so. To the employee, the strongest form of communication is not management's words but its actions.

Supervisors often fail to keep their ears to the ground and assume that no news is good news. Their failure to show interest by deliberately seeking out employee opinions discourages the employee from seeking them out. Through upward communication, a clearer picture of the work, accomplishments, problems, plans, attitudes, and feelings of employees can be gained; and the individuals, policies, actions, or assignments that are likely to cause trouble can be identified. By welcoming upward communication, management taps a fertile resource of ideas. Employees should understand that they can depend on you—that they will get the correct information from you as soon as it is available. Let them know by your intent and follow-up actions that you are the best source of information. The better you keep them informed, the better they will keep you informed.

Suggestion Systems

Many companies use suggestion systems to encourage upward communication. The technique contains many desirable features: an opportunity to get a message to someone who can take action; assistance in making suggestions; a specific form on which to make them; acknowledgment of all suggestions; rewards for those that are usable; a specified time limit within which the employee can expect action; and the knowledge that management welcomes and encourages this type of communication.

A suggestion system is effective because it offers benefits to both the employee and the company. It is a creative outlet for employees, since it affords an opportunity to contribute ideas and opinions. It may also increase their job security, improve their chances for promotion, and be a source of financial reward for worthwhile suggestions.

A favorable and cooperative attitude by supervisors is essential in promoting suggestions from the employee. Supervisors should acquire a thorough knowledge of the system's rules and policies so that they will be able to answer questions about the process. Many of the suggestions will pertain to their own departments. Supervisors should actively promote regular use of the suggestion system by encouraging the employees to submit their ideas.

Developing the Skill of Listening

Most people are not good listeners because they do not stop talking long enough, or because they do not know how to listen. Most managers spend the major part of each working day trying to communicate with others, and most of this time should be spent listening. Failure to listen—and learn from what the other person has to say—wastes valuable time.

Father Theodore V. Purcell of Loyola University conducted an 18-month study of employee attitudes at Swift and Company in 1965 and reported in the *Harvard Business Review* that year that "of all the sources of information a foreman has by which he can come to know and accurately 'size up' the personalities of the people in his department, listening to the individual is the most important."

But listening is not simply waiting passively for the other person to stop talking so that you can begin. It is an active process that requires that the listener be receptive and interested, pay careful attention, and ask questions or take appropriate notes. And once the message has been received, it is important that the supervisor give full credit for suggestions and information rather than claim credit for the ideas. To do otherwise eliminates a source of future information and antagonizes the employee at the same time.

Listening brings about achievement and understanding, but it enriches the individual as well. Skilled listeners develop a sensitivity that enables them to share the experience and emotions of others.

Guides to More Effective Communication

We all admire the person who is able to say the right thing at the right time. This is not simply a matter of intuition; it is the practice of skills developed through experience. No two people communicate in exactly the same way, and all have to adapt the techniques to their own particular personalities and abilities. But a sincere effort to apply the guides that follow and to work at sharpening communicative skills will result in improved human relations.

Plan your communications. Build communications planning on facts, straight thinking, valid conclusions, and mature judgment. Develop a clear concept of what you want to communicate. Keep your immediate and long-range objectives in perspective. Know the people who are to receive the communication—what types of people they are, how receptive they are, what they are most interested in, what their personal values are, and what approaches will be most effective.

Know your own abilities and limitations and compensate for them in determining your most effective approach. Plan your approach as carefully as you would plan any other aspects of your job. Make notes—don't leave important details to chance. Aim for lasting results. A response is no proof of understanding and, without understanding, nothing has really been accomplished.

Clarify your ideas before trying to communicate them to others. Clarence Randall has said, "I don't advise you to start talking until you have begun thinking. It's no good opening the tap if there is nothing in the tank."

Consult with others. If your communications could affect others outside your department, it would be wise to seek their advice before proceeding.

Communicate for tomorrow as well as today. Although it is necessary to meet today's goals and needs, supervisors should not ignore long-range goals, nor should they delay unduly in communicating disagreeable information, as delay only makes it more difficult and distasteful.

Be consistent with follow-up action. How much you convince people of your sincerity depends more on what you do than on what you say you will do. This means that clear assignment of responsibility, adequate delegation of authority, fair reward for effort, and consistency in policy enforcement are more important than expressed good intentions.

Communicate the right information in the right amount. Saying too much serves to confuse the receiver. Saying too little fails to supply all the needed information.

Make it original, colorful, and interesting. Use the most effective tone, words, media, time, and occasion to ensure the most effective reception.

Gain attention and interest first. Remember that before you can communicate, you must have both the attention and the interest of the receiver.

Execute thoroughly. Plan and execute communication with great care in order to convince and to elicit response. Communication is not an end in itself; it is only an instrument. But if it does not achieve the desired result, it has served no useful purpose.

Communicating is like eating in the sense that today's intake will not satisfy tomorrow's hunger. Communication must be an everyday affair to be successful. It should not be something the supervisor concentrates on at intervals when time is available. Employees must believe that they can depend on the supervisor and on management to furnish correct information. Management states its intent through its communications, but demonstrates it through follow-up action. The better employees are kept informed, the better they will keep management informed.

If the policies and philosophy of management filter down to all employees and through them to the public, and if all the people who get the message have a full understanding of what is going on and how they fit into the picture, then communication has in fact been successful. The final test is favorable response.

20

The human mind contains reservoirs of vast power and potential which, when tapped, can enrich both the individual and the company.

Creativity:
Pearl of Great Price

A philosopher once said, "Man is the greatest thing on earth, and the greatest thing in man is his mind." Another called an idea "the pearl of great price." Both were saying that an individual's mental capacity is a vast resource of priceless ideas and creativity.

In 1935, at the age of 29, Chester Carlson set out to invent a pushbutton copying machine. During the years that followed, he worked almost day and night, used his own meager earnings to buy materials, developed a machine that worked, and approached more than 20 companies that turned him down because they saw no practical use for his crude and toylike process of copying. He received his first royalty payment in 1947—the start of the millions that were to come his way because of this one invention. This came about because a man had an idea, he believed in it, and he exhibited remarkable persistence in working it out and eventually selling it to others. This is but one example of what can be accomplished through the creativity, belief, and persistence of just one mind at work.

Business and industry today hunger for ideas and are ready to reward the people who can supply them. Ideas are the foundation of progress: Without an infusion of new thinking, no business enterprise can succeed for very long. Idea people are rare, not because ideas are so difficult to conceive but because, if they are to be developed, hard work is usually involved. An idea can originate in a flash of inspiration, but before it benefits anyone, it has to be developed, sold, and applied. It is at this point that too many bright ideas lose their luster.

A young advertising executive stood before a group of California orange growers in 1918 and said, "I have an idea. Let's teach people to drink oranges." Consider for a moment the thousands of growers, shippers, and processors, and the millions of consumers who have benefited from this one idea.

A man spent a summer in an area where the ground remained frozen. He observed that when scraps of food were thrown out the back door, they lay preserved and didn't rot. The man's name was Birdseye. A whole new industry was created because his observation was followed up.

Within each person, ideas lie dormant, capable of bursting forth into fruition. Ideas are not the exclusive property of mystical men. The talent for creating them exists in every individual, but the use of certain techniques is necessary to ensure a fuller development of this potential.

Ideas Don't Just Happen

Creative and constructive thinking, like any other skill, can be developed to a high degree. The key to the creative process is the individual. No group or committee ever had an idea. Generally speaking, though, most of us are more creative when working with other people, at least part of the time.

Ideation and creativity are important to every company. To firms such as advertising agencies, they are the very lifeblood of the business. This critical dependence on new ideas and creative thinking has prompted many firms to conduct training sessions in the creative process. Because of the success of these deliberate attempts to be creative, businesses of all types are now making the techniques of creativity a part of their management training programs. Although these techniques are highly variable according to specific needs, the following guides will provide a reasonable approach to individual ideation.

What is the problem to be solved? The first step is to identify and write down the problem that needs to be solved, the product that needs to be altered, or the process that needs to be improved.

Make a start. With the problem before you, bombard it with ideas.

Don't let your mind drift—keep it directed to the problem. Use your mind like a laser beam whose tremendous power stems from the concentration of rays on one small area.

Write down the ideas as they occur. It has been said that a pencil can serve as a crowbar to move our minds. Write down the ideas immediately. Don't stop to analyze or evaluate them. Continue looking for more ideas.

Use a checklist. Jot down all the changes that can be made in a proposal. How many different ways can the product be used. What additional groups can use it? Saturate yourself with background information and knowledge about the problem so that your checklist will be meaningful.

Choose a time. Set aside some time each day for thinking—then stick to the plan. Make thinking a part of the daily routine. If you wait until you have time for creative thinking, you will never get around to it. If you want to develop new ideas badly enough, you will provide the time.

Pick a place. Ideas can and do occur everywhere—in the midst of busy activity, while traveling, or while working on an unrelated subject. But experience shows that certain surroundings can be more conducive to ideation than others. Find the place that is best for you, and spend some time there.

Ask yourself questions. A curious mind opens many doors. Repeat the who, what, when, where, how, and why every step of the way. Use these questions regarding every product, use, and technique. Can it be made bigger or smaller? Can it be divided or combined? Can it be reversed or changed? Ask yourself questions to stimulate your thinking.

Set a goal. If new ideas are important, set a quantitative idea goal that is ambitious but realistic. The very fact that you have a target will help stimulate ideas.

Give yourself a deadline. For too long, the creative process has been relegated to a corner of the mind. Utilize the pressure of a time schedule to force yourself to concentrate on the problem so that you will produce ideas.

For the mind to produce, it must be put into forward gear. It must be challenged, stimulated, exercised, strained, and forced to act. But ideas have to come from someplace—they cannot be produced from a complete vacuum. Ideas will have a much better chance of coming into being if certain stimulators are applied to the process. These include travel, personal contact, creative hobbies, reading, and writing. Borrow ideas and improve them. Combine two or more ideas. Change ideas. Associate new facts. Try to apply techniques and ideas from different fields. Talk with people—ask them what they are doing and why they are doing it that way. Think of ideas as thousand-dollar bills—good ideas really are worth money—and you'll be persistent in your attempt to find them.

The employee group can be a rich source of ideas and creativity. Tap this reservoir of creativity. If the supervisors are willing to recognize the tremendous potential of employee ideas, they will make every effort to utilize this potential for the benefit of their department. Remember to give appropriate credit for employee contributions.

Employees will communicate their ideas to supervisors only after supervisors themselves have demonstrated that they are receptive to ideas, are willing to give serious consideration to them, and will make every effort to share the benefits of the ideas with the employees who present them. This receptiveness must be communicated in daily relationships, because an employee's idea can be killed by a sneer, a yawn, a quip, or by a supervisor's frown.

Brainstorming: Group Ideation

One popular method for developing ideas is called brainstorming. It is basically a technique for discovering and developing new ideas through the group approach. Several days prior to the session, an idea or cluster of ideas will be given to participants, who will be told certain things about the problem and about the rules that will be observed during the session. They will be told to think about the subject ahead to time, to write down any ideas in advance, and to apply the various approaches that were listed earlier in this chapter. They will probably be given the following four rules:

1. Judicial judgment will be ruled out. No attempt will be made during the session to evaluate the merits of ideas.
2. Freewheeling will be recommended. Go as far afield and be as wild as you like, as long as you keep to the subject.
3. The more ideas, the better. The need is for quantity. The greater the number, the greater the likelihood that good ideas will be presented.
4. Combine one idea with others. Improve on the ideas of other people. Attach one idea to another.

Participants are usually asked to come to the session prepared to enjoy the fun. The ideas presented during the session are usually written down or tape-recorded. It is the leader's responsibility to keep ideas flowing by preventing criticism or evaluation of ideas and by attempting to keep the ideas focused on the announced subject.

Experiments have proved that ten individuals working on an idea together usually produce more and better ideas than the same ten people working individually. Brainstorming has the advantage of enabling participants to alter one another's ideas, triggering new ideas based on what other people have said, and producing a beneficial atmosphere from the mental stimulation of others.

If it is not feasible to get a group to brainstorm an idea, it can be done individually by following the same basic rules. The object is to produce a quantity of ideas and to worry about their evaluation at a later time.

Usually, in the case of group brainstorming, some person who is familiar with the subject will evaluate the ideas suggested and bring the best ones before the appropriate individual or group for possible action.

Selling Ideas

A company does not benefit simply because it has manufactured a product. Customers must be sold on the product and must purchase it before the seller can benefit. Similarly, an idea that is not sold or used has no value. The supervisor who has originated ideas should also know how to sell those ideas. Getting the acceptance of others is the critical problem for most people. Ideas too often wither and die for lack of customers. The following guides should be helpful in selling ideas to others.

Prepare the idea. Countless excellent ideas have died a sudden death because they were exposed to critical examination before they were strong enough to endure. Whatever their possibilities, they were unacceptable because they were presented prematurely. Thus, the potential of the ideas was lost and the originators were discouraged from future attempts.

To a great extent, the future of an idea depends on the thoroughness of its development. Have all angles been considered? Has the idea been used before? Is the idea good but impractical because the cost or consequences are too great to make it acceptable? Is the idea well organized? Are you prepared to communicate everything about the idea that is necessary in order to sell it to your supervisor? Are your facts accurate?

Present the idea. Get the attention of the person you want to sell. Make an effective presentation. Know more about the idea than you will need to present. Be prepared to answer all pertinent questions. Don't be put in the embarrassing position of having to say, "I'm sorry, I can't answer that—I didn't think of it from that angle." Be able to prove the advantages and to present adequate ways for overcoming the disadvantages.

If the idea is a good one, don't give up. Some of the most significant ideas have been turned down many times: "The thing will never fly." "The world is flat." "Television will never work. It just isn't practical." There are dozens of examples of things we take for granted today that were once thought impossible. If you believe sufficiently in an idea, stick with it, but never be ashamed to admit that your idea was wrong. It was Santayana who said that "a fanatic is a man who redoubles his efforts after he has lost sight of his objectives."

Fly High on Jet-Propelled Ideas

Ideas are based on facts accumulated through years of experience, work, and study. Since facts are available to everyone, so are ideas. Edison was a prolific inventor, yet the wonders he developed were not the result of sudden flashes of insight. He created from vast resources of information. He assembled and reassembled facts available to all the scientists of his day.

Form the thinking, searching, and writing habit. Many executives who are convinced of the importance of ideas keep a pencil and notepad handy at all times—when they travel, or read, or attend lectures or business conferences—lest they forget an idea or the germ of an idea.

If you make time available, you can start looking for ideas. You can be as creative as you are willing to be. You will find no greater source of growth and improvement than your own fertile mind. Idea people are rare—no wonder they command so much respect, prestige, and salary! An important responsibility of leadership is to use ideas to solve problems, to make the department and company more successful, to get more done, and to make your own job easier. Work for ideas so they can work for you.

21

Einstein did not convince the world of his genius by saying he was a genius; his public image was created by what he did, not by what he said he did. A company's public image is what it does, not what it says it does.

Guides to Favorable Public Relations

WHO in your company is responsible for public relations? You are—and it doesn't matter who you are or what your position is. Every employee is the molder of the company's public image. Public relations is what people think and say about your company because of the impression it has made on them.

You may have heard of high-powered word magicians who sit in Madison Avenue offices and work miracles of public relations. The fact is that a company image is not created artificially. It is based on what people experience about a company for themselves.

Kinsey M. Robinson, chairman of the Washington Water Power Company, has said, "We may talk in print until we are exhausted; our lawyers and publicity men can make the most logical statements on earth. But unless our employees are enthusiastic about what we do, they can neutralize our motives by the single comment—'baloney.' "

The supervisor has a special interest in good public relations as well as a prime responsibility for its success. A good reputation enables the company to attract and retain a better workforce. People like to work for the company that has the best reputation—morale is higher and good employees stay longer, because they can take pride in the place where they work. Productivity is greater and the quality of the product is higher when employees are proud of their company.

A good public image helps give the company's salespeople access to places that might otherwise be closed to them. And if the company sells a product or service directly to the consuming public, good public relations can influence the public's decision to buy.

Good community relations assure the business a fair shake. Municipal governing bodies, such as the city council and county commissioners, make decisions which vitally concern the company, including tax evaluations and assessments, zoning, the routing of streets and highways, and the authorization of railroad sidings. These decisions are more likely to be favorable to the company if it maintains good relationships with community and employee groups.

During times of crisis, misfortune, or emergency, the community's reaction often determines whether the company can remain in that community. Goodwill and good public image are like insurance when the company needs community friends.

The company's ability to stay in business is dependent on its public image. Public choice is the purest form of democracy. The public's feelings about a company, as reflected in the cash registers, ultimately determine the success or failure of the business.

Creating a Favorable Corporate Image

The increasingly competitive nature of most business and industry, the greater mobility of customers, the speed of transportation, and the ease of communication mean that every company is competing with every other in the field, regardless of location. It is not always the best products or services but those that are most effectively linked with public relations and advertising programs that receive the greatest acceptance.

For this reason, many businesses are now giving the same careful, systematic, and thorough attention to the total area of favorable public relations that they formerly applied only to production and sales. This new emphasis has led them to employ experts, spend large sums of money, and engage in elaborate training programs for supervisors in order to promote a favorable image. At the same time, increased attention is being given to employee benefits, employee activities, company publications, and other considerations that affect what the employees and the public believe and say about the company.

The first step in favorable public relations should be to determine the current status of the company's reputation or image. Then, a program must be planned and implemented to bring about the desired improvement. The following are recommended steps for creating and maintaining a favorable corporate image.

Favorably influence the people who shape your company's image. It has been estimated that every employee influences approximately 50 people outside the company. What will the employees in your department tell their neighbors and friends about the company? Remember that outsiders will believe what employees say because the employees work for the company. If each employee influences 50 people, you as a supervisor should influence twice that number. In addition, you represent the company to the employee. If you are fair and understanding, so is the company. If you are unreasonable and unreliable, the company is, too.

Get your house in order. Public relations is doing a good job and getting credit for it. What type of job are you doing in your department? Is your house in order? What treatment do your employees receive? Do you set an example of loyalty and pride, and do you constantly tell the employees that they are working in a fine department and for the best company around? Do you encourage employees to keep their gripes and complaints inside the firm rather then airing them on the outside? Do you urge your employees to speak well of the company because they are part of it? Remember that the foundation for good public relations is good internal relations.

Be a good housekeeper. Hosts like to be proud of the appearance of their homes, so get your employees interested in making a good impression on customers and company visitors. Many companies consider their spotless plants one of their most important advertisements. Create in each employee a sense of pride in the appearance of the department.

Promote safety, courtesy, helpfulness, and friendliness. The potential customer's only contact with the company may be through one employee. Will that contact improve or harm the firm's reputation?

Maintain favorable relations with community groups. This includes news media, law enforcement agencies, governmental units, and civic associations. Every community has scores of civic groups which need a place to meet, speakers on special subjects, and experienced leadership. Opportunities to win their goodwill are tailor-made for the alert and responsive company. Warm relations with these community groups can foster the image of an organization that is concerned with people and with the welfare of the community.

Practice good communication. Keep your employees informed so that they can keep the public informed. The community has a concern for the welfare of the company and an interest in what it is doing. Press releases can be instrumental in supplying this information, but perhaps the most effective way is through the employees.

Protect the company's reputation. If the company claims to maintain top quality, its quality control program should insure this in every item that leaves its factory. If it advertises a liberal return policy, every employee should conscientiously strive to carry out this policy. If it stresses service, it must give service in full measure. One major food producer considers its most valuable asset to be its reputation for the quality and freshness of its products. In order to protect this reputation, the route salespeople are instructed to pick up leftover products that have reached a certain age. These items are not sold at reduced prices or given to employees. They are cut open and destroyed, so that the company label can be protected and its reputation guaranteed.

If a company claims a liberal employee benefit program, then the program must be available and it must be administered fairly. If the company prides itself on its concern for its employees, then it should demonstrate this concern during illnesses, personal emergencies, discharges, and retirements, as well as in its employee activity programs.

Go the Extra Mile

Perhaps in no other activity can a company get as much mileage from its efforts as in public relations. If the company goes all out because of its genuine concern for people, for the community, and for its own best interests, then it can make great gains in public relations. The following are steps it can take in that area.

Corporate community citizenship. Community citizenship means support of community projects; taking good care of company property; maintaining favorable employee and public relations; and the active support of business, cultural, educational, and religious activities. No business can function on its own, completely isolated from the interests of the community. The company is part of the community, and as the community goes, so go the fortunes of the business.

One large electrical utility company maintained a number of substations throughout the city, consisting of unattractive cold gray masses of transistors and transformers surrounded by steel link fences. By planting rose bushes around the fences and putting up attractive circular signs bearing the words "Citizenship and Service," the company not only improved the appearance of its substations but also improved its corporate image.

Promote mutual friendship. Every organization should take the initiative to make certain that its employees know the community, its people, its facilities, and its needs. Greater stress should be placed on this when a company is new to a community or when some of the management group has been transferred into the area.

It is up to the company to enable the community to get acquainted with its facilities. This can be accomplished to some extent through written communications, booklets, and talks by company personnel, but the best method is to hold an open house and conduct tours of the plant. Businesses are often surprised at how little the community knows about their operations and how much the feeling toward the company improves after people have had an opportunity to look for themselves. Even such businesses as banks and department stores have many interesting behind-the-scenes activities which are largely unknown to the public.

Provide community leadership and talent. The purpose of a business is to operate successfully and make a profit, but it should never lose sight of the fact that it should also enable its employees to have more satisfying and constructive lives. One of the best ways for accomplishing this is through individual participation in community groups and activities. Business executives have already proved their leadership and organizational ability, and civic groups need their special talents. A real service can be rendered by the company employee who is also willing to be a community leader.

The company should both permit and encourage its people to participate in community affairs, within the limits set by their work. Before employees accept community responsibility, especially if it requires time during working hours, they should check with their supervisors—and they should be careful not to commit the company in any way without prior authorization.

Participation in community activities not only benefits the community, but it also benefits the company and the individual. Many leaders have refined their management skills, learned to work more effectively through people, improved their public-speaking ability, and increased their value to the company as a result of their community activity.

It should be remembered that all employees are representatives of the company and cannot divest themselves of this identification. The good that they do benefits the company. But if employees don't do a good job, are uncooperative, fail to follow through, seek positions of leadership but do not work, or make enemies, then the company will suffer. Hence, if employees do decide to participate in community affairs, they should make sure they do the best job possible.

Public relations consists not of major promotions but of a steady, step-by-step approach. The result is influenced more by action than by stated intentions. The very nature of the free enterprise system leads each company to promote its own best interests with its employees, its customers, and the general public. This activity deserves the same management attention as do other vital factors affecting the success of the company's operation.

All people are the architects of their own achievements, but only the successful are willing to admit that the result is of their own design.

22

Moving up the Management Ladder

THE casual observer is often puzzled why promotions don't always go to the brightest people but often to those considered less likely to succeed. The reason is that the successful ones know what they want and go after it. They have a plan of action; they have determination and drive; they compensate for their deficiencies with purpose and tenacity that cause them to outstrip their more talented but less dedicated competitors.

There is as much care and planning in building a successful career as there is in designing and erecting an outstanding building. Successful executives recognize that the odds are against accidental successs, so they decide what they want and commit themselves to paying the price. They put first things first. They develop a sense of values and decide how their time could be spent more profitably—both on and off the job. They set their sights on ultimate goals rather than settling for momentary pleasures.

The keys to accomplishment and success are conviction and follow-through. Many people have a small amount of success, and exert small influence, because they think, plan, and act small.

One brilliant newspaper reporter was distressed when a less talented staff member was promoted to assistant city editor. The man who was promoted wasn't especially gifted or even well liked, but he

224

had done something the brilliant reporter had failed to do; he had planned a course of action that would make him the logical choice for promotion when an opening occurred. Every free moment he had was spent at the city editor's desk, watching how the job was handled, helping whenever he could. He was not asked to do this and he received no extra pay for it; what he did was to take the opportunity to learn about the higher job. In time, he became a sort of unofficial aide at the city editor's desk, and because of this invaluable training he was the obvious choice when there was an opening for an assistant city editor.

The important ingredient was that he knew what he wanted, and developed a plan of action to get it. The brilliant reporter had just as much ambition, but he didn't have a plan of action. He had failed to recognize that success is dependent on three factors: desire, determination, and a plan of action.

One of the country's leading educators, remarking on the technological revolution that has taken place in American industry during the past decade, said: "Whatever we're teaching three years from now ought to be different from what we're doing today. Otherwise we'll be wrong."

All executives, regardless of their position, must keep up with developments in their own fields and in related areas. Every supervisor who expects to grow in responsibility must be willing to acquire additional knowledge and skills.

It can be assumed that you are qualified for your present job. But are you qualified for the next job up the ladder? Perhaps that job requires knowledge that you don't possess. It probably involves the practice of techniques and skills that you are not now using. It certainly requires the handling of bigger problems. What plans of action do you have to increase your qualifications and move up?

The story is told of a big, lumbering young man who took a job in a heavy production industry. A few years later, fellow employees and friends were heard to remark that it was a shame that, although he had finished college, he was still running the same machine. After he had been on this machine about three years, he was promoted over several other people and given a supervisor's job. Everyone seemed surprised about the promotion—except the plant manager, with whom he had talked about his plans to move ahead; the manager's secretary, who had been asked many times about the books and reading habits of the manager; and the local librarian, who had checked out dozens of books to "Big Ox." He knew what he wanted, had a plan, and kept working at it.

Are you satisfied with your present position, pay, status, and career? Are you content to stay where you are for the remainder of your working life? Will the company be willing to let you stay where you are and go on making the same contribution even though the company as a whole must improve or go out of business?

If the answer to these questions is "no," then time is short. You need a personal plan of action that will qualify you for promotion. The first step in drawing up a plan is to decide what you want to accomplish. What are your assets and shortcomings in relation to your goal? How have others achieved the same goal? What action will move you toward the goal?

Keys to Executive Progress

Management experts generally agree that the pendulum of specialization has swung too far and is beginning to swing back. Specialists can perform within the confines of their limited areas of expertise, but they have difficulty in managing activities that require judgment beyond their narrow specializations. The supervisor who rises in management in the future will have to be concerned not only with the technical aspects of the job, but also with management organization, salesmanship, personnel, public relations, and many other areas. This requires broad general knowledge about many things. The leader who expects to be part of a highly complex and smoothly functioning management must be versatile. The following factors should receive the attention of the supervisor who seeks to move to higher levels of responsibility.

Develop an executive attitude. This factor will play a vital role in your success or failure as an executive. It will shape your attitude toward other people and theirs toward you. A negative personality can cause the best plan of action to fail. It can doom the most carefully devised scheme, because you must create a good impression if you expect to move ahead. From the start, you should learn to look, think, and act like an executive. Naturally, you won't try to take on executive authority before you have the job, but you can be management-minded by showing your interest in seeing that the company is successful and by being concerned with eliminating waste and increasing profit. In this way, you can demonstrate that you have the necessary mental capacity and attitude to qualify you for the management team.

To determine the traits of a good executive, the University of

Chicago's Committee on Human Development studied the personalities of 300 executives. From the results, Dr. William E. Henry has drawn this composite picture of the best executives:

- They have a strong desire for personal achievement. They get as much satisfaction from achievement on the job as others get from winning at golf or football. They are never satisfied with what they have already accomplished but feel compelled to move on.
- They are not content to stand still, but must constantly move upward. If their present jobs do not offer them the opportunity to move up, they will seek that opportunity elsewhere. They need proof of progress in the form of pay increases, new titles, and greater responsibility.
- They must advance socially. Their ambition extends beyond their jobs to their personal lives. They seek symbols of success—a fine home, a big car, and a place in the prestigious social circles of the community.
- They respect authority. They are good followers because they look to those in positions of influence as a source of help for their own advancement. They realize that to run afoul of the power structure is to jeopardize their own futures.
- They are decisive. They know how to make decisons and are not afraid to do so, even though some of these decisions may be wrong.
- They are assertive. They have the courage of their convictions. They aren't afraid to stand up and be counted, even if their opinions aren't popular.
- They constantly fight failure. They know that yesterday's successes will not help them deal with today's problems. They never assume that success will be automatic. They fight to do an excellent job and to keep the respect of their superiors. They know that the company has a right to expect constant improvement. They are realistic about what they must do to achieve success, and are critical of their own accomplishments.
- They are mentally and emotionally mature. They stand on their own two feet and accept responsibility for their own actions.

Be knowledgeable on a broad front. Even first-line supervisiors must possess a wide variety of information and skills in order to carry out their duties and responsibilities effectively. They must know about the company, its products, its manufacturing and marketing processes, and about the economic and labor conditions in the community.

A prominent businessman once told a meeting of training directors: "Most executives are receptive to new ideas if they're good. But those who have the final decision in management are cautious. They have to be. They can't afford to go off half-cocked. Therefore, when you make recommendations to them, you must be sure they are well thought out and are useful to the company as a whole. Perhaps it is not management that is rigid in its views. Rather, we make no special effort to learn the other functions of management. If we had a comprehensive understanding of all the problems of a company, maybe we would be better training men."

Specialists have a place in business and industry, but that place is seldom in top management—at least not until they acquire a diversity of knowledge and skills. Specialists often limit their interest as well as their knowledge to such a narrow field that they are unable to grasp the overall management picture.

Recognize that learning should never cease. The executive who expects to grow must make knowledge a constant pursuit. The humanities should be given an appropriate place in the continuing acquisition of knowledge. General cultural enrichment gives an individual knowledge that may be usable in unforeseen ways; in addition to direct benefit on the job, it can enrich a supervisor's life. As a case in point, an advertising woman who spent two hours on the commuter train daily always carried paperback books to read while she traveled. When an associate in the company commented on this "waste of time," a coworker replied: "Well, I don't think it's a waste of time; she writes the best and most original copy of anyone in the agency."

Remain young in spirit and eager for new experience. The mark of a truly great mind is that it never grows old. It remains young in spirit, eager to learn and to enjoy new experiences. The habit of study will keep leaders identified with the mainstream of dynamic activity. If they become too set in their ways and too conservative in their thinking, they will not advance. Companies need the active and inquiring mental posture that is constantly looking for newer and fresher ideas. Learning and vitality are a matter of attitude and effort, not of chronological age.

Make time available for what is important to you. It seems reasonable that leaders ought to spend their free time doing the things they enjoy. After all, it is their own time: They work hard on the job and are therefore justified in devoting their off-the-job time to off-the-job activities. But how this time is used can have a significant impact on their careers.

One university professor has said, "Any man or woman who is willing to devote 15 minutes a day to the acquisition of knowledge can secure a cultural background that is superior to that given by any college in the country." Time is one of our most precious and perishable resources. Each of us has as much time at our disposal as others who seem to accomplish twice as much as we do. One of the most common supervisory complaints is, "I'm too busy—I don't have enough time." Yet it is not so much a matter of amount as of organized use of time. First, make a complete record or audit of how your time is spent for at least a week, and identify the amount of time spent in each area. Next, decide what can be eliminated. You will no doubt discover that considerable time is spent on unnecessary things. If these are dropped, more time will be available for essentials.

An analysis of what remains will reveal that some of the things you now do can be delegated to someone else. Letting other qualified people make some of the decisions and do some of the things you have been doing will release more of your time for more essential activities. Establish a priority system for the use of your time. List the things that must receive your attention, and arrange them in order of importance. Discipline yourself to follow your plan. Intelligence and ability vary with individuals, but every individual has the same number of hours each day. Whether you waste your time or use it to improve your executive stature and enrich your life is a choice only you can make. There is a direct relationship between the use of time and career accomplishment.

Resources for Self-Development

An almost unlimited reservoir of resources and assistance is available for self-development, much of it at no cost. Many companies offer courses during working hours or pay tuition for certain courses that are available at schools and colleges. Most national organizations conduct training and development programs designed to meet their specific needs. If supervisors are really serious about wanting to get ahead, they will be willing to spend their own time in increasing their value to themselves and the company.

Learn from your own supervisors. They will probably be able to offer many suggestions for increasing your qualifications for executive growth. Ask them for recommendations regarding courses of study. Analyze the duties and responsibilities of their jobs to determine what additional skills you must acquire before you will be qualified to move up. Their advice will be authoritative because it will be based on experience.

Learn from top management. Most executives are quite willing to talk about how they got to their present positions. Not everything they say will apply to you, but their decisions and philosophy on company operation and management will indicate what you must do to gain their approval. Let them know of your interest in getting ahead and what you are doing to prepare yourself for a bigger job. If you can also back up your expressed ambition with results, you will be given special attention and promotional consideration.

Take advantage of all training offered by the company. Many company programs are planned and conducted by the best trainers in the field and are often superior to those available in colleges and graduate schools. Most businesses recognize that appropriately qualified supervisors and executives cannot be hired from the outside; often, they must be developed and promoted from within. How eager are you to take advantage of training when it is available? Do you have to be forced to take courses that have been designed to help you move closer to a promotion? The most competent managers are always present at company courses—ample proof that success goes hand in hand with the acquisition of new knowledge and skills.

Modern communication and transportation have brought most of us within reach of vast resources for self-improvement. Among those usually available are organizations of personnel and training directors, executives, foremen, purchasing agents, and many other special-interest groups whose primary function is to keep their members abreast of development in their own specialized areas, improve their qualifications, and enhance their professional standing. Also available in most communities are evening colleges, industrial schools, trade courses, or other adult education programs. Fees are usually reasonable, and in many instances employers will pay all or part of the tuition. These courses offer opportunities for professional as well as cultural and personal development. Many trade associations, such as the American Institute of Banking, have professional development programs which may be conducted locally or through correspondence courses. In addition, many large universities and a number of national companies offer correspondence courses.

Books, magazines, and training aids can be found in public libraries. Executives who do not make use of their local library are ignoring a rich resource of professional and cultural assistance. Successful executives also subscribe to technical and trade magazines in their special field of interest; some companies have a policy of paying for these publications. A large volume of valuable printed material is also available through trade and other associations.

Make no mistake: Your company is interested in more than just your present ability. Management development is one of the fastest growing areas in industrial training, for there is increasing realization that an efficient management team is more important to the survival and growth of the organization than any tangible item on the balance sheet. As a part of the management team, you can depend on the firm to take an interest in your development and to plan formal programs to accomplish this purpose. But the fact remains that development is up to each individual. If you expect to rise faster and go further, you will have to develop the competitive edge.

Don't depend on the company to manage your own personal and professional development. Remember that you have more at stake in your future than it has. If you falter and fail, you can be replaced—you, not the company, will suffer most if you do not seize the opportunities afforded by the company environment. All you have to offer is your knowledge, skills, and leadership contribution. How much is it worth today? How much will it be worth next year? If you don't make a more valuable contribution next year, you won't deserve more pay or responsibility.

Executive Development: Whose Responsibility?

A business deliberately engages in a program of research to determine what products or services it should offer to the public. It then develops the products as efficiently and quickly as possible. But before the company can benefit, someone must be willing to pay for these goods or services. Similarly, executives should analyze their own strengths and weaknesses, discover their potential, seek to develop it to the fullest extent, and then fully utilize these skills in the organizational environment that has the greatest need for their contribution.

23

A Program for Executive Growth

THE thousands of executives who have reached the top rung of their companies, and the thousands of others who are on the way up, have a wealth of information to share. Their stories of how they achieved their positions and how they moved up are most revealing.

No executive or management expert can develop an infallible guide that will guarantee success. There is too much variation among individual personalities and circumstances for any one set of rules to be infallible. However, a look at the characteristics and behavior patterns that usually lead to success will be beneficial to ambitious executives seeking to chart their own rise to success. Smart managers learn all they can from both the success and the failure of others.

Building Blocks for Executive Growth

Executive success arises from many factors which must be integrated and coordinated into a smoothly functioning whole. Here are some guides for the ambitious individual who seeks to become a promotable executive.

Plan a specific program for self-improvement. Include adequate provision for budgeting time, developing good work habits, planning and scheduling things that must be done, and evaluating and improving your own performance. Work hard at being liked by others. Acquire more poise and become a more effective speaker. Try to improve your leadership attitudes and develop habits of mental alertness. Always be sure to adjust your present and future plans and to keep your sights aimed high.

Your specific program for growth should be constantly refined and revised. Miracles can be accomplished by the supervisor who does the job a little better and accomplishes slightly more each day.

Improve your relations with your own boss. Besides yourself, the most important person in your business future is your boss. The type of executive hir proves to be, and what hir thinks of you are vital to your future.

On first consideration, the suggestion that you pick the right boss may seem a little ridiculous, but on deeper analysis the idea has merit and is not so farfetched. Not only does a company select the individual for the job; the applicant can also analyze the company to determine whether it offers the best opportunity. For the same reason, ambitious executives should try to pick the right boss within the organization. It is certainly true that managers don't always have the prerogative of choosing their bosses; but in many instances, requests and desires will influence their placement or transfer within the firm.

What type of boss is the right boss? Hir is the manager you would like to become. Hir is the trainer who will guide you to more skillful performance. Hir is the executive who has confidence in other people, who is willing to delegate responsibility, who is constantly seeking improvement, and who is willing to develop your executive potential. The ideal boss is a manager who likes to see people get ahead, doesn't stand in their way, and is the first to say, "This employee is ready for promotion." Aside from your own attitude and application, this type of leadership will have the most decisive influence on your executive progress.

Be the type of executive you would want working with you. Every executive must be three people: supervisor of hirs department, associate of those on the same organizational level, and implementer of the programs of hirs own supervisor. Every manager has a boss, whether it be an executive at a higher level, stockholders, or customers. The loyalty and support you give your boss will be an indication of your qualification to move up the ladder. How can you be an effective and valuable contributor to your supervisor's needs? Consider these possibilities:

- Give supervisors the information they need and have a right to expect from you. Don't embarrass them by not letting them know what is taking place.
- Exercise initiative. Don't wait to be told—demonstrate that you can see what needs to be done and follow through to get it done.
- Don't try to win arguments with them in front of others. You don't gain by forcing them into admitting mistakes. Nor do you enhance your own opportunity by belittling them or by trying to show how much better you could have done the job.
- Be quick to support their programs. They probably know more about company plans than you do. Give them the benefit of the doubt—ask discreet questions, seek information, but always try to support them rather than oppose them.
- Think before you speak. Impulsive talk can do great damage to carefully calculated plans.
- Don't try to grab the limelight. Your recognition will come from the help you give them. If you try to outshine them you will be cut down to size. They appreciate your support, but don't want to be overshadowed.

An announcement in the paper was headlined: "Assistant Credit Manager Named Operating Manager." A few weeks later, the executive vice-president who had made the announcement was having lunch with several of his business friends, and the conversation got around to the promotion. One man remarked, "I knew you planned to fill the position, but I was very surprised that Frank got the promotion—which in essence makes him your assistant. I know you have several key executives who've been with the company longer and who had higher positions than Frank's. I imagine that a couple of these men were expecting to receive the promotion. What gives?"

The executive vice-president replied, "I can understand why it may seem surprising to you, but let me explain. I've never asked Frank to do anything that he didn't do well. I've never had to go back to check whether he had carried through on a job. When I've asked him to accept a responsibility, he has always been available. Frankly, he has made my job a lot easier for the past several years. As you know, we've had several projects in the company that I got credit for, but Frank did a lot of the spade work on them and pushed them forward. He has been of tremendous assistance to me in helping get things done. I felt that I needed this sort of man to help me more of the time, and I can assure you that he deserved the promotion. Truthfully, he has helped me more than any of the others, even though he had less opportunity because of his limited authority."

Your boss wants the type of support and cooperation that will make hirs job more effective and successful. The individual who is best able to carry out this responsibility is likely to be considered best qualified for promotion.

Build friendships. There is a tremendous difference between what other people must do for you and what they are willing to do if they like you. The manager who has friends, not just associates, in the company and the community at large can be a far more effective executive. Executives cannot function in a vacuum, but they can accomplish almost anything when they have a team of loyal supporters who want to see them succeed. Personal friendships with people in the community can have a decisive effect on the operation of a business. But it is even more important for a manager to be on good terms with employees who cooperate willingly and work toward mutually beneficial goals.

Building friendships is the result of having genuine concern for others. It means giving them confidence in themselves and encouraging them to face challenges. It means building people up instead of tearing them down. It means making them feel comfortable around you and giving them confidence in your integrity.

Maintain an inquiring mental posture. We learn most of what we know from others, but tremendous opportunity still exists for original thinking and for the individual who questions traditional theories and seeks better ways. Progress is made by those who question general assumptions, who don't resist new theories, and who don't dislike new ideas. Thought has become so standardized that the reaction of friends and competitors to any given proposition can be anticipated. This gives original thinkers the edge in anything they want to do. Lack of new insight is often the reason that one business fails while another succeeds—the business that fails is so set in its ways that its competitors can anticipate its every move.

While he was Secretary of Defense, Robert S. McNamara used an effective technique in managing the largest enterprise in the world. He asked such questions as: Why? Why is it done this way? Why isn't it done a different way? Why is it necessary to follow this procedure? Why can't a better way be found? Often, the only reason a procedure is performed in a particular way is that it has always been done that way. Startling changes and improvements can be made by using the questioning technique. The purpose of a questioning attitude is to produce a manager who can step back and look objectively at the total activity. The executive who develops an inquiring mind is the one who makes the greatest contribution and therefore deserves to move upward.

Expand your influence. As executives move up in management, they increase their sphere of influence. First, they influence only themselves, then a department, then several departments. They must recognize that people change and so do their needs, and that executives must constantly adjust to these changing needs.

Supervisors can expand their area of influence through sympathetic counseling, effective resolution of complaints, and realistic service to others. Executives who cannot modify people's behavior or actions cannot supervise them. And if the extent of this influence is not enlarged, those executives do not deserve to move up the management ladder.

Maintain perspective. To be effective, executives must organize their own duties and responsibilities and be able to function effectively in other company activities. The best starting point and the best permanent reference point for doing this are a good perspective on the job itself and a realistic overall view of the entire company.

Know what your job really covers and the results expected from your department. Analyze the potential of the position and what constitutes ideal performance. The scope of your job may well be larger than the job description. Jobs have a way of changing with time and shifting with the talents of the individual occupying the position. Don't be satisfied with merely meeting the minimum requirements. Instead, develop your own list of the key results you expect, and then exceed your own projections. Be systematic in analyzing what is now being produced, and develop long-range plans which will improve results.

Maintaining perspective means keeping the various aspects of the position in proper balance. Most executives have likes and dislikes with regard to their duties and responsibilities. Some like the mechanical or statistical part of the job, which can be measured precisely, and prefer to ignore the less precise areas—those pertaining to training and personnel, for instance. Yet to disregard any significant aspects is to lose one's essential perspective. Effective executives must keep the whole job in view, as well as its individual parts. This perspective allows them to keep all aspects of the job moving forward and to guarantee that a good relationship is maintained with other company activities.

This problem of job balance has been of concern for years in planning middle-management development programs and in promoting people to higher levels of management. At beginning levels, supervisors deal with only one department and with restricted responsibility. But most top managers have to be concerned with at least seven major areas of responsibility: purchasing, production, finance, personnel, sales promotion, expense control, and community and customer relations. If they neglect any one of these areas or fail to do an effective job in any one, the entire operation will be affected adversely. If they expect to grow in management, they must make up their minds to be both knowledgeable and effective in all these areas. The higher they advance in management, the truer this becomes. This is the job perspective that will be necessary if they are to grow into the full responsibility of top management.

Moving Forward and Upward

How does the executive keep moving forward and upward? Simply by recognizing that growth in responsibility and compensation is dependent on increased value to the organization. This value can only be the result of making a greater contribution and carrying a bigger load of responsibility.

No company president or chief executive has ever been known to complain of having too many capable executives. Rather, the question is: Where do we find enough talented leaders? For the supervisor who seeks to move upward in management, the following steps deserve attention.

Appraise and improve your own job performance. If your position and the position above yours do not have realistic descriptions of duties, responsibilities, and expected results, the first important step is to develop these descriptions. When this has been done in cooperation with your supervisor and with others in the company, you will have a reasonable picture of what you are expected to do and how well you are expected to do it.

After standards have been developed, evaluate and appraise your job performance in relation to these standards. Be realistic and not shortsighted in your own self-evaluation. Whatever advantage there may seem to be in trying to fool other people, there is none in trying to fool yourself. Be your own severest critic. Deal harshly with areas where you are not meeting expectations. Discipline yourself to bring about the improvement which the evaluation indicates is needed.

Ask your supervisor to evaluate your performance and assist you with a plan for improvement. Remember that hirs appraisal is important to your future. If hir feels that you are not meeting requirements and that you need to improve in some areas, this is the most important information you can receive. And when hir indicates that a change is in order, respond in full measure. No good purpose is served in discovering where an improvement is needed unless the improvement is made.

Be guided by facts. Questions are usually more effective than orders. Many people resent being told what to do. However, when asked their opinion and how they think a job can best be handled, they are eager to cooperate. Supervisors can get their programs accepted through the effective technique of asking questions. Certain pitfalls should be avoided—prying, asking embarrassing questions or questions the individual may not be able to answer, cross-examining people, or implying that you know something the other person doesn't.

Improve your ability to accomplish results through others. The supervisor's responsibility is to weld a group of individuals into a capable and enthusiastic team. When this is successful, people will give more service, get more pay, and derive more pleasure from the job. The supervisor must be able to see possibilities in people who are just on the edge of failure, to search for and discover the things that are holding them back—lack of training, inadequate knowledge, a need for better direction of energies—and guide them skillfully from failure to success.

A technique for getting results through people was expressed in the following way by Charles H. Brower, when he was president of Batten, Barton, Durstine & Osborn, Inc.:

> What you and I have to do, patiently, and day by day, is to teach those over whom we are given supervision that work can be fun—that the only real reward that life offers is the thrill of achievement, and that the place where achievement amounts to most is on the job. A hole in one isn't half as thrilling as landing a big order—a piece of furniture built in your basement workshop will never be as thrilling as a sales plan that works—a sailfish mounted on your wall will never be quite as exciting as a well-earned promotion.*

Increase your contribution through better decision making. Decision making is the critical test of management—the ability and the

*Speech before the National Sales Executives Association Convention, Washington, D.C., May 20, 1958.

courage to reach the right conclusions and take the right course of action, skill in persuading others to cooperate with total commitment, and then follow through to successful results.

Decisions must be based on factual information, not hearsay or personal opinion. When factual information is not available, the validity of the decision must depend on the judgment and experience of the person making the decision. To the casual observer, many decisions successful executives make appear to be snap judgments, because there has not been time to gather and evaluate the facts. Yet what looks like snap judgment to the inexperienced may actually be utilization of experience, superior knowledge, and the skill necessary to coordinate both experience and knowledge.

How do you rate when it comes to decision making? Several negative choices are available: Do nothing; do nothing right; let someone else decide; appoint a committee; delay; or check the decision with others so, if it is unpopular or doesn't work, there will be someone else to blame. On the other hand, you can take the firm and positive approach: Accept the responsibility; recognize what needs to be done; make the decision when it needs to be made, without undue delay; and, once it has been made, set in motion the action necessary to ensure its success.

Fortune magazine has listed business executives, politicians, and military officers as the principal decision makers in the world. A specific technique for decision making was first developed by the military. A former colonel in the Air Force has described the military method as consisting of these five steps:

1. Determine the mission. What is the goal? What is the objective to be accomplished?
2. Describe the situation and courses of action. What supplies, men, and resources are available? What are the possible courses of action?
3. Analyze the various courses of action. What would each require? What consequences and results can be anticipated?
4. Estimate how the opposition will probably react. (Napoleon's generals had all gone to the same military schools and their decisions could always be anticipated by the opposition.)
5. Make the best decision. At this point, a decision is not a snap judgment but a calculated decision based on experienced judgment, evaluation, and analysis.

Many executives cannot describe their technique for decision making. Some even say that when they think about a problem too much, they are likely to make the wrong decision. It is certainly true that the athlete and the military leader do not always have time to stop and ponder every move. Their reactions result from training, drills, and practice. Then, when a situation calls for an almost automatic reaction, the ability to react is there.

The business executive can learn to make decisions by the same techniques. Undue dependence on stereotypes or rigid procedures is inadvisable, but the supervisory training technique of role playing and the case method of problem solving provide practice in decision making.

Make your leadership more positive. If department heads have difficulty getting the people in their departments to follow instructions, it may be their own fault. The very manner in which they give instructions and communicate their decisions may suggest a lack of confidence in their ability to lead. To be successful, leadership must be positive. Requests should be made and instructions should be given with the full expectation that there will be a definite response. An apologetic approach to leadership is doomed to failure.

Learn to manage yourself. Successful managers of others begin by managing themselves. Those who lead must obviously have some general knowledge of what the position requires. But the real test of growth is whether leaders practice sufficient self-management to bring their fullest potential to bear on the duties and responsibilities of their positions. The failure of most supervisors to reach the top rungs of leadership is not caused by lack of ability or of knowledge, but by lack of self-management. Managers who can discipline and manage themselves can usually manage others.

Be the uncommon man or woman. Herbert Hoover had this to say about the common man:

> Among the delusions offered us by fuzzy-minded people is that imaginary creature, the common man. This idea is a cousin of the Soviet proletariat. The uncommon man is to be whittled down to size. This is the negation of individual dignity and a slogan of mediocrity and uniformity.
>
> The common man dogma may be of use as a vote-getting apparatus. But the greatest strides of human progress have come from uncommon men and women. You have perhaps heard of George Washington, Abraham Lincoln, and Thomas Edison. They were humble in origin, but that was not their greatness.
>
> The humor of it is that when we get sick, we want an uncommon doctor. When we go to war, we yearn for an uncommon general or

admiral. When we choose the president of a university, we want an uncommon educator.

The imperative need of this nation at all times is the leadership of uncommon men or women. We need men and women who cannot be intimidated, who are not concerned with applause meters, not those who sell tomorrow for cheers today.

Much can be said for the organization man or woman, the leader who fits nicely into the stereotyped mold of the executive. But it must also be said that opportunities for such managers are extremely limited, because there are so many of them. The higher positions in management are filled by uncommon leaders who are willing to apply uncommon devotion and effort to their jobs. No company president can draw straws to decide which of five average supervisors to promote; rather, hir must find the one who has demonstrated the potential for making an uncommon contribution.

Dare to be uncommon. Be willing to work harder, plan better, think clearer, and achieve greater results. Recognition, prestige, and compensation await the manager who rises to uncommon accomplishment.

People who are dedicated to climbing the executive ladder, must not be lured into the fatal sleep of averages. Remember that the average executive is the worst of the best and only the best of the worst. Statistically speaking, the manager who has one foot on a hot stove and the other on a block of ice should by the law of averages be comfortable. The ambitious executive remains constantly aware that promotions do not beckon those who are just average.

Executive leadership can be exciting, challenging, and rewarding to the man or woman who is willing to meet its challenges in an uncommon way.

24

Conclusions Worth Applying

EMPHASIS has been placed on the supervisor's responsibility for results. There can be no real compromise with this obligation—it is the primary function of the position, and it is what the company expects from its supervisors. However, supervisors must recognize that the degree of employee response to training, motivation, and leadership is dependent on how fully the job meets the individual needs of the workers. Supervisors must not overlook their human responsibilities—to be interested in the people they work with, to share their employees' joys and accomplishments, and to help them find in their jobs a source of fulfillment. If supervisors are to achieve results through people, they should remember that people must find satisfaction in their work if they are to give their best efforts to the job and meet its requirements.

The supervisor who misses this point is missing one of the most significant aspects of the job. It is this factor that gives the final dimension to leadership. Few other positions offer the same opportunity for helping people in their personal and professional growth.

Supervisors should never assume that leadership is for their benefit alone. Supervisor and supervised should form a partnership. Appropriate leadership benefits the employee; employee performance benefits the supervisor. Each should understand that the achievement of departmental objectives is of mutual benefit. Supervisors who can establish the concept of partnership with their employee group will be gratified by the overall accomplishment it fosters.

The Moral Responsibilities of Leadership

The most important obligation of leadership is teaching by example. Just as the parent cannot escape the responsibility of personal example, neither can the business leader. The attitudes, the work habits, and the very spirit of the supervisor often set the pattern for the employees.

Both doctors and lawyers have a professional code of ethics, and so should professional executives. They must not disregard the feelings and rights of others, and should be constantly aware that they hold in their hands the livelihood and an important part of the life of each employee. Just as the minister treats information given to hir as confidential, so must the supervisor. Hirs code of ethics must include keeping promises: Hir should not make promises lightly, and once made, hir is morally obligated to keep them.

The ethical code of managers also means accepting responsibility for decisions and actions. They should welcome responsibility and not attempt to shun it or shift it to the boss or to employees. Certain duties and responsibilities are assigned to their positions, and they should meet these to the limit of their abilities.

As Americans, we recognize that people are entitled to dignity and consideration, and deserve an opportunity for full development. People want to be remembered, recognized, and considered in such a way that their importance and status are clear. Most people enjoy conversation, especially the opportunity to talk about their accomplishments, as well as the accomplishments of those who are close to them. This need gives the supervisor the opportunity to keep in touch with hirs people—not just with the details of their work, but with other aspects of their personal lives.

Casual conversation and free exchange of information can make both supervisor and employee seem more human. Keeping in touch in this manner not only serves individual needs but certainly enhances each person's goal achievement. The supervisor should welcome every opportunity to talk with the employee and to both receive and communicate information of mutual interest.

The Goal of Involvement and Participation

Employee participation is one of the most overworked phrases and most underdeveloped activities in the area of leadership. There is little doubt that when employees feel an involvement and are allowed to participate fully, they are better satisfied and put forth greater effort. Yet supervisors excuse their failure to involve employees by saying that it takes too much time, or that it's easier just to make decisions and give orders. This practice reveals that supervisors often misunderstand or misinterpret the real meaning of individual involvement, which encourages participation in establishing and achieving group goals and sharing responsibility. Involvement and participation are not limited to overt gestures. They include the whole person—hirs personality, hirs need to be heard, and hirs desire to participate in those decisions which affect hirs life.

Management's concern with employee participation is not solely one of meeting human needs; there is ample evidence that it results in improved job performance. Training sessions are more effective when employees become personally involved. Safety campaigns are more successful when employees feel that they are participating in the planning and decisions.

There is no implication here that all decisions can be made by employee consensus. But supervisors can take the time to sound out employee feeling. They can encourage participation in training. They can take advantage of countless opportunities to encourage employees to satisfy their innate desires to be creative and to function as full-fledged members of the team.

Unlocking the Doors to Future Growth

An executive's only valid claim to growth must be that of rendering genuine service and producing results in the areas of hirs responsibility. The following factors are essential for executive growth.

The master plan. No structure can be any more attractive or functional than the blueprint that was used for its construction. A master plan deserves the careful, systematic, and thorough attention of the ambitious manager. It should be sufficiently detailed and of wide enough scope to afford a view of the finished product and to furnish detailed specifications to ensure that work can move steadily toward the ultimate goal.

The formulation of this plan should be coordinated with those managers who have functional responsibility for its overall results. The plan should be ambitious enough to assure improvement and growth, but at the same time be realistic enough to be attainable.

The tools and techniques of achievement. The builder first views the task before hir as a whole, but then separates it into specific steps, each to be completed at the right time and with the tools best suited to each step.

Supervisors, too, are builders in a sense. Their task is to structure a productive team. It can be said of their jobs that the identification and mastery of the tools and techniques of leadership constitute the decisive factors in success or failure. If leaders are to be successful, they must use the right combination of leadership tools and techniques.

Understanding and influencing people. Understanding others begins with an understanding of ourselves, and it continues with a recognition of the basic needs and desires of people. Only when there is an understanding of individuals and human relationships can supervisors be effective in their daily job of influencing people toward specific goals.

The factor of human leadership. Every team needs a captain. The direction and distance traveled by any one group are determined by its leader. Top management recognizes that departmental leadership is the most decisive single factor affecting the accomplishments of the department.

Leadership consists of what managers are and what they do; it is the trait they possess and exhibit to others; it is the enthusiasm and inspiration they are able to infuse in others; and it is the confident and willing support they are able to elicit from others. Expansion of this leadership is the most reliable test of executive growth.

Prescription for job-related problems. Unresolved problems can be damaging to the goals of a department. Attitude, motivation, correction, complaints, and change confront the supervisor with potential problems. Once these arise, resolving them requires constant attention, early diagnosis, and skillful handling.

Although their influence can be negative, problems can also be used by the supervisor to exert a positive influence on job performance. As in the case of every other job influence and resource, the supervisor has the responsibility of turning these problems to the most favorable advantage. But the best way to deal with problems is to prevent them.

Growth through the development of people. The installation of new machinery often necessitates the expenditure of large sums of money, and the overhaul of procedures may require major and often complex changes. However, the daily gradual development of people involves a modest outlay of cash and a limited disruption of routine. Everything employees learn and every improvement in their skill should result in improved performance. This can be one of the most dependable and economical keys to departmental progress.

Enlarging the span of leadership. Not every supervisory job can offer enough growth at a rate that will satisfy ambitious executives. Perhaps their growth needs can be realized only through transfer to a larger department, supervision of two or more departments, or promotion to a higher level of responsibility. In preparation for promotions of this type, the supervisor should pay particular attention to delegating responsibility to others, training an assistant, and improving communication. To disregard these vital areas of growth is to squander the opportunity to continue moving up the executive ladder.

The executive in the mirror. It is common knowledge that "it's not what you know but who you know" that determines whether you get ahead in business. But the "who" is the individual in the mirror. This person more than any other will determine the future growth and progress of the executive. All people must shape, control, and determine their own job performance and executive growth. Get to know yourself, recognize your strengths, and identify those traits and handicaps that will interfere with your executive growth. Discipline yourself in accordance with your own needs. And develop self-confidence in order to keep moving forward. You hold the keys to your own success—don't be satisfied until your goal has been reached.

The future. Time offers benefits, through experience gained, for those wise enough to be guided by its message. The future is opportunity itself. The present is the time when executives must improve their skills and acquire new ones; now is their opportunity to show proof of executive ability. Time cannot be borrowed, stored, or stopped, but it can be ignored and squandered. If people thought of time in terms of the future being chopped off hour by hour and day by day, and forever lost, they might have a more realistic appreciation of the value of time. Each day wasted is one less in which to make of the future what we want it to be.

Ascending the Steps to Success

The great wall of China was built thick and high to keep invaders out. Those who built it considered it insurmountable. But invaders had only to build steps in strategic places, and they could quickly scale the wall that took thousands of men countless years to build.

Similarly, from some points of view the problems of leadership appear insurmountable. From others, these problems are only walls which must be scaled. One person comes to such a wall, stops, sits, and contemplates hirs cruel fate; another builds steps. The individual who scales the walls is discharging the responsibility of leadership. To the capable executive, *problems have a way of becoming goals and opportunities.*

Success is not available at discount prices. More people could be successful if they were willing to pay the high price in painstaking preparation, long days of hard work, and perhaps even a few sleepless nights of problem solving. Creative genius and leadership success seldom result from strokes of luck; they are more often built on the basis of effort, tenacity, and determination.

Admiral "Bull" Halsey said about heroes, "There are no great men, only great challenges that ordinary men are forced by circumstances to meet." Opportunity enables ordinary men and women to rise to greatness. There can be no better proving ground of greatness than a position of leadership in business and industry.

Index